SOARING

WITH DESTINY

Cover Photo:
SR-71 Blackbird #17952 refueling from KC-135Q #58-0054 (Circa 1968)
Lockheed Martin Photo Copyright Notice: @2009 Lockheed Martin Corporation
Unclassified and Approved for Public Release

Published by Mindstir Media, LLC
45 Lafayette Rd | Suite 181| North Hampton, NH 03862 | USA
1.800.767.0531 | www.mindstirmedia.com

Printed in the United States of America
ISBN-13: 978-0-9600237-0-7
Library of Congress Control Number: 2018964995

SOARING
WITH DESTINY

A USAF PILOT'S MEMOIRS
of Challenges, Experiences & Accomplishments

LT. COL. CHUCK MILLER, USAF (RET.)

CONTENTS

CHAPTER 8

INTRODUCTION

DESTINY- defined Merriam Webster Dictionary

1. "What happens in the future: the things that someone or something will experience in the future"
2. "The predetermined or inevitable course of events considered beyond the power or control of people".

As human beings we seldom have any idea of *our destiny*, until we look back at it from the many paths that we have experienced and lived, and through the wisdom of the eyes that these experiences have provided. Only in compiling these many anecdotes and stories over the years, did I begin to recognize that I have literally "Soared" with my Destiny. This writing helped me to identify certain formative experiences and pathway diversions that gave me a renewed vision that my life and career were guided and overseen by a much "higher power" than mere coincidence and random events would indicate. I hope that this story can successfully point out some of these moments of epiphany and revelation, and the valuable lessons they provided along the way.

I have written these memoirs to serve several purposes:

1. To provide to my children, family, former military compatriots and friends an expanded perspective of the many important challenges, experiences, and accomplishments of my life's path. And to provide them with the insights of how my personal destiny developed and unfolded, along with the significant and important "gateways" of experience that caused or re-directed me along my destiny's many paths.
2. To document for posterity in the Library of Congress'

"Veterans History Program", a record of the history of my career(s) that can be researched to provide insight into the eras of the Cold War and the Vietnam War in which I participated and influenced operations and policy, both as an individual officer and pilot, and subsequently as a senior USAF middle management representative with considerable responsibility for a specific Weapons System, budget, and policy that impacted the US capability to fight and win wars, to efficiently manage complex assets and resources, and to make major contributions to the National Defense of the United States during my years of involvement.

3. To hopefully provide interesting and entertaining reading and insight into some of the many complexities of flying (piloting and instructing), maintaining and upgrading these complex systems, and an understanding of the importance of technically detailed knowledge of those complexities in order to grow in management through knowledge, responsibility and authority.
4. To provide an insight into many of the significant differences between a military career and a (parallel similar) civilian career, in terms of advancement potential, challenges, opportunities, and philosophical attitudinal variations between the two.

With these objectives in mind, and knowing how diverse and complex the subject is in many areas, you can understand how difficult it was to write for my "intended audiences". ***["In order to communicate with another, you must have <u>a common core of experience</u>", according to USAF communications training.]*** Being essential to tell my story to this diverse audience, it was often necessary, for full understanding and appreciation, for me to set the stage with background details, technical insights, or spotlight the results of the actions undertaken. If the reader has experience as a "heavy-aircraft" pilot (or crew member), for example, he may already be acutely aware of the terminology, or the complex forces that are at play. For him there may be far too much extraneous detail explanation. For the inexperienced (a youngster; a non-flying family member, or child, for instance), the detail may not be understandable and be of no value. In between those opposite ends of the experience spectrum, my narrative hopefully may provide a good learning explanation with some degree of interest.

Also to add to the insights provided, I have tried to use illustrations, graphics, and photographs to help the level of understanding. If I refer to a C-47 aircraft, or T-33 trainer, or any other military vehicle, I have tried to include a photo, or another image, so the reader can relate to visuals to tie the words into meaningful comprehension. This book includes over 115 color photos, graphics, and charts in that attempt.

In any event, I apologize in advance, if I have overwhelmed the reader with too much detail, or too little visual material in describing the complexities of the subject matter.

I have tried to add colorful and entertaining anecdotes, and descriptions of what flying entails, as well as the sometimes-intense effort involved in getting the job done. But the intent was not to make the flying effort sound too overwhelming to do, because the effort was the result of gaining experience in small bites with further accomplishment after an earlier effort was mastered. I have told my story in terms of the time line of my experiences, so the reader can connect the lessons learned earlier and how those lessons and experiences proved helpful in later experiences and challenges. And I have separated time intervals of assignments into time-sequenced Chapters with sub-heading divisions for events within those subject challenges and experiences. If you get bogged down in undesired details, then just scan through each of the sub-titles sections for the "meat"... the stories, which satisfy your specific appetite and don't get bogged down in the details.

There are many, many more stories and anecdotes of my experiences covering 20-years of my time on active duty and several years beyond. But I could only relate some of what I considered most meaningful in my life, or the most interesting to relate. The many colorful stories of others that I encountered in my career would take another volume to capture in this book, and then limit the added "war stories" that I might relate in other venues.

At the end of the book, you will find my email address. I will be happy to receive any comments, questions and especially any corrections that you feel I should make for accuracy (especially if you have first-hand knowledge that is more recent or more detailed than the memory-drawn descriptions that I have included in my narrative.

Privacy and anonymity — In order to protect the privacy of the many individuals who were a meaningful part of my career over more than three decades, yet provide a recognizable hint to the identities of those who were a part of the story, I have reduced their identities in this text to their Rank (where applicable) and First name and Last Initials. For example Colonel Adam Smith, would be abbreviated as "Col. Adam S", and Mister John Jones, would be identified simply as "Mr. John J". (Generally, family member names are not abbreviated, nor are well-known celebrities.)

Sources of info — Details of my career were written and compiled in anecdotal form originally over a period of more than 20 years after my military retirement, for the purpose of journaling the events accurately while they were still relatively fresh in my memory. They represent the details as I perceived them and have not been reviewed and coordinated with the other principals identified because of their lack of availability, or in several cases whom are no longer alive. Several of these related stories or anecdotes have been published on various History websites on the Internet (www.ec47.com; http://www.wvi.com/~sr71webmaster/sr-71~1.htm, etc.), and too many others to note. Some have subsequently been deleted from the Internet as the site operator passed away, or lost the ability to keep them on-line. Other of these anecdotes have been published in printed periodicals such as the quarterly "Friends Journal" of the National Museum of the USAF, and other national and local military organizations, to which I have belonged.

I began the compilation of these anecdotes and commentaries into a single contiguous autobiography at the request of my two adopted daughters in 2001. During the most recent compilation, through encouragement of our local library Director, I updated and amplified many of the details, for interest, clarity and accuracy, and with continuity of data and events researched from the Internet, and other available records. This final version, was researched, compiled, proofed, and finalized in November 2018 for self-publication (after my 80th birthday) with limited distribution anticipated by end of 2018 to family and close friends.

CHAPTER 1

Childhood Formative Years

In the Beginning — I was born in late Oct 1938, in "Tom Sawyer – Huck Finn", Mark Twain country, at the extreme southern end of Illinois, where the Ohio River and the Mississippi Rivers converge, in a small town – now a virtual "ghost town" – named Cairo, IL. My Dad, Donald Austin Miller, Mom, Grace Eleanor (MacDowney) Miller, and my older brother, Harold, lived initially in a moderate-sized two-story frame home built at the beginning of the 20th century on a lot next door to my paternal grandmother, Charlotte, "Lottie" Miller, (a widow). Her home was on the corner lot and was an anti-bellum style two-story frame home, but larger and architecturally more ornate than ours. My paternal grand father, Charles "Carl" Sumner Miller, passed away (in 1939) from abdominal cancer less than a year after I was born, so I have no direct recollection of him. He was the Illinois Central Railroad corporate attorney and also the Pulaski County Judge, where Cairo is the County seat.

I vividly remember several of my very young events from my story-book early youth in the "Tom Sawyer" environment, where I learned the culture of the paddle-wheel steam boats on the river and the small town picturesque atmosphere of the early 1940s. A middle-income household, at that time, typically had only one-telephone and one automobile; very few had air-conditioning; some of my local cousin's homes had no indoor plumbing nor in-door toilets; and with no TV we had only a big console radio that we sat around and listened to for news and entertainment. Computers were non-existent. We did a lot of family activities like playing board games; outdoor picnics and the kids occasionally enjoyed a Saturday matinee in the only air-conditioned movie house watching double-feature Westerns preceded by "Movie Tone" news-reels and cartoons. In the post-Civil War "anti-bellum" southern town of Cairo, we had a hired loving and wonderful "black-nanny" named "Woolina" who cared for my older brother and I, and assisted Mom with house cleaning and laundry over the course of our pre-school years.

My Dad was the only boy and second oldest among four female siblings. He was a sportsman who loved exploring in the beautiful outdoors, fishing, hunting, picnics at a local quiet lake, and canoeing on the rivers. All of my dad's four sisters were very musically talented, played the piano and/or electric organ, sang in the choir (including Mom and Grandma Miller), and one sister was proficient in all the wind and string instruments you might find in a concert orchestra. She never married, but gained a PhD in music and became a college music teacher. Dad also loved music and he played the "licorice stick" clarinet, and saxophone. From these surroundings, I inherited the love of music and the desire to play piano, but never had the training (at this young age) to read music. It was a common summer event for the whole family, including my aunts and grandmother, to gather around the baby grand piano in Grandma Miller's parlor and have family sing-alongs on Sunday afternoons to the entertainment and enjoyment of the neighbors, who observed through the open screened windows.

> *At one Sunday dinner, when I was three, (according to one of my aunts), just after the "Grace" was completed, I got up from the dinner table, went to the piano and did several choruses of "bang the keyboard". When I returned to the table, as she told the story, one of the family-members asked me what that was all about. To which I replied, "Oh, I just had some music in me that I had to get out before I ate my dinner"!*

At the age of about five, in one of our week-end outings, we went with the family to a local private grass airfield and as I watched the Piper Cubs fly around, I became enthralled with airplanes, and decided I wanted to be a pilot. I was also very good at tinkering with and repairing mechanical things, and with subjects relating to science, math, and physics, as I progressed through grade school and high school in following years.

> *One if my earliest memories involving these gifts prior to age six (marked in my memory, by the death of my father before the time I had reached that age), occurred when I found an old alarm clock in the trash bin. My curiosity led me to take the clock out of its metal case using Dad's toolkit, to see how it worked. As I moved the gears and springs, which somehow dislodged a particle of dirt or realigned some piece, the clock began to run again! As a result of this success I put the clock back in its case and it was restored to normal use.*

Dad, as a high school student had been very mechanically inclined. He loved making carpentry projects with crude power equipment (of the era), and his puttering no doubt kindled my interest in machinery and building things by hand. He had a tiny workshop in our dirt-floored basement, next to the coal bin, and I enjoyed (at age four or five) "helping" him work on his various projects. He campaigned in his high school years with his parents to enroll as a mechanical engineer at the University of Illinois, in Champaign. Once there he also wanted to participate in the social life of the university and joined a fraternity. His first several semesters' grades suffered from the socializing and he learned "the bad habits of smoking, drinking beer and chasing skirts". His father (the Judge), after observing Dad's several mediocre semesters, finally went to Champaign, and took him out of the school because of his "misbehaviors" and transferred him to Grandpa's Alma Mater, John Marshall Law School in Chicago saying "he had no intention of paying for Dad to learn all those bad habits, while ignoring his studies". While enrolled at Marshall Law School in Chicago, Dad met my Mom, Grace, (a student elementary school teacher) and they subsequently married. They started a family in Chicago, with the birth of my brother in 1936, (2-years my senior). After Dad's graduation they returned to Cairo and he entered a law practice with the Judge, who helped him to purchase the vacant house next-door. I was born to the young family in Cairo, in Oct. 1938.

Dad, at age 34 – although a college graduate, a member of the Legal Bar and draft-exempt by age and family status, and qualified to be an officer candidate, volunteered to do his part fighting in WWII, and enlisted in the Army as a Private in the spring of 1944. During infantry boot camp, due to the rigors of fatigue and bad environment, he came down with double pneumonia and was hospitalized for several weeks. This detached him from his original assigned unit. Once released from the hospital he came home on 2-weeks of recuperative leave and then was re-assigned to finish boot camp with a new unit, which subsequently was assigned to the ETO (European Theater of Operations). Ironically his original unit never went overseas. He was killed on Dec 8, 1944 on the French-German border, just 8-days before the commencement of what became known as the "Battle of the Bulge" — less than two months after arriving in theater. I had just turned 6-years old, two months earlier. After Dad's death, Mom relocated the family (she, my 8-year old brother, and me). Concerned to provide a paternal positive roll-model for her two father-less sons by their grandfather, we moved back to Chicago to live with our maternal grand parents, while Mom found full-time administrative employment, with United Air Lines, at Chicago's Midway Airport to support us. My idyllic Tom Sawyer life-style had ended, and I learned the miserable existence of the impersonal and hostile childhood of the big city. After three years living with our maternal grand parents, Meta and Morris MacDowney, Mom made a down payment on a small 2-bedroom bungalow in Oak Lawn (1948), on Chicago's south-side, which was a more suburban and likeable lifestyle than Chicago offered. She later remarried (in Dec 1952, at my age 14) to a divorced lawyer and law school alumnus of my Dad's, who brought two children (a boy of 13, and a girl of 11) into our "merged family".

> *Many years later, I recognized that my father's premature death, and our family's forced relocation to Chicago was one of* ***destiny's*** *first major life alterations that made a profound effect upon my life, my personality, and my later career. Having been charged at Dad's funeral service that my brother and I were now the "men in the family" and had to take responsibility to help and care for our mother (in the very male –centered culture of the mid-1940's).*

High School Years (1953-1956) — After elementary school, I joined my older brother at Blue Island Community HS (another suburb on Chicago's south side). This seemed a natural choice since my brother had already attended Blue Island Community High for two years, and had his own car, thus eliminating the need for dependence on the daily school bus for me. I enrolled in "College Prep" courses at BICHS, which was highly rated, where I could obtain college credit for nearly a whole semester of college-level courses. (Oak Lawn had a new local High School, which had just opened at the time that I began high school, but was not yet college accredited, partially explaining why I did not want to go there. Both of my younger step-siblings, however, did later attend Oak Lawn High). I excelled in math & science classes and graduated number 14 out of 414 seniors. While in high school, I held several near-full-time jobs after class and on week-ends, including counter waiter, cook, and general janitor in a small truck-stop restaurant, followed the next summer at the next-door archery range, arcade and mini-golf amusement park, and then on to assistant store manager (only employee under the owner) of a local Western Tire Auto Store. The pay was good at Western Tire, and the management skills and responsibilities proved valuable later.

College years (1956-1961) — Being always mechanically inclined like my Dad, and enthralled with aircraft, I felt it logical to pursue a degree in aeronautical engineering. *[As an aside, my college counselor informed me that my entrance aptitude exams indicated that I had better analytic skills and should work toward a degree in engineering physics. Boy was he proved wrong, when I found I had major difficulties with the higher math, analytical thermodynamics, and aerodynamics courses.]* I received a full tuition scholarship at any state college from the GI Bill, due to my veteran father's death. When I attended the first day of enrollment, at the Univ. of Illinois (a federal land-grant college), I discovered that it was mandatory for all male students to participate in 2-years of basic ROTC. ***[This was a second life-changing event that redirected my life path into a military career, which I had never even anticipated in my earlier career considerations.]*** Naturally of the three services available, I chose Air Force ROTC. My USAF StaNine ("Standard Nine", a Pilot Screening Aptitude Test) qualification scores were in the 98th percentile, and I subsequently continued with high acceptance into the Advanced Corps through my senior year.

The Advanced ROTC program also provided a monthly stipend to supplement cost of my books and some of my housing expenses. I found Military Science and related AFROTC subjects, as well as Drill and Ceremonies (as a Cadet Colonel Wing Commander) a pleasant no-homework break from my other 18-20 course-hours of science, math, and complex aerodynamics courses. One of my Advanced AFROTC Professors of Air Science mentored me, helping me with my difficulties with the advanced math and aerodynamics issues, and offered to obtain a nomination for me to the Air Force Academy (which, had I been better informed, I could already have had from my Dad's WWII status). I declined this late Junior-year opportunity, because that meant I would have to restart my college for 3-more academy years after already completing two-plus at U. of Illinois.

As an unrelated issue from AFROTC, instead of the anticipated 4-years for graduation, it took me 5-1/2 years to battle through my advanced math courses and complete my degree. During this time I already had acquired 30-hours of ROTC logged flying-time in the Aeronca 7FC, "Tri-Champ" aircraft (a more powerful Piper Cub-sized aircraft, with tricycle landing gear) during one month of my Junior year summer semester. The same summer, I also completed a second month of ROTC boot-camp training at Craig AFB, AL.

Aeronca 7FC "Tri-Champ"

Flying the AFROTC Cadet Pilot program, in the Tri-Champ was a very intense summer month at the U of I airport. It was 4-weeks of five-days per week activity, consisting each day of 3-hours of ground school and 2-hours of flying and flight related activity. Flying included basic emergency procedures and landings, air maneuvers, radio procedures, cross-country navigation, night flying, and solo flying, once qualified. The flying activity was so intense that the Cadet students hardly had sufficient time to review the flying techniques and lessons learned, much less apply those lessons to the next day's flying activities. The TriChamp was well equipped and provided not only basic flying skills training, but also an introduction into minimum instrument flying skills. But with only a 90 hp engine and a fixed pitch prop, it was still basically more related to a Piper Cub than an Air Force airplane.

The program was intended by the Air Force, to be a preliminary qualification for "pilot hopefuls" to expose the students to air sickness, high stress learning demands and other pilot qualities, and efficiently led to about 30% of the enrollees either quitting, or getting washed out, before expending the big bucks on true USAF Pilot Training enrollment for 12-months in Undergraduate Pilot Training. I successfully passed.

Upon graduation from the university, I received my BS degree in aeronautical engineering, plus a 2nd Lieutenant Reserve-Commission, and by then had a bride of 7-months. Surprisingly, my bride, the former Patricia VerSchave, had lived just a block away from our family home in Oak Lawn and was a classmate of both my step-siblings at the recently opened Oak Lawn High. But since they had different last names (McGee vs. Miller) than my brother and I, at 16 Pat had never known of the Miller family existence as neighbors, just two blacks from her home.

Pat and I first met during the summer after my second year at college, introduced by my former boss, Al, at the Miniature Golf park where I had previously worked the year before. I had stopped by to visit Al and show off my newly acquired 1956 Pontiac Star Chief convertible. Al had promised Pat's dad that a safe ride home for Pat after work would be provided, after closing at midnight. Al had asked me to fulfill his pledge. After obscurely checking her out from a distance, I told Al I would be happy to give that cute girl a four-block ride home. This Pontiac convertible, was instrumental in our path leading, to marriage … But that is not what you think and will not be revealed here. We were married at a U. of I. campus chapel two and a half years later (March 1960).

1956 Pontiac Star Chief Convertible

Wedding Portrait – 1960 –

[Are we starting to see the hand of "higher powers" guiding me as I progressed down destiny's path?]

Pat and I lived just off-campus in a minimally furnished 300 sq.ft., one-bedroom apartment rental on the second story of a mid-1940s farmhouse located on the edge of Urbana, surrounded by about 20-acres of cornfields. Our home-owner and landlady was an 80-year old widow and retired fraternity housemother, who had been gifted the fraternity's equally old African McCaw parrot, which could out-cuss even the worst frat-boy, or sailor, you could imagine. During the warmer months, he lived in a cage on the screened porch, just below our bedroom and kept us entertained with his "screeches and frat-boy diatribe". For my entire college years, I held meal jobs working either in fraternities, or sororities, which I continued through my final semester. Pat had her own car — a graduation gift from her parents — and worked at a local department store to supplement our meager income. Our Best Man (a former campus room mate of mine, and aeronautical engineering student, too), and Matron of Honor (his wife; Bob and Rosemary P.), lived a mile or so away in a similar meager apartment, so we had some local good friends to share our skimpy beginnings. Life was good with an exciting life to look forward to.

Supplementing My Way (Sep. 1956 – Jan '61)— I returned home to Oak Lawn each summer during vacations from college, until our marriage. I held summer employment to supplement my tuition, initially returning to the place of high school employment at Western Tire in Oak Lawn. Then in my second year vacation I found employment on a one-month labor position at the Real Lemon-Puritan Co. as a shipping department worker on a bottling line, in Chicago. (You probably remember the "Lucy Ball Show" on TV and the ever-faster, "never-get-tired" bakery-line conveyor skit? This was my occupation for the early part of this new job.) There, I was also unloading & loading pallets on boxcars, until I was laid-off in late-summer on a labor strike; my first and only experience with labor unions. That was hard and hot summer work, which provided strong motivation for using my education, rather than "blue-collar" skills and union controls for employment. After being laid-off from Real Lemon, I worked door-to door marketing of Collier's Encyclopedias, where I became top salesman in the Chicago area, for the final month of my 6-weeks on the job. My third summer, I found employment at the business owned by my step father's friend, in a TV sales and service store in the neighboring suburb of Evergreen Park, doing non-technical handyman type of work, installing roof top antennas, pulling TV chassis from their metal cabinets to assist the technician in making repairs, and installing stereo speakers in car rear seats. The final two summers, I sold home-installed water softeners on a commission-only basis from telephone generated sales leads, in communities near the U of I campus. This was also very successful for added income since the water hardness in central Illinois was very high. Each of these several summer jobs provided great experiences with management, marketing, and mechanical tasks which proved formative in my later career.

Enough background... On to USAF Pilot Training and the beginning of my military career.

CHAPTER 2

USAF Under-Graduate Pilot Training

Pilot Training (Apr 1961 – May '62) — Once my orders arrived 3-months after graduation, I went to the 2nd class of UPT (Under-graduate Pilot Training, all USAF manned), Class 62-G at Moody AFB, Valdosta, GA., reporting to Active Duty in Apr. '61. I trained in the T-37 Primary trainer and T-33 Basic trainer jet aircraft, graduating #13 of 33 students upon completion, in May 1962.

T-37 "Tweety Bird", (Primary)

T-33 "T-Bird" (Basic)

First Impressions — Flying the T-37A was like driving a Jaguar sports car, compared to the Tri-Champ, which was more like a garden tractor! The "Tweety Bird" had two internal fuselage mounted

Continental J69-9, 880-pound thrust, single-stage centrifugal compressor engines, which ran with a high-pitched scream, thus earning it the name of "Tweety Bird" (or "flying dog whistle"). It had a maximum gross weight of approximately 5,500 pounds, and a top speed of about 400 mph, and a range of 930 miles. The student pilot and instructor sat in ejection seats placed side-by-side in a non-pressurized cockpit requiring that both wear oxygen masks and fighter-style hard helmets at all altitudes, for ejection protection and supplemental oxygen above 10,000 feet. This non-pressurization limited normal operations to below 25,000 feet, even though it had a service ceiling of 39,000 feet. The aircraft was so low to the ground, that the pilot could easily stand on the ramp and clean the windshields.

Compared to the prop powered aircraft I had flown in, the inflight cockpit noise level was almost whisper quiet, there was no engine vibration and the action was very fast paced. On my first few training flights, I thought I would never be able to keep up with the frantic and rapid actions required to do an overhead pitchout and break at 1,000 feet above the ground over the end of the runway while flying at 250 kts. (~290 mph), then while banking at 30°, maintaining level flight at 1,000 feet through the first 180° of the turn, dropping the gear and then the flaps, and starting the 300 foot per minute descent to the runway while continuing the turn around the 360° descent. After several days and a lot of "muscle-memory" training, I finally got the rapid drill down to a reflex action and could finally make a "360° overhead break and pitchout by reflex habit as good as any proficient student.

Conducting a two-ship formation take-off with two aircraft on opposite sides of the runway centerline, with number two about half a length behind the lead, was the most awe-inspiring experience of my early career. The image in my memory, of maintaining exact spacing and watching the smooth acceleration and lift-off of both aircraft, as though welded together, was a major image of beautiful coordination. This was really flying!

My best and most loved subject became formation flying, though my initial attempts at rejoining formation caused both me and my instructor, some concern if I would ever get it safely accomplished! I finally "got the picture" and mastered the technique, and then totally enjoyed doing two and four-ship aerobatics (just like the Thunderbirds)! I also seemed to get more than my share of flying Instruments, when the weather was bad. I guess my instructors found me just needing more instrument instruction, than others in my class. Or maybe, I was better at it than my tablemates. My instructor never told me why he chose me for the worst weather in which to perform. This was a total exercise of hard work and much frustration, because ALL the work had to be attended to by just one pilot – working the radios and writing down the lengthy detail flight clearance instructions, flying on instruments with little or no outside visual reference, maintaining altitude, compass direction and airspeed, as well as situational awareness, while keeping touch with Aircraft Traffic Control or Departure/Approach Control. It seemed that there were just too many constantly changing distractions that had to be addressed. It was really hard work, especially when turbulence and precipitation were added into the mix. This was the true reality of flying a fighter-type single-crew aircraft.

After successfully completing a lot of sweat, stationary simulator training, mastery of inflight maneuvers and landings, emergency drills and book learning, I finally passed the 125-flight hour mark and the last "primary" check ride, which was followed by graduation into "basic training" in the T-33, "T-Bird". This was truly a fighter-type aircraft and was the dual cockpit, trainer-version, of the first operational USAF jet fighter; the 1948 single-seat version designated the Lockheed F-80. The T-33 still had the machine gun ports (blocked over) in the nose, and the same basic cockpit configuration as the F-80. It was powered by a single Allison J-33 centrifugal compressor jet engine, which was rated at 4,600 pounds thrust. The aircraft had a max. gross weight of 15,000 pounds (slightly 3-times more than the T-37; a top speed twice that of the T-37 (600 mph; or 521 knots.); a range of 1275 miles, and a service ceiling of 49,000 feet. It had a pressurized tandem 2-pilot cockpit (each with an ejection seat) that offered only about two to three inches space for my shoulders at the canopy rail and stood a little over 7-feet to the sill (bottom) of the closed canopy, which was where one's shoulders were positioned in the cockpit. This gave the true impression of being a much bigger and heavier aircraft, which it was.

With the greater mass (weight) compared to the T-37, the T-33 was slower on acceleration and heavier in the control response to pitch and bank inputs. This made it more complex to fly formation because of its slower response to power changes from its inertia. But flying 4-ship acrobatics was even more challenging and exhilarating to accomplish. Basic training was a refinement of all the things we learned in primary, and really began to demonstrate the skills needed to fly heavier aircraft. The T-33 was also much less forgiving to improper handling, and less sophisticated in its control systems, as compared to the much more refined and simplified, later vintage T-37. Moving the throttle too rapidly or jerkily could cause the large diameter engine to flame-out. And the pilot had to know instantly what switches to activate and throttle position to set to get a quick re-light.

When we arrived at Moody there were only a handful of T-33s on the base. They were being scavenged from bases all over the USAF to replace the T-28 prop powered, former Basic Trainer from the 1950s. When originally collected it had dozens of different cockpit configurations. On some, pressing the side button on the control stick would jettison the tip tanks; on another the same button would engage the nose-wheel steering on the ground. Few were equipped with the latest instrumentation, and the newly implemented "Tiger Start" system, which would do a rapid start, during an engine flame-out with single-switch activation of properly sequenced actions for fuel pump, ignition, and reset of the engine fuel control. Every newly arriving T-Bird had to be sent through a cockpit standardization modification so that all were configured the same. The Basic Training class, 62-F, just four months ahead of ours, was the first to get the T-33 upgrades, so they worked out all of the "bugs" before we moved up to Basic.

The "Triple Nickel Curse" Incident — One "bug" that was missed, created an exciting training flight for me. I was on an instrument flight mission where one of my tasks was to fly some instrument aerobatics "under the hood". The cockpit was configured with a hood, or canvas canopy liner over the aft (student's) cockpit, so the student could not see outside the cockpit and had to rely solely on his instruments (as if flying in the clouds). The maneuver I was challenged to demonstrate was to fly an aerobatic loop solely on instruments. The procedure was identical to what I learned on normal visual (VFR) aerobatics, but had to be flown without any outside visual references. My instructor demonstrated the maneuver from his clear unshielded front cockpit, and talked me through the instrument references that I needed to concentrate on, to do it on instruments alone. Then he told me to perform the maneuver. I added power (from level flight), lowered the nose five degrees on the attitude gyro while maintaining level wings and constant heading on the gyrocompass. Upon reaching entry speed of 400 knots, I pulled back steadily to 6-Gs (grunting to keep from passing out as the forces tried to drain the blood from my head) and maintained wings level (no bank) with the stick straight back all the way into my gut. As the aircraft went through the vertical climb position and the Gs were at +6, the attitude indicator sphere had to do a controlled roll of 180° to maintain a wings level precession as we went upside-down over the top and I checked my heading gyro to assure we came out the bottom of the loop wings level, on original heading. But to my dismay, the heading at the bottom was about 30° off. My Instructor critiqued me that I had failed to apply correct straight back control over the top, as the attitude indicator had done its design-required precession-flip.

He demonstrated the maneuver again (but of course he had the benefit of having all the visual outside cues). I noticed when he did the demo, that he was pulling the stick back diagonally into his lap, rather than straight back. I then mirrored his control movements while paying especially close attention to the wings level indications through the straight up precession-flip. It worked perfectly, but didn't make any sense. I argued with him about this point in the after-flight debrief, but as far as he was concerned, I was just making excuses for my poor initial performance.

"The rest of the story…" A couple weeks later, we heard that a student had encountered a minor incident when he overbanked on landing and had scraped and dented the wingtip tank when it struck the runway. It was the same aircraft — tail number 0555, "Triple Nickel" — that we had flown with the strange high-G roll characteristics. Subsequent maintenance inspection of the aircraft determined that the fore and aft wing spars at the fuselage were both broken, explaining that previous incident we had incurred. Under the high-G pull up, the wing was actually twisting due to the broken wing spars causing the whole wing to act as an aileron! Under more similar forces, a further center spar failure might have caused the wing to completely break off, resulting in a catastrophic accident. The aircraft was judged as uneconomical to repair, or "Class-26" and retired to a monument pedestal at a nearby former WWII Georgia training base. Some of the more senior students in our class told us that in MAC (Military Airlift Command) there was a fable that aircraft with "Triple Nickel" tail numbers were accident prone, or cursed.

Beginning to look like there really IS an angel on my shoulder!!

Missed Limited Fighter Pilot Opportunity — On my final flight in the T-33, I had a once-in-a-lifetime opportunity. Since our monthly pay had an additional flight pay of $125, we were required to fly at least 4-hours each month in order to earn it, and that amounted to about 25% of my pay for any given month. Since graduation was scheduled to be in mid-month of May, I had to fly at least 1-hour and 50 minutes (1+50) to gain my pro-rated adjusted-flight pay, and there was no guess as to how long after graduation, before my next flight duty might occur, while having to move family and household somewhere across the country and get established in my next assignment, before reporting for duty. I had completed all the other requirements for graduation to be awarded my Pilot's wings, but the training squadron made provisions for everyone to get their flight pay for (at least) the final month. I dug into the "Dash-1" Pilot's manual and computed the maximum endurance flight time I could achieve (with regulatory fuel reserves) and determined that the maximum endurance was 2 hrs +10 mins, but required climbing to 40,000 feet and operating there at a slow "maximum endurance" airspeed (about 225 knots). In other words, any acrobatics, or low-level operations would consume extra fuel and reduce the time aloft, which would cause forfeiture of flight pay.

Shortly after taking off, the yellow engine "Fuel-Ice" warning light came on. Based upon the "Dash 1" Emergency procedures, it stated that unless the pilot could confirm this was a false Warning, he should lighten the aircraft fuel load (i.e. Jettison the external wing-tip fuel tanks), and land as soon as practical (before the potentially iced fuel caused the engine to flame out). Located about 12-miles from the Moody AFB Runway was an abandoned WWII training base with its cross-shaped runway, at the edge of the Okefenokee Swamp. The Moody SOP (Standard Operating Procedure) in such an emergency was to dive on the abandoned Runway and try and drop the wingtip tanks onto that field, so that the fuel tanks would cause no damage to public or inhabited property, and the wreckage of the tanks could be recovered. This was the closest a student could ever get to "dropping bombs" and was probably on every student's "bucket list". Now I was confronted with a hard decision. I could either realize my desire to drop the tip-tanks as if bombing an enemy, without any repercussions of destroying Government property or breaking the rules, but that would prevent me from earning any portion of my May flight pay. Or I could continue to climb to altitude and fly out my flight pay requirement. Considering that it was a hot day and that it was unlikely that I had ice in the fuel lines at low altitude, I let my greed for meager flight pay over-ride safety precautions, knowing that I could remain close to the base at 40,000 feet and still have a margin of safety. So I opted to forfeit my opportunity to punch off the tip-tanks, and save the taxpayers for the several hundred dollars cost of these surplus WWII tip tanks!

The assignment tradition, at that time, was that each graduating training base would get a list of assignments equal to the number of graduates, with a wide variety of aircraft-types, and with their matching Base locations from which to be chosen. The highest scoring student of the class would draw first choice. Each following class members would draw according to his placement in standings from the remaining assignments. Days later, after receiving the list of 33 aircraft assignments for post-graduation, my classmates and I did a mini-selection the night before, so members might know what was left when their official selection turn came around. Graduating #13 of 33, I chose the last F-100 fighter assignment rather than spending another year or more at Moody as a T-33 Instructor (the only "single-seat" assignment left to choose). The next day the student directly ahead of me changed his mind at the last minute and selected the last F-100 fighter assignment. (Ironically, he was killed in Vietnam two years later in that aircraft! —"There but for the hand of God, go I").

[There's that angel on my shoulder again, keeping me on my destiny's path, and safe from harm!]

CHAPTER 3

First Operational Assignment (1962 - '67)

Aircraft Assignment After UPT Completion – I selected my secondary choice, a TC-47 Navigation trainer at my hometown of Chicago (O'Hare Field, on Chicago's northwest side, about 15 miles from Oak Lawn) betting on the upcoming upgrade to T-29s (a converted late '50s twin-engine airliner), projected to be soon replaced by jet-powered Nav Trainers thus causing the T-29s to replace the TC-47s for the Reserves. (The C-47, the Stearman, and the P-51 had always on my "bucket list" to fly, so my alternate TC-47 choice, combined with returning to Pat's birthplace and my former family location seemed an obvious good choice. And having 5- "more-senior" pilot trainees in my UPT Class, who were former USAF navigators, that were cross-training from multi-engine aircraft to Pilot wings, we had been exposed to their recommendations that flying the multi-engine aircraft offered better flying experience, more hours, better global opportunities, and more stable promotions).

Convair T-29 Navigation Trainer

TC-47 Pilot at O'Hare International Airport – After being awarded my Pilots Wings, Pat and I were on our way to our first assignment — *back to Chicago*. We at least had a place to stay upon arrival, and we moved in with my parents in Oak Lawn, for about 3-months until we could move closer to O'Hare. While still on leave before my report-in date, I travelled to the "military base" at O'Hare Field to find the location, get acquainted with my new unit, and get a tour of the facility. The Air Force Reserve and the Illinois Air National Guard had airport property amounting to long-term custody of the nearly 230 acres, (about 12% of the O'Hare field acreage), at the northeast corner of the 2000-acre airport real estate.

O'hare Field — Originally called Orchard Place ("ORD", as its FAA designation), the site of Douglas Field, had a long history dating back to WW II, and began as a location for a WWII Douglas Aircraft Plant that manufactured the USAF C-54 (DC-4), 4-engine transport. Of the total of 1,170 total C-54s manufactured during WWII, 655 – about half – were manufactured at the Orchard Place, Douglas Field plant. The Douglas manufacturing facility included a ½-mile long wooden beamed, L-shaped hangar facility large enough to hold an assembly line of approximately 100, C-54 aircraft, at a time. The Douglas plant ceased operation in 1945, and the airport property was subsequently renamed with the construction of Chicago's O'Hare International Airport in 1949 to honor Edward O'Hare, the U.S. Navy's first flying ace and Medal of Honor recipient in World War II.

Douglas C-54 (DC-4), 4-engined Big-sister of the C-47

After the closure of the Douglas Plant, the military facility became home of a Continental Air Command (ConAC, later renamed "AF Reserve Command") Troop Carrier Group flying C-46 "Commando" aircraft and then C-119 "Flying Boxcar" transports, plus (up until 1960), a squadron of F-86D Air Defense Command fighter-interceptors. Tucked into the corner of the condemned old Douglas L-shaped hanger was the 3-aircraft TC-47 Navigation Training detachment, Det 4 2223rd Instruction Squadron (Det 4, 2223rd INSTRON), where I was assigned. It was in a refurbished Douglas flight line office building that comfortably accommodated the 25 active duty personnel assigned, and had classrooms, locker rooms and office space for the up-to-250 AF Reserve Navigators assigned to the Civil Reserve Air Fleet's (CRAF) Midwest sector.

The CRAF organization was a post-WWII Department of Defense (DoD) program that had paper-assignment of a large fleet of commercial airline passenger and cargo transport aircraft, to support a future wartime contingency, and was originated after the Berlin Airlift operations ended in 1952. Its purpose was to place military trained and proficient Navigators on board commercial aircraft with commercial crews to fly emergency global military airlift in the event of war. And it was the mission of fourteen Navigator Training Detachments of ConAC, located all around the

Continental US, to train and maintain proficiency of these "weekend warrior" Navigators, and maintain their administrative and training records.

Although the Douglas manufacturing plant was mostly deserted and condemned when I arrived, the original larger separate Douglas Office Administration building had been refurbished into an on-base Officers Housing Apartment Building and small Officer's Club. However, it only contained about 10 apartments and there was no occupancy available or foreseen when I arrived (especially for a 2nd Lieutenant). So Pat and I found a nice little 850 sq.ft., 2-bedroom home with a detached 2-car garage and workshop, located in the northwest suburb of Rolling Meadows. It was only about six miles, by road, from the military gate (and three miles out on the glide slope of O'Hare's busiest, Runway 14R). With no air-conditioning, and windows open in summer, we seldom got to see a full TV program due to the 500-foot fly-overs of commercial jets and prop aircraft on short final with the included noise and horizontal rolling of our TV picture.

But life was good. We were moving into a cute 5-year old pre-owned home. We had also purchased, from the sellers, a lot of needed furniture, appliances and even garden tools and lawn furniture and I had a new job that paid me a take-home salary of $405 per month, which included $105 for housing allowance and $150 for flight pay, not to mention 100% medical care for myself and family for life. (Unfortunately, Congress reneged on the medical portion of the recruiting incentive in the '70s when they converted retirees (veteran and family) to salary-contribution Medicare at age 65). Pat found a job at O'Hare as a Hertz Rent-a-Car sales representative, which more than doubled our monthly income.

Detachment - 4 Operations – For me, as a new USAF pilot, it was a great opportunity to gain a lot of unique flying experience (for a first assignment, flying out of the world's busiest airport), plus orientation and knowledge of all the functions of running a squadron. My primary duty was as a pilot with the opportunity for personal

OJT (on the job training) and flight experience to rapidly upgrade from copilot to pilot-in-command. Plus every crewmember had multiple additional duty responsibilities to perform – duties that would normally be done by dedicated assignees in a 100-man squadron consisting of leaders, administrators, NCOs and airmen (Commander, Operations Officer, Navigation Training Officer, Administrative Officer, etc.).

TC-47 Navigation Trainer (Early 1960 Paint Scheme)

C-47 Aircraft Impressions — I had gained my pilot's wings through "all-jet UPT" Training. I suddenly found myself flying in a vintage WWII fleet of three TC-47s. The C-47 was of mid-1930's, pre–WWII design *(before my birth)* and was a relatively simple, "seat-of-the-pants" airplane to operate. These TC-47 aircraft at O'Hare were all 1942 Tail Numbers. They had twin 1200 hp double-row, 14-cylinder radial, air-cooled, reciprocating engines (Pratt & Whitney R1830-90Ds) each turning a hydraulic variable-pitch, constant-speed 11.5-foot diameter Hamilton-Standard paddle blade propeller. The aircraft was a "tail dragger" with a cruising speed of 140 mph (125 knots), and range of approximately 1,500 miles. It was unpressurized and carried only minimal onboard oxygen for the flight crew, so was nominally restricted from altitudes above 12,000 feet, but was physically capable of cruising up to 25,000 feet with built-in engine superchargers (left over from WWII modifications for flying the CBI – China, Burma, India

"Hump" – but now locked permanently into the "low blower" configuration). With this totally "obsolete" equipment configuration and performance, I found myself basically having to learn how to fly all over again, after all-jet training.

The aircraft systems were antiquated, and even "unsophisticated", due to their design parameters and pre-WWII engineering technology. Instrumentation consisted of engine manifold-pressure driven vacuum (suction) gyros. An autopilot containing two vacuum driven gyros (one for heading the other for pitch) that were non-integrated and not stabilized by magnetic flux gate (compass), nor altitude hold (barometric) features. These gyros were tied to hydraulic servos that moved the flight control surfaces – a very rudimentary system. An autopilot turn required the pilot to rotate three control knobs simultaneously to generate a "coordinated" heading change of inputs to aileron (bank), rudder (yaw), and elevator (pitch), so it was seldom used except during essentially straight and level flight, for long duration intervals.

The system gauges (hydraulics for landing gear, flaps, and engine-cooling cowl flaps) were round boiler gauges that read pressure, which the operator (copilot) had to observe – hydraulic pressure when static, then pressure drop (when the component was actuated) and then return the valve handle to an intermediate position to lock the actuator movement when the gear or flaps stopped in the selected position. The landing gear also incorporated a mechanical device to physically lock the handle down, when the gear was down.

The fluid lines behind the instrument panel, also were not "Murphy-Proofed", but all used common diameter tubing and common fittings, so there was no built-in mechanical safety against maintenance actions inadvertently mixing pitot & static pressure lines (airspeed & altimeter indicators), with manifold suction sources (for gyros), or hydraulic lines – a potential for disaster after instrument panel gauges were replaced or disturbed.

Other cockpit instruments were also "boiler gauge" indicators for hydraulic quantity, fuel and oil indicators, with valve hardware that looked like it belonged on a steam locomotive. It seemed to be designed (obviously) by civil engineers – i.e. "Rube Goldberg" – (prior to the specialized aeronautical engineering style of my background), and with little or no implementation of ergonomic designs, and with system designs more typical to its origins of the 1930s and '40s, rather than of the mid-1960's when I was trained.

The flap indicator was a linear slider about 10-inches long, which originally was mounted vertically along the left side of the Pilot's instrument panel. The slider was moved along the scale, marked in 1/4 flap increments, by a push-pull cable mechanically attached in the wing to the flap actuator mechanism. This was logical in that the slider moved UP toward zero flaps (flaps UP) and downward (to flaps FULL down). But over the years, as the instrument panel became more crowded, the indicator panel was rotated 90° clockwise to a horizontal position along the bottom of the instrument panel. Then flaps FULL was to the left end, and flaps UP was to the right (neither intuitive, nor ergonometric).

The C-47 maximum take-off weight, for a transport, was light, (originally 31,000 pounds, but restricted to 25,000 in the late 50's due to age and structural concerns) with a payload of 6,000 pounds, (measured after basic weight and operational equipment and fuel are excluded). The basic C-47 had 25 passenger seats in the cabin, but the TC-47 had only eight to accommodate 8-navigators and their work tables.

Most significantly, the use of a tail wheel – common to all early aircraft – required new pilot techniques for me to learn during take-offs, landings and taxiing. On the ground, because of the high nose attitude, the pilot could not see directly forward, and had to zigzag in order to keep sight of visual obstacles ahead, pavement edges, and painted taxi or runway lines. With this configuration, obviously the aircraft center of gravity, had to be aft of the main gear, which then set up a natural tendency to cause the airplane to ground loop like a castoring action if the tail deviated very far left or right of the direction the nose was pointed. (This is known as directional instability – the farther the deviation, the more it wants to deviate further in the same direction.) Being a "tail-dragger" meant that upon entering the aircraft from the standard entry door located on the left side about 20-feet forward of the aft tip of the tail, the pilots were facing an approximately 15° uphill climb to the cockpit, which was about 40 feet forward from their entry point. This meant that loading baggage, briefcases of flight manuals, maps and charts and large coffee urns and other cargo was all the more difficult. It felt like hill-climbing before every flight!

C-47 Flying Impressions — Operating a "low-and-slow" aircraft, intermingled with commercial jet and heavy prop aircraft, at what was then the world's busiest airport, was quite challenging and provided lots of lessons, which few other USAF pilots ever had the opportunity to experience. O'Hare was the first airport to have dual parallel runways operating simultaneously under IFR conditions. It was the first airport to test and adopt the ATIS system (Automated Terminal Information System) to eliminate the amount of radio chatter regarding runway, wind, altimeter and weather broadcasts. It was the first airport to implement abbreviated clearance delivery on a separate ground frequency, and was the first to implement a surface-control radar in the Tower for handling high volumes of ground aircraft taxiway-traffic.

TC-47 Navigation Trainer (Mid-1960 Paint Scheme)

That being said, the C-47 was a very relaxing and nostalgic airplane to fly. Despite its 25,000 pound limited maximum gross weight, it was an airplane that could still be flown be "the seat of the pants" with little or no need to spend any time computing "Take-off and Landing", or "Cruise Performance Data". I learned very quickly that it burned an average of 100 gallons of fuel per hour at cruise for both engines (50-gal each engine), which gave it a maximum full to dry tanks of about 8-hours. The approach speed on final (compared to the jets) seemed to take as long to fly from the final approach fix to the touchdown as to provide enough time for a last cup of coffee. And it was completely forgiving and docile when in flight under most any wind or weather condition. And it could readily be landed on a grass field or unpaved runway, with its large balloon tires. However, it could be a real handful on a crosswind landing, and like all "tail draggers" had a potential for unexpected ground loops.

I will never forget my first supervised take-off at O'Hare. Without any before-flight review or counseling by my Instructor Pilot, I attempted a rolling take-off (like I had learned in the T-37), advancing the throttles from taxi speed to full throttle more rapidly than wise. With the different inertia between the two engines, each accelerating the big diameter props at a different speed, I found the aircraft suddenly careening toward the runway's edge. My rudder input was too rapid and over-controlling and we careened toward the other side as the aircraft accelerated and the rudder became more effective. Sitting in the left seat, my left knee was trapped by the bottom of the control yoke arm which was canted at about 30° over my knee when I pushed the right rudder in. Although the tail wheel swivel-lock had been engaged before take-off roll, that only provided a spring loaded limit to the amount that the tail wheel could swivel from straight ahead, and I found myself initially swerving from runway shoulder to opposite shoulder before I finally understood the error of my lack of experience and caught up. I obviously gave the commercial pilots in the jets behind me a chuckle of amazement at my incompetence and poor handling!

(That surely didn't reflect a high degree of experience from my Instructor, either.) But I still had a lot to absorb and a lot to learn about flying this otherwise gentle lady.

Additional Duties – My principal additional duties were largely oriented to utilize my College training as an Aeronautical Engineer, and my recent AFROTC military training. They included being Detachment Flying Safety Officer, and Maintenance Liaison Officer for the aircraft. (Heavy maintenance was provided by the Air Reserve Technician maintenance unit that handled the C-119 Group aircraft, and later the KC-97 Tanker Squadron aircraft assigned on the base). I also was trained in the Detachment to become an aircrew ground and flight Instructor, and had leadership responsibilities for supervising the 5-Flight Mechanic NCOs and overseeing their scheduling, discipline and performance evaluations, over the entire term of this first assignment. *[More about Additional Duties later.]*

Working primarily with the "week-end warriors", our workweek was Wednesday through Sunday, with Monday and Tuesday as our normal "week-end" days off. On Wednesday our work was oriented toward active-duty type of administrative responsibilities (office paper work) and ground school training, plus various non-flying types of duty. It was also a flying proficiency day for those of us that were active-duty crew members to train by flying a 3 to 4 hour flight – usually over to Greater Rockford Airport, 30-miles NW of O'Hare, or Navy Glenview 15 miles NE of O'Hare, for traffic patterns, emergency procedures, instrument approaches, and touch-and-go landing practice, and general proficiency. (O'Hare traffic was unsuited for local proficiency-practice training).

Thursdays also provided time for more deskwork, but most weeks Thursday afternoons were set aside for physical training consisting of optional golf, indoor volleyball (during cold or inclement weather), or boating & water skiing at nearby small lakes. (Only two of us had outboard boats, which was a popular diversion when the weather was nice, but too hot for golf. And since our regular "week-end" off time was Mon. and Tues., we seldom had to deal with the usual crowds of the standard weekend when off-time boating was also done).

Friday afternoons we flew one or two aircraft on day-night navigation training missions typically of 5 to 6-hours duration. A typical navigation proficiency mission was a triangular round-robin flight, giving up-to-8 onboard navigator "trainees" the opportunity for three navigation legs using basic map reading, celestial navigation, dead reckoning planning, and nav-logging experience. Our missions preferred VFR conditions (Visual Flight Rules) so that we could fly without being required to fly on designated electronic airways, which were less flexible and were pilot oriented navigation, rather than Navigator (student) controlled.

Saturdays we again flew two similar missions, one in the morning and one in late afternoon/evening. Often, the weather would require instrument conditions so we would try to fly out of O'Hare under IFR (Instrument Flight Rules) clearance to another location where we could get some time using VFR flying with more navigation flexibility.

Sundays we flew again starting about noon with one or two aircraft. With a Navigator contingent of up to 200 navigators, we had that group broken down into smaller "Flights" so that we could have both ground and flight activities for different manpower "Flights" each weekend of the month. All Reservist Navigators had to fly at least once per month for flight pay and currency.

Special Missions – Six times per year we would do an incentive-flight of 5-6 days for the Reservists (and ourselves) where we would do long overwater flights that would go either to Bermuda, refueling at either Dover AFB, DE or Charleston AFB, SC with 48 to 72 hours spent in Bermuda. When the weather was unfavorable at Bermuda (too cold, or during hurricane season) we would fly to Ramey AFB in Puerto Rico with port of entry/departure at Homestead AFB, FL. Or alternately, we might do a trip to Biggs AFB, TX (El Paso), for a visit (by ground) to Juarez, Mexico for shopping, duty-free liquor-purchase, and sightseeing. (Fortunately, this was long before the time of drug cartels and illegal immigrations). These special trips were always popular and provided a break from the heavy at-home routine of flying and training.

Other Personal Anecdotes Flying the C-47 (TC-47)

Low-Level Desert Departure — The great thing about any kind of flying is that you are constantly being challenged, and constantly learning new lessons (at least, if you want to survive!). In one of my earliest days in the C-47 — while I was still only co-pilot qualified — our unit had a mission to take one of our three aircraft into a depot facility for an IRAN (Inspect and Repair As Needed) depot overhaul. The contractor that had been selected by headquarters was located in Hondo, TX in the west Texas desert. We departed Chicago mid-week with two airplanes — mine for depot input, and the second to bring the first crew home. After dodging weather and flying over seven hours we arrived in Hondo in late afternoon. After signing over the aircraft to the contractor, the "lead pilot" (the onboard Detachment Operations Officer, Maj. William S – a cigar smoking Gen LeMay look-alike – and also rated Instructor Pilot) had decided there was nothing worth visiting in Hondo and we were going to fly over to El Paso for an overnight crew rest, a relatively short distance away

Since I was still in training for the left seat, and we had two instructor pilots between the two involved crews, it was decided that I would fly the left seat as an instructional ride in the aircraft that would carry both crews to El Paso. There was a sense of hurry to get to our "fun-destination" as we walked across the ramp to our waiting aircraft. My instructor pilot divided up the exterior preflight saying that I should do the aft portion of the outside inspection, the other instructor would check the front half, and "the boss" would do the preliminary cockpit copilot preflight.

Then once I arrived on the flight deck, together we would run the "Before Engine Start" checklist and those items that followed.

As I performed my aft half of the exterior preflight, I noted that, in the landing and shutdown haste, the crew flying this aircraft had failed to return elevator trim to the neutralized position (reset to zero-nose-up trim). But I didn't have much experience, so that little detail was of no real significance to me (yet!). When I arrived on the flight deck, I was rushed to get the engines started for departure from the left seat. At the point when the checklist challenge on "Elevator Trim" was made, I didn't quite hear what was asked and, my response was, "Say again". The instructor, assuming the "habitual" correct reply, advanced to the next checklist item. *(That's the second procedural deviation. Did you catch the first? — <u>The bad decision to split "team work" of the exterior checklist items between multiple pilots</u>)?*

Completing all the rest of the items, we started engines, taxied for take-off and began our take-off roll. At this point I had only performed a handful of left seat take-offs, but something seemed strange. Normally, shortly after starting the take-off roll, the tail of the C-47 automatically starts to fly (at about 30 knots), bringing the fuselage deck angle close to horizontal. Then once reaching flying speed (at about 80 knots) the aircraft becomes airborne with little elevator input from the pilot, even from the beginning of the roll. In this situation, however, the aircraft accelerated normally, but the tail never came up, and suddenly we became airborne at about 50 knots just barely above the stall speed. Almost instantly the mis-trimmed elevator observation flashed into my mind and I began pushing the controls forward with my left hand as I struggled to roll the trim wheel (next to my right knee on the throttle quadrant) forward with my right hand. Simultaneously, the instructor pilot started yelling "I have the aircraft", and also reaching for the trim wheel with his left hand.

Murphy (of "Murphy's Law") was quick to jump into the fray, because as the instructor in the right seat became preoccupied with the elevator trim wheel, he let go of the throttles that he was guarding in the (full-throttle) take-off-power position. The throttle friction, being tired and worn on these 20 year-old aircraft, was not operating up to par and the right throttle slid back to about 65% power. Here we are with excessive nose up trim, flying in a nose high attitude barely above the stall speed only a few feet off the desert and in an asymmetric power-induced right turn off the runway heading. Thank God for the vast empty desert at Hondo, Texas! *[There's that terrific angel on my shoulder again!]*

"High Speed" Instrument Approach — At the time of this incident, I had been checked out as aircraft commander (left seat pilot in command) for only a few months and had very little actual weather time on instruments in the C-47. As we returned to O'Hare on that cloudy and drizzly fall Sunday afternoon, in 1962, the field was operating at near IFR minimums, and it was during peak take-off and landing times for the week-end flying at O'Hare. Landings were being conducted on their primary instrument runway, 14R, and the other parallel runway, 14L, was being used for simultaneous departures. The arrival traffic was heavy and stacked up more than 20 aircraft out. After having been airborne for nearly 5-hours, we were given our first holding pattern about 125 miles to the west of Chicago. We spent about 20 minutes "in the soup" with light turbulence at 9,000 feet and then were sequentially cleared into a closer holding fix and were gradually working our way down to lower altitudes at the bottom of the stack. After over an hour of bumpy and very fatiguing IFR holding, in the typical heavy Sunday afternoon peak commercial traffic, we were finally number one for the ILS (Instrument Landing System) precision self-guided beacon approach. Approach Control asked if I could maintain 140 knots to the marker for traffic separation with the heavy-jets. I advised (with a verbal smile) that the only way we could sustain that speed was in a power-on dive, but that I could give them 120 to the outer marker, if that would help. Approach thanked me and cleared me for my first real IFR approach to minimums, since pilot training.

I crossed the outer marker on glideslope at 120 knots, a speed too high to allow lowering approach flaps (104 knots limited). As I called the "marker Beacon" passing to Approach Control, they asked if I could maintain 120 to the threshold (just above runway touchdown). I explained my flap limitation and told the controller I could give him 100 knots on final. This really increased my normal descent rate to remain on the ILS glide path. The turbulence and tension had me soaking with sweat, but I was flying on their turf in a slow bird, so we were trying to be accommodating (not to mention my anticipation that they would send us out of the sequence to hold some more while they gave priority to the gas guzzling commercial jet traffic).

A similar C-47 with tail still flying to fast, immediately after touch-down.

As I crossed the threshold at about 50 feet in the air, with throttles in idle and nearly twenty knots above take-off speed, O'Hare Tower advised me there was a heavy 707 on short final behind me and requested that I make the first high-speed turn-off, which was only about 2500 feet from the touchdown point (and I was already forced to land long by my faster approach speed)! As I neared the turn off, we were still doing almost 60 knots indicated – barely above flaps-down stall speed – and I made the turn off with the tail still airborne and both feet hunkering down hard on the mushy brakes. As I looked over my shoulder, I saw —sure enough — the 707 in the "squat" of her flare less than 2000 feet behind me (and at about twice my turn-off speed).

Boeing 707 in Landing "Squat"

I had never experienced, or been trained in a "tail-dragger" to do such a maneuver, and had not ever even considered the potential for making a high-speed ground loop if I didn't literally "fly the airplane around the corner" with the tail still in the air! ***[There's that angel on my shoulder again, keeping me out of harm's way!]***

When my tension finally settled down and I got back into the Squadron Ops area, I picked up the hot-line to the Tower and informed them of the potential hazard they had created by "directing" the high-speed approach followed by their "direction" that I should make the first turn-off.

The Tower response was to inform me that they had no authority to "<u>direct</u>" the pilot in flight to do anything out of the ordinary, that this was only a <u>request</u>! *(Didn't sound like a request to me! — <u>Lesson Learned!</u>)*

Twin Engine Glider — Nearing the end of another 6-1/2 hour Sunday afternoon VFR navigation mission, we were in a gradual descent from 7,500 feet, heading into O'Hare from the west. I was flying co-pilot and the Squadron's grizzly old cigar smoking Operations Officer, a former WWII B-17 pilot, named Major Wm S, (the same Instructor from the Hondo incident) was in the left seat. The TC-47 we were flying had been experiencing somewhat high fuel consumption rate on the right engine, and throughout the flight we had been using periodic abnormal fuel sequencing to keep the fuel weight in the wings equalized to eliminate a heavy wing.

Suddenly, in the midst of the letdown, both engines went silent without as much as a surge or a pop. I was surprised to learn (several years later) that the constant speed regulated props, combined with normal airspeed, kept the engines turning at near normal RPM. But the sudden silence was deafening! Many of you have heard the off-color joke about what causes the fastest romantic four hand movement in the world — well I'm here to attest that I saw the fastest four hands in action that day, with both mixtures rapidly advanced to Rich, both boost pumps switched ON and both fuel selectors repositioned to a different tank (ones with fuel in them)! Almost as quickly as they had quit, both engines returned to their usual noisy and comforting rumble before more than 100 feet of altitude (and probably only a couple seconds) had been lost!

To better understand this incident, one needs a little bit of insight into the "Rube Goldberg" C-47 fuel management system. The airplane was designed and built long before ergonomic considerations were invented. In fact, I think "Rube Goldberg" was one of the principal designers of the aircraft! There are two identical five-position bat-handled mechanical fuel tank selector valves, located one on either side of the throttle console down near the bottom of the instrument panel — one for each engine. (See picture below). Due to their location neither pilot could see both valve selectors from their normal seat position, without leaning over toward the center of the aisle to see around the obstructing throttle console. Each valve could select, for its respective engine, either OFF or fuel from any of the four tanks — left, or right inboard wing-tanks, and left, or right outboard wing-tanks. In this way, the pilots could feed fuel from any available tank to any operating engine. Adding to Rube Goldberg's unique design concept, there was a mechanical four-tank fuel quantity gauge that rotated like a central-mounted 4-bladed fan blade behind the glass instrument face, with only one blade visible at a time. This multiple gauge was rotated by means of a control knob permitting the pilots to view the quantity of only one of the tanks at a time.

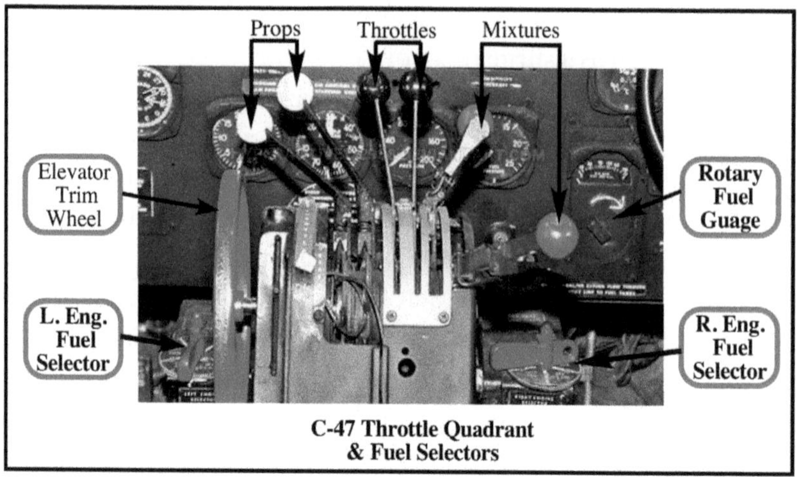

C-47 Throttle Quadrant & Fuel Selectors

Normal procedure was to make initial take-off on the fullest tanks (usually the inboard mains) with the **left** engine selected to the **left inboard** and the **right** engine to the **right inboard** tanks, respectively. During the flight normally the tanks would be checked and switched every hour to the alternate tank on the same side as the engine — after rotating the quantity gauge, through all its four positions, then setting the engine mixtures to Rich and the boost pumps ON, (*i.e.* **left** engine from **left** inboard main tank to **left** outboard main, and **right** engine from **right** inboard main to **right** outboard main tank).

With the right engine having a higher than normal consumption rate, on this particular flight, as we neared the sixth hour tank change, the "boss" said, "I'll put my engine (left) on my outboard (left) tank, and you put your engine (right) on the left inboard". Since we were entering O'Hare's arrival zone things started getting busy and I got preoccupied from doing my periodic fuel readings. Unbeknownst to either of us, we had inadvertently both selected the same left inboard fuel tank, while the rotary fuel quantity gauge had ended up being selected to the left outboard tank. With both engines burning from the same left tank, all of that tank's fuel had been depleted and both engines had been simultaneously run out of fuel! ***[Only a small assist needed from my Guardian Angel!]***

Inflight Engine Failure — We were on the second half of an over-water mission returning to home base (Chicago O'Hare) on a day VFR summer's day from Bermuda. The 6-hour flight to the east coast had been uneventful to Charleston AFB, SC. where we made a refueling stop. The aircraft was fairly heavily loaded since all 4-primary crewmembers, plus all 8-Reserve Navigators had taken advantage of their periodic Customs benefit to buy 2-cases each of twelve quart Duty-Free bottles of alcohol, liqueurs, or other alcoholic equivalent, as well as some souvenir furniture, and jewelry. The take-off from Charleston was normal and we had planned an extended dog-leg to fly northwest over Lansing MI, and then a dog-leg across Lake Michigan so we could maximize our training with a second short overwater leg before home. Departing Charleston, the ambient temperature was in the low nineties, and with the extra 2 to 3,000 lbs of duty-free spirits and cargo, the TC-47 climb was very listless and slow. We climbed to 8,500 feet for our VFR westerly heading and set cruise power. After several minutes, I detected an irregular shudder of the airframe. I quickly scanned all of the engine instruments, and all looked symmetric and normal between the two engines. I visually checked the front of the left engine from the pilot's side window, then I leaned forward looking across the copilot's position and scanned the right engine. I could see the right engine cowling twisting slightly and then releasing, like an over-wound clock spring. The visual "torqueing" of the cowling coincided with the shudder that I felt and heard. Another check of the engine instruments showed everything remaining unchanged, except for the right engine cylinder head temperature, which was slightly reduced from that of the left, and there was a slight loss of cruise airspeed and a slight yaw to the right.

By this time we were over 100 miles from Charleston, and that meant 100 miles closer to home, but still over 4 hours to go. We shut down the right engine, declaring and emergency and altering heading for a direct course to O'Hare, eliminating the dog-leg. As we tried to maintain our 8,500 ft altitude our indicated airspeed gradually fell from 115 knots to 100 knots and continued to degrade. We notified ATC of our problems and changed our destination to Wright Patterson AFB, Dayton, OH. There was a lot of grousing from the Reservist Navigators wondering if they were going to be forced to jettison their precious bargain cargo of liquor and souvenirs, and speculate what would have happened if the engine failure had occurred over the Atlantic.

We began a slow 200 to 400 feet per minute descent in order to maintain our 90 knot adjusted cruise airspeed and to protect the left engine from overheating. Once in range of the Wright-Patterson Tower, we confirmed our emergency for a preferential handling and made an uneventful single engine landing. The maintenance folks there found metal shaving in the oil sumps and filter and determined that a piston or cylinder had failed from the heat and prolonged time at climb power. We contacted home base in Chicago, and they dispatched another TC-47 to come and recover our Reservists, so they could get back to their civilian lives the next day. We left our flight mechanic NCO with the airplane at Wright–Patterson while it was undergoing an engine change. Four days later, we returned with two pilots on the second TC-47 and picked up the repaired aircraft and flight mechanic for flight back to O'Hare.

In my total C-47 experience (including that in my subsequent Vietnam assignment in the EC-47) for a total of nearly 3,000 hours, this was the only true inflight reciprocating engine failure that I ever experienced. This spoke exceedingly well of the reliability and durability of the vintage WWII Pratt & Whitney R-1830, 14-cylinder twin-stack air-cooled radial which powered many WWII fighters, bombers and transport aircraft. 173,600 of these engines were produced from 1932 to 1951, powering such renowned aircraft as the C-47, B-24, PBY Catalina, and over 65 more international transports and bombers.

Uncontrolled Prop Feathering Incident — During the five-years that I flew the vintage WWII C-47 at Chicago O'Hare Airport in the mid-1960s, I accumulated nearly 2,000 hours of flight time, during which I experienced only two engine failures — one of which proved to actually be a prop feathering solenoid failure and NOT an actual engine failure.

It was shortly after take-off on a very frigid night departure, when I noticed an asymmetric thrust–induced yaw and noted the number 2 (right) engine RPM winding down. I assumed an engine failure caused by congealed engine oil in the oil cooler due to the frigid ground cold-soak prior to take-off — a not unknown precautionary condition. I called for completion of the Engine Failure Checklist, while I shut down the engine. To my amazement, after the propeller went into full feather and the right (#2) engine RPM dropped to zero, the propeller began turning again as the prop cycled out of feather on the "dead" #2 engine. Initially I couldn't understand this because the magneto and fuel for that engine were, by this time, both OFF from the Emergency engine shutdown procedure. And since the engine was not running, but rather cycling between zero and normal wind-milling RPM, we were still losing airspeed and had to descend to maintain speed above stall. *According to the aircraft Dash 1 (operations manual), in the event of an engine failure where the prop cannot be feathered, only a controlled descent can be achieved.* Fortunately, we were not much above traffic pattern altitude and were still within a couple miles of our departure and we quickly declared an Emergency and returned to our take-off base (Chicago O'Hare).

On the post-incident investigation, I confirmed that the engine had not failed, but that the prop-feathering solenoid (located on the forward wheel-well bulkhead just above the oil cooler) had suffered an age related mechanical/electrical failure. The solenoid of this vintage 1940's design was nothing more than a big electromagnet coil, that when activated pulls a plunger, that in turn pulls the arm of a contact switch to the "contact-closed" position. This switch in-turn applies power to the prop-feathering oil pump. Once the prop blades go to the full-feathered position this switch is automatically tripped. And the pump stops running. A second activation of the system, trips the switch closed again, which turns on the pump and returns the blade position to what the prop-governer RPM was set for. This solenoid had a large electrical coil (about 2-1/4 inch in diameter and about 3 inches tall) and was bolted together to the contactor switch with four long external rod-screws at the four corners of the electromagnetic coil spool running the length of the coil with the switch contacts at the top. The Bakelite housing, through which the four vertical bolts passed, had cracked due to age and vibration, bringing a bolt in contact with one of the electrical terminals, which in turn had shorted and fused the contacts closed. The result was that the feathering motor was activated ON at the instant of failure and was running continuously regardless of the feathering switch position in the cockpit, thus continuously recycling the prop from cruise RPM to full-feather (zero-RPM) and then back to unfeather, again and again. I subsequently made close examination of this solenoid as part of all of my future pre-flight inspections.

This condition was actually more serious than an actual engine failure. In that case, had the prop successfully feathered with the engine shut down, and remained feathered, we could have maintained flight on one-engine without difficulty!

Had I better understood at the time, the characteristics of the prop governor on a constant speed prop, I would have realized that a normal engine failure would NOT induce a significantly decreasing prop RPM as long as there was sufficient airspeed to windmill the prop, and the engine hadn't seized from mechanical fault or lack of lubrication. Then I might not have been as quick to diagnose the problem as an engine failure. Although, getting it on the ground ASAP was still the proper procedure.

[I subsequently participated on crash investigation of a fatal AC-47 gunship off Nha Trang Vietnam in 1967. There were strong indications that the crash may have been the result of a similar prop feathering failure during slow flight orbit at night just offshore when there was no visible horizon reference.]

Startling C-47 Snap Roll! — After becoming checked-out

as Pilot in Command and in the additional duty capacity as the Detachment Maintenance Officer, I occasionally was called upon to fly maintenance related Functional Check Flights. On one FCF, after an aileron change had been accomplished, I was tasked as pilot in command to perform the test flight. Our flight was to verify the rigging by doing in-flight approaches to stall, both "clean" (gear and flaps retracted) and "dirty" (gear down, flaps full down). Our actual stall speed buffet observations on the test flight would then be compared to those predicted by the flight manual for our in-flight gross weight to verify that the airplane performed within flight manual parameters, thus verifying there was no major rigging (drag) discrepancy.

The initial approach to stall was entered at 5,000' in a clean configuration, making a gradual transition from wings-level cruise into slow flight and then into the stall buffet. When the buffet was encountered (typically a couple knots above the actual aerodynamic stall), I experienced a normal and distinct stall buffet or burble that could be felt in the airframe and control wheel as the airspeed gradually decreased, just above flight manual predicted values. The recovery was made by easing back-pressure to lower the nose slightly, and adding full power.

At that point, without much thought, and still at a relatively slow recovery airspeed (~ 75 knots), I called for "gear down and full flaps" while still holding about 65% power. With all the drag out and less than about 15 knots to lose to the stall, I ended up with the throttles still substantially open, with rapidly decaying airspeed as I maintained level altitude and continued to apply back pressure (level flight) waiting for the stall buffet.

The buffet from the extended flaps and gear (as compared to the previous clean configuration) very effectively masked the rapidly approaching stall buffet, and I suddenly found the aircraft in a semi-inverted 120-degree roll to the right. I saw startled Capt. Todd C, my co-pilot's hands dangling over his head and our lap charts were headed for the ceiling of the cockpit, with dust and debris flying everywhere"! As any experienced twin-engine "prop jock" knows, doing power-on stalls is a sure fire way for the prop wash to create asymmetric lift on the wings and flip the aircraft on its back. *(I later learned that many twin-engine C-123 "Ranch Hand" aircraft were lost in Vietnam in this very way, when they were flying tree-top spraying missions and lost an engine due to enemy ground fire or bird ingestion and reflexively pulled up into an engine-out power-on stall).*

Subconsciously, there were two questions that flashed through my mind, to which I had no time to consider answers. How long would it take for the engines to become starved for fuel in the inverted position, and how long would it take before inverted flight caused negative-Gs, which could cause potential structural failure of the wings from inverted lift? Rapid recovery to upright flight was critical to eliminating either of these concerns.

Of course the recovery was almost instinctive — throttles to idle and ailerons to the left until we were wings level and upright again while holding neutral elevator, and applying max throttles to regain airspeed. Wow, whoever thought we would do aerobatics in the Gooney bird? It was then obvious why we started this test routine above 5,000 feet altitude. It never crossed my mind, at the time, that I had just learned a very important lesson that would probably save my life several years later while flying in Vietnam! (Story to follow). This was definitely NOT in the training syllabus.

Flying with a Cross-over "Fighter Jock" — After about two years at O'Hare, a new pilot, more senior in rank and time-in-service than I, named Maj. Vance L transferred into the unit. He was a seven + year prior fighter pilot, who had never flown a multi-engine transport, much less a "tail-dragger" Gooney bird. But he was low in total flying time due to the short mission duration (typically 2-hours per mission) of fighters over his history, and was threatened with being grounded if he did not accumulate more hours quickly. He had a very difficult time adjusting to flying with a crew, and to the nature of flying slow tail draggers.

Due, I suspected, to his lack of "aircrew operations", he had never been exposed to, nor experienced the close aircrew coordination, proper verbal communication techniques, delegation of crew tasks and responsibilities, and consideration for the comfort of the crew by smooth and non-abrupt control inputs. The major was usually designated as my Aircraft Commander when ever we flew together since I was two grades his junior in rank, even though Aircraft Commander qualified. I watched in amazement as he "over thought" every crosswind take-off and landing, trying to use differential power rather than cross-controlling rudder and aileron to keep the wings level during the crosswind departures and arrivals to the runway. The method taught to multi-engine pilots for handling crosswinds on landing was to fly down the initial glide path with the aircraft longitudinal axis crabbed into the wind (heading was not aligned with the runway centerline, but the flight path centered on the runway extended centerline). Then on short final the pilot would apply bank into the crosswind wind with opposite rudder to align the aircraft axis straight and parallel to the centerline. It was taught that although use of differential power could be used in steady state crosswind conditions, that it used far too many power adjustment and the other flight control inputs to be smooth and effective in variable winds and gusty conditions. His use of power differential was adding the extra components of speed and pitch (altitude) variations. He also tended to be excessively harsh on control inputs to put the aircraft where he wanted it during crosswind flight and taxiing. I watched more than one approach of his from the ground in gusty crosswinds and observed the obvious over controlling and raggedness of his flight path, only to observe another aircraft landing in the same conditions immediately behind him with a smooth and apparently wings level approach.

On one interesting trip we were crewed together on a summer week-long simulated wartime exercise at an inactive air base in South Carolina. While there, it was very hot and our specific mission was to fly courier missions during the night-time hours carrying senior commanders and intelligence documents to and from other "friendly" bases in the mock tactical exercise. So we slept during the days, amongst the loud and continuous take-offs, engine checks, fighter after-burner pre-take-off run-ups, and landings. It was too hot to sleep in the canvas tents, so we frequently slept outdoors under the shade of the C-47 wing and close to the edge of the runway, where the noise was at its worst, and restful uninterrupted sleep near impossible, but the temperature and breeze more bearable. Since we were flying one of our TC-47s, we did not have the usual complement of 28- passenger seats, but had only student table-seats for 8- passengers. At the end of the exercise, we were assigned to carry the most senior commanders to Greenville AFB, SC for them to catch other transportation home to their individual bases. When departure time came there were dozens of aircraft lined up, nose-to-tail on the taxiway, waiting for individual clearance to depart, and long distances to taxi before reaching the runway, while sitting in a hot aircraft with virtually no airflow through the cockpit windows, nor especially through the passenger cabin.

After stop-and-go taxiing and waiting for over a half an hour, I suddenly became aware of a couple arms leaning on our cockpit seatbacks as a bird-Colonel poked his head into the cockpit. He was impatient about having such a long and uncomfortable wait to get airborne. He challenged Major L. about his rough handling of the aircraft during taxi. After the Major explained how difficult the Gooney bird was to handle (compared to a fighter) the Colonel informed him that he had piloted the Gooney Bird and ridden in a lot more, and that he had never experienced any pilot as rough and heavy handed on the controls. Needless to say, this was a very embarrassing public critique for the Major.

Night Icing Inbound from Bermuda — Another chilling event occurred (no pun intended), during a winter night return-flight from Bermuda, (our vintage aircraft were not equipped with radar). We became walled off by a solid wall of a winter squall line, and thunderstorms and lightning over the North Atlantic Gulf Stream current, about 50-miles parallel to the eastern US seaboard. This prevented my pilot-in-command (Maj. Vance L) from making landfall during over an hour of tiring hand-flown turbulence. The inexperienced Maj. was so unnerved that after all this time in the weather (blind of any ground assistance) he called for the Instructor Nav in the cabin to come forward and give him heading course reversals to fly back out the way we had come into the frontal system. The Instructor Nav (also a Major) had a very difficult time convincing him that without radar there was no way to "thread the needle" out the way we came in, because the whole system was moving continuously. Unable to successfully penetrate a thick wall of thunderstorms – detectable only by trying to fly between the flashes of lightning and avoiding the heavier turbulence – he had turned parallel to the coastline on a southerly heading, and I had become concerned that, as conducted, we could run out of gas before ever reaching landfall. While flying near the freezing level at 6,000 feet in the heavy precipitation, we encountered as much as four to five inches of rime icing on the nose, windshield, antenna masts, and airfoil leading edges, while the fuel-remaining was falling to a critical state and radio communications were intermittent, at best, from the iced antennas.

[By this time I had learned that I had an angel guarding my safety and felt compelled to rebel against seniority in the name of safety. Seniority of rank didn't necessarily make one smarter than his juniors!]

I finally determined that I had to take the initiative with common sense and direct that we turn into the wall of weather and take the shortest distance westbound to the coast or face running out of fuel and not even having a good fix on our location, much less any traffic control communications. It was then that I realized how inexperienced this fighter jock was in the type of flying that were routinely accomplishing with the C-47.

Adding to the nerve-wracking experience, I had to activate the propeller de-icing system periodically to remove ice from the prop blades. The alcohol spraying on the prop would cause chunks of ice to be thrown off of the blades, which would hit the side of the aircraft about 6-feet aft of the pilot's seats with chunks as big as Coke bottles, which also caused shaking and vibration from the out-of-balanced props. It sounded almost like artillery shells hitting the plane. We finally landed at Dover AFB, DE after quite a fright. We were encrusted with several hundreds of pounds of excess ice weight, lost lift and increased drag from the ice, which caused aerodynamic degradation of the wings. We had to leave the aircraft parked outside on the freezing ramp until the next morning before deicing could take place.

The following morning, after a good night's sleep, we were informed by our Flight Mechanic that while deicing the aircraft on preflight, he was using a broom handle to bust the rime ice free of the leading edge of the wings and had accidentally shattered the left landing light lens on the wing. The supply folks had located a spare acrylic lens to replace the broken one – a 15-inch wide plastic panel about ¼ inch thick that was molded to blend with the curvature of the wing leading edge. This lens was held into place with an aluminum frame that surrounded the lenses and was attached to the wing skin with dozens of short Phillips–head sheet metal screws. However the screws could not be budged due to the ice and corrosion and cold. So the Flight Mechanic had obtained a 6-inch wide role Typhoon Tape – also known as Duct Tape – and had formed a giant sized "band-aid" over the lens, so we could continue home to Chicago where more permanent repairs could be made after several hours warming in the hangar!

Back in those days, with much less sophisticated airplanes, and slower flight regimes, aircrews had to be very ingenious to keep the airplanes flying. Now you know one example why "duct tape" is so popular with mechanics for its versatility in making temporary repairs!

Lasting Leadership Example — One of my most valuable and formative experiences in this original USAF assignment was the good fortune to have an excellent unit commander during the last half of the assignment. He was a highly regarded Major, Maj. Nelson H, who had come up through the enlisted ranks and had learned from both sides of his commissioned career about leadership by example and the responsibilities of command.

In many units there was an ingrained attitude that at the end of the fiscal year, any budget remaining, both in funds and in annual unit flying-hour allocations, that the unit should use up all those resources by fiscal year end in order to guarantee a full allocation for the following year. In each year, these budgeted funds and flying hours always had a built-in "pad" to accommodate unforecast contingencies – such as weather systems or mechanical failures, that made it necessary to repeat a failed accomplishment. Using the prevailing attitude – like watching Congressional Budgets that have ever-spiraling inflationary increases –it was obvious why this attitude was counter-productive, even at the lowest level. Our Detachment Commander, Maj. Nelson H, had a different attitude, and never hesitated to respond to his higher commanders when the orders came to be sure and use up all of the current budget resources nearing the end of the year, stating that he would use only those resources needed to get the mission done, and pass any surpluses forward to others who might have fallen short. He also recognized, that in planning for next year's requirements, we had to add some extra reserve, and that was just good planning. He refused to accept "punishment" for surpluses, caused by good management of our resources, which in-turn would prevent our unit from uselessly spending those resources up by "flying around the flag pole" at year's end just to use up the budget. Under his example, our Detachment typically performed 100% of its mission with an annual surplus of 10 to 15% of budgeted resources. If we should run out of resources, due to unplanned exigencies, he knew he could always honestly justify a request for an end-of-year supplement, because he had developed a reputation of not "playing the game" of wasteful consumption. And his firm example was honored several times during his command, during my tenure. This was a very formative example of good stewardship of public resources, for the entirety of my USAF career. *[I detail a specific example later in Chapter 6. relating to the Pentagon's "Super Skirt".]*

He ultimately earned promotion to full bird-Colonel before retiring, and we remain good friends through email contacts and occasional visits, to this day, 50-years after first working together!

Three Special, Additional Duty Projects —

1. Flight Safety Enhancement & Aircrew Fatigue

The **TC-47** configuration (like its military C-47 cousins) had little or no insulation (neither thermal, nor acoustic) on the inside of the fuselage, and minimal insulation in the cramped cockpit. The side windows in the passenger cabin were thin ¼-inch Plexiglas, which made the cabin reverberate in flight, and mechanical noises sounded like the inside of a cookie tin. The aircraft operational noise was well above suitable levels for spoken conversation. The pilot and copilot had to fly with one ear uncovered by their headphones (the pilot's on his right ear, and the copilot's on his adjacent left ear) and still shouting was required even with less than two feet separation between seats. The aircraft had only rudimentary manual intercom systems requiring use of hand-held microphones for intercom use and for radio transmissions, and used archaic headsets over the ears. At Detachment 4, (O'Hare), I initiated a project to modify our three aircraft using a rocker-switch, added to each pilots' control wheel, which could be toggled with one side for intercom and the other for radio transmitter. This modification used Mil-Spec transformers for matching-up to modern boom-mic equipped headsets for all crew members. This relatively inexpensive project (probably about $150 per aircraft, plus the cost for individual boom-mic equipped headsets, for each active duty aircrew member), was a small step toward modernizing the World War II electronics.

The benefits of this modification provided *enhanced safety* by drastically enhancing the communications of the "front-end crew, without the necessity for leaving one ear uncovered and shouting over the cockpit and engine noise while leaning closer to the person being shouted at, while simultaneously hand-flying the aircraft in any weather conditions encountered. This also had the added benefit that commands or critical communications would be less unlikely to be heard incorrectly, or mis-understood (i.e. *"Gear Up" vs. "Cheer-Up" – a classic take-off crash-scenario in C-47 history*), and provided long-term protection of the crewmember's hearing. It also lowered the fatigue of working long periods under high perceived noise levels, and improved crew efficiencies by keeping more of the crew aware of what was being said (on intercom and outside radio transmissions). Unfortunately, these benefits were not easily translated into monetary value, when trying to justify the cost over a substantially larger number of aircraft.

I made a formal proposal to ConAC headquarters to implement this local mod across the entire fleet of 14-Detachments nationwide (42 total aircraft), but was unsuccessful in getting higher approval "due to cost and safety/efficiency benefits analysis" of need, by uninvolved and non-crew bureaucrats who didn't comprehend the problems of the noise environment!

2. *Utilitarian and Health Related*

Another project I accomplished in my capacity as Detachment Maintenance Officer, addressed a winter-related problem. At O'hare, we had no inside hangaring capability for our aircraft, except that shared with the AF Reserve Troop Carrier Wing when major maintenance was required, and when their facilities could be made available. As a result, when minor engine maintenance was required between missions (e.g. the frequent need to change spark plugs, change oil, or perform carb. adjustments or leak inspections), the engine cowling had to be removed outdoors and the work performed in sometimes arctic winds and temperatures with blowing snow – without shelter. This was accomplished from elevated rolling work-stands (a form of portable scaffolding). On a warm day this task typically required about 2 to 3-hours per engine. In unsheltered winter conditions it could take 8-hours or more with two to three mechanics each, threatening extreme conditions of frostbite and other potential injuries. I coordinated with my mechanics and we designed and implemented – with the assistance of the fabric shop and metal working shop – two sets of two each modified portable elevated work stands with added metal framework, all with canvas covering. Each set could be configured with the canvas and additional framework in about an hour and could then be set-up around the front of the engine (propeller outside the canvas) and the cowling removed. A ground heater/blower with flex duct could be inserted under the skirt of the apparatus that could heat the entire area to nearly room temperature, while sealing out cold air and wind from the work area.

A second winter modification was done: Without aircraft pressurization, there were many leaky and drafty hatches and panels that kept a constant airflow circulating in flight. Operations from Chicago in winter months during sub-zero temperatures, the cockpit could be kept moderately comfortable with heated air ducted from inside the engine cowlings. But the aft cabin, where the Reserve navigators had to operate could readily become a literal deep-freeze during the 6-hour flights at inflight temperatures of -30°F, and worse – so cold that the 2.5 gallon thermal insulated coffee jugs would freeze solid after only a couple hours flying time. With my Maintenance Officer responsibilities and supervisory responsibilities of the 5-aircrew Flight Mechanics, I initiated a project during these very cold days of using ground heating blowers to pre-warm the fuselage interior before flight, and gave the maintenance crews permission to fabricate interior-fuselage canvas zippered bulkheads, just forward of the crew entry door in the fuselage side, for each aircraft, and we fabricated several 10-inch diameter vertical canvas tubes that could be secured to the single overhead center-line heating duct, which would provide an exhaust of heated air down at floor level which better warmed the aft cabin.

3. Recreational & Morale

I also initiated and accomplished a special project where I acquired the entire inventory of a wood working shop from another Detachment that was vacating its facility. I arranged for the equipment to be packaged up and we flew one of our aircraft to the losing Detachment and transported everything back to O'Hare. In the meantime I located some vacant space in the old C-54 plant adjacent to our building, set up the shop and then went about largely single-handedly refurbishing all of the power bench tools – which were 1945-vintage Sears Craftsman equipment – by stripping, cleaning, repainting, and replacing worn & missing parts. These tools included a 10" table saw, a 15" band saw, a floor mounted ½ HP drill press, power-jointer, a thickness planer, and a substantial amount of hand and portable-power hand tools.

I set-up and negotiated a special account with Sears, so that the Detachment members could buy – at a 10% discount – Craftsman equipment repair parts, obtain repair/user manuals, and purchase member-paid Craftsman brand tools for their personal tool kits.

Self-designed & Built 7-foot Stereo Console

As the first user of this refurbished and stocked wood-working shop, I designed, integrated, and built my first major piece of furniture – a walnut veneer 7-foot wide stereo cabinet on tapered-leg base with large stereo 12" tri-axial speaker boxes at opposite ends. In the three-foot center section I designed and fabricated a pair of bi-fold doors, behind which were a built-in vertical stereo tape deck, AM-FM hi-fi stereo amplifier, 3-speed record changer on a slide-out drawer, an integrated central system timer clock, and vertical storage for 3-dozen LP records.

This was the beginning of a long hobby for me with design and fabrication of custom cabinetry and furniture in our subsequent homes. This hobby shop became a much used focal point for the many personnel of Det 4, and their families.

Squadron Officers School, SOS (May 1964)— As part of my Professional Military Education (PME) program, I went to Squadron Officer's School for 3-months on TDY (temporary duty) at Maxwell AFB, AL., during the summer of 1964. I took advantage of the existing regulations to generate a TC-47 training flight from O'Hare to Montgomery, AL about three weeks in advance of my course date. The aircrew of volunteer officers required to round-out the crew (including myself) volunteered to contribute to pay the Flight Mechanic's per diem expense (lodgings and meals), while the rest of the volunteer crew (without personal reimbursement for travel expenses) had a day of golf at Maxwell, while I went rental-house hunting. I found a totally furnished, beautiful secluded (but somewhat dated) 3-bedroom rental ranch nested on a wooded 1-acre lot belonging to an NCOs' widow. The price was spectacularly inexpensive, because we discovered the Master Sergeant's former owner had recently committed suicide in the master bedroom and the bullet hole was still in the wall behind the door. His widow was still in town, but couldn't bring herself to live in the house any longer!

Being current and proficient and an instructor in the C-47, I was a very popular available pilot to take a plane load of multi-engine recip. aircrew members out for their monthly 4-hours of flight currency pay at any time I was available. This was typically done by flying an out-and-back, four-hour, "round-robin" loop. The main downside to that was that generally, I was the only pilot on board who was truly fully qualified in the C-47 aircraft. Often my various co-pilots on any given flight, had zero time in the C-47 and were qualified to be my copilot based upon their C-123, C-54, T-29/121, or C-124 pilot or co-pilot time.

This occasionally created some interesting episodes, like when I had to go back to the tail to relieve myself at the urinal while leaving the aircraft on auto-pilot. (It was a simplistic vacuum 3-gyro with hydraulic servos, non-integrated three-axis system, previously described, could easily be over-powered manually if needed. My copilot for the flight had received no auto-pilot familiarization on his mini-check-out and felt compelled to physically "brute force over-ride" the auto-pilot when needing to change altitude for VFR avoidance of another opposing aircraft! His abrupt maneuver, momentarily oscillated my weight in the tail cone lavatory from +0.5 Gs to +1.5 Gs, leaving me with P-streaks down the front of my flight suit and the lavatory wall!

Looking back — My first operational assignment, as I anticipated, was certainly a better-than-expected choice. Fortunately the anticipated retirement of the T-29, as primary USAF Nav Trainer, did not materialized during the time I was flying the TC-47 (not until 1971). Had it done so, I would not have likely followed the TC-47 experience into the EC-47 following assignment. And that would have negatively affected the experience – chain that formed the rest of my USAF career (as described in the following chapters).

Our new family addition – In December 1965 after 5-1/2 years of marriage, Pat and I concluded the lengthy adoption procedure through Catholic Charities in Chicago of our first daughter, Caryn, at the age of two weeks. I continued at this O'Hare assignment for almost 5-years, was offered and accepted selection to a Regular Air Force commission —a career oriented move— and was rewarded promotions to 1st Lieutenant, and subsequently Captain, while stationed there.

CHAPTER 4

Vietnam Combat Tour (1967-'68)

Top Secret EC-47 Electronic Reconnaissance —

While stationed at O'Hare for 5 five years, I had accrued nearly 2,000 C-47 (TC-47) hours flight time, including a few instructor hours. I received notification of pending orders to Vietnam in October of 1966. I was directed to initiate application for the lengthy Top Secret security clearance process for "Project Phyllis Ann" to fly the R/EC-47 variant of the C-47 "Gooney Bird". These aircraft were a fully refurbished electronic reconnaissance version – highly classified because of its state of the art special antenna array system, the updated precision navigation equipment, and the computerized radio spectrum tuning and direction finding technology. In addition to the normal 4-man flight crew, the EC-47 also carried an onboard mission crew of up to six Security Service NCOs whose mission was to detect, collect, record, decipher, and pinpoint enemy data and transmitter locations.

I was designated to be a one of three pilots on the augmented ferry crew of a newly refurbished and modified Phyllis Ann aircraft (#37 of 45). We were to ferry the modified aircraft across the Pacific Ocean during the first two months of 1967, from the equipment modification center at Sanders, Inc., Grenier Field, Manchester, NH, to a final undetermined destination in South Vietnam. From October '66, until the following February, I was relieved from my TC-47 duties, and was on almost continuous TDY (temporary duty) status, awaiting the backlog of modifications and checks on the complex and unproven equipment and "bug-ridden" advanced software to finally be approved for this 37th modified aircraft, before our departure. The scheduled had already slipped by a couple months before we were finally ready to get under way. ***[This fortunately provided some much desired time to spend with our newly adopted baby before I had to depart. She was just 14-months old when I departed. Pat and Caryn would remain in Chicago-land, in our Rolling Meadows home, which was about 30-minutes from Oak Lawn, where Pat's and my extended families lived.]***

The "Million Dollar Gooney Bird" — Top Secret Project "Phyllis Ann" consisted of three Squadrons of highly refurbished and modified World War II vintage transport C-47 aircraft. These original forty-five C-47 aircraft (subsequently expanded to sixty-nine aircraft under various added project code names and Mission Designated Series, M/D/S) were all 1943 to 1945 original vintage C-47A or C-47B versions. They were first taken to a contractor overhaul facility in Miami, FL where they were essentially "zero-timed" through extensive overhaul and renovation activities, designated "IRAN" – Inspect and Repair As Needed – which included standardization of their configurations (mission equipment, wiring, engine configuration, etc.). This created a total of three new M/D/S configurations, RC-47N, RC-47P and RC-47Q. The subsequent additional EC-47Q were originally "Super DC-3" US Navy configurations that included larger engines and retractable wheel fairings over the main landing gear, and could accommodate several more mission consoles and personnel in the main cabin (i.e. higher payloads).

EC-47N "Snoopy" - #37 of 45 EC-47s Ferried to Vietnam

Skins were removed from frames and stringers; corrosion was treated or metal replaced; engines and propellers were overhauled; landing gear was removed and overhauled; the entire electrical system and wiring was gutted and replaced; wings and fuel tanks were removed and refurbished; fabric-covered control surfaces were re-skinned and painted; and the aircraft finally was given a new coat of jungle-camouflage paint. The black rubber wing and tail leading-edge de-icing boots were retained for the winter ferry flights and were subsequently removed after arrival in tropical Vietnam. In preparation for the upcoming Trans-Pacific ferry flight, two temporary 400-gallon ferry tanks were installed with appropriate venting, servicing and interconnecting fuel valves & plumbing, thus doubling the basic fuel capacity and range of the aircraft. This safely extended the ferry range to over 1600 nautical miles, with reserves. These tanks were located along the right side of the fuselage in the main cabin just aft of the cockpit bulkhead.

In addition to the basic total refurbishment, the cockpit systems were extensively modified in preparation for their special mission equipment role of ARDF (Airborne Radio Direction Finding). The antiquated and high-maintenance vacuum-hydraulic autopilot was removed and deleted from the center of the instrument panel. In its place a Bendix monochrome-display weather-avoidance K-band radar was added with the oscillating radar antenna located in the replaced black-painted nose radome. Secondly, all of the vacuum driven gyro instruments were removed and replaced with alternating current (AC) electrical gyro instruments. A duplicate set of primary instruments was installed in the co-pilot position. The original vacuum attitude indicators (gyro horizons) were deleted and replaced with units in both left and right panels that were the same or similar to the electric gyro-horizon found in the T-33 jet trainer. The original 3.5-inch non-slaved vacuum directional gyro compass instrument, in the pilot's panel was replaced with a highly precise, six-inch diameter magnetic heading instrument with a slaved magnetic fluxgate system adapted from the B-52 bomber (The C-12 Compass System).

The aircraft was also equipped with a Doppler Navigation System (DNS), a Loran-C (Long Range-Computerized) navigation system (primarily intended for the long ferry flight) and its computer. *[As a note of technical interest, Loran-C navigation system never became operational because, in the haste of the project development, the system engineers failed to recognize that the Loran-C system chosen was designed for aircraft with 115 volt AC* ***three-phase power****, but the installed AC inverters could supply only* ***single-phase power.*** *These Loran C systems were deleted shortly after arrival in Vietnam].*

Also added was a gyro-stabilized optical drift meter at the Navigator station (similar to a bombsight's stabilized cross-hairs). The drift meter, mounted atop a vertical viewing tube through the floor, would allow the navigator to optically verify when we passed directly over any discrete ground map reference (a bridge, road intersection, conspicuous mapped landmark, etc.), which he could use to periodically update the Doppler position in order to maintain absolute accuracy in the aircraft's ground mapping location. Also included were updated UHF, VHF, (Army-tactical compatible) FM and long range HF radio transceivers as well as two secondary dual needle RMI (Radio Magnetic Indicators) that were linked to the "back-end" mission equipment. Additionally, the aircraft had an advanced intercom system that permitted hot-mike inter-cockpit communications (a luxury almost never seen on the DC-3/C-47, but similar to what we had locally improvised on our O'Hare-based TC-47s), with an isolated intercom system for the back-end operator crewmembers, for "need-to-know" classified crew intercommunication).

Electrical power for the aircraft systems was provided by main and alternate AC inverters that were located in the tail lavatory. These inverters were basically 12 volt DC powered motors that drove 120-volt AC single-phase alternators.

After each aircraft refurbishment was completed the aircraft was re-designated as an RC-47 series and was test flown in Miami. The aircraft was then ferried to the Sanders Electronics facility at Grenier Field in New Hampshire where the "Phyllis Ann" mission equipment was installed, flight-tested and calibrated. This original designation was changed within a year (after all "Phyllis Ann" aircraft had arrived in Vietnam), to EC-47 (the "R" designation implying passive photo-reconnaissance, and the "E" indicating a higher level of Electronic Intelligence gathering, or "ELINT"). The total cost of the refurbishment and system installation contract reportedly averaged **$1 million per aircraft** before each aircraft was released for duty in Vietnam. *(The original C-47D from which it was derived had a USAF inventory value in the ballpark of $50,000, so this was a substantial degree of modification and upgrading.)*

Delayed Departure for Vietnam — While waiting for my aircraft to be prepared for ferry, my SEA (South East Asia, Vietnam) assignment required that I complete the C-47 Conversion Training syllabus, at England AFB, LA, then SEA Counter Insurgency (COIN) Training at Hurlburt AFB, FL and then proceed to Grenier Field, NH, to ferry aircraft number 37 to Viet Nam. By the time my training blocks were all completed, the Sanders people were still running well behind delivery schedule due to technical system problems and they were only ready to ferry aircraft number 30 by the end of November 1966. The subsequent aircraft ferry crews were sent TDY back to their previous home stations to await recall, and complete monthly flight currency flights at their losing organizations, if possible.

Newly Learned Combat Assault Landing Technique — A bit of levity was provided during my required "C-47 Conversion Training" at England AFB when it was discovered that my designated instructor pilot there had 400 hours of logged experience in the C-47 and I had nearly 2,000. Although, he did have one new technique to teach me – that of doing "assault steep-glide-angle power-off landing approaches in a combat zone (to minimize exposure to ground fire during descent and landing). On my final proficiency flight at O'Hare, prior to departure for Vietnam, I was riding with my former unit Commander, Maj. Nelson H (the Instructor Pilot), as a third pilot on a regular proficiency flight mission. At the end of his mission he allowed me to get one approach and full-stop landing. I asked if he'd like to see the combat approach technique I had learned at England AFB. He agreed.

I was in the left seat, he was in the right; I flew the typical left downwind leg level at 1,000 ft, but at a tight, close-in position (parallel and about 100 feet right of the runway, but opposite the landing direction, with gear and flaps retracted, and about 105 knots). Upon passing abeam the end of the runway, I reduced power to *idle*, advanced the propellers to max RPM (minimum-pitch for landing) and rolled abruptly into a 30° left bank, 180° course reversal to align with the runway heading on centerline. Simultaneously, I pushed the nose over to maintain a rapid descent (about twice the normal descent rate of a standard approach angle). Then half-way around the course reversal turn, I called for "Gear Down", followed by "Full Flaps".

Meanwhile, we were descending at 600 feet per minute with the engines remaining at idle. Approaching 100 feet from runway elevation, I started back-pressure on the controls into the landing flare with the engines still in idle and bled off the airspeed as we came into ground effect. Then as I decreased the descent rate, the airspeed bled off to a perfect three-point, full stall "squeaker"! The Engines had remained in idle from the beginning of descent, and the flaps arrived at Full Down about simultaneously with the touch down. The landing roll-out was probably less than 300 feet! All the while, Maj Nelson H was holding his breath. The landing could not have been better (purely by stroke of luck). He looked over at me and breathlessly said, "That was the most amazing landing I have ever experienced … ***but don't you ever do that again in my aircraft*"!!**

Calibration Flight Test Mission — I was finally notified to report to Grenier Field on 2 January 1967. ***(Thanks to my Guardian Angel for permitting Christmas at home with the new baby and extended families!)*** When I arrived at Grenier Field with numerous other aircrew members, due to the security classification, I had only a very vague idea of what I would be doing in Vietnam. *[At the same time, I was amazed to learn that the technical magazine, "Aviation Week" had just published a several page article, which described in detail the "Phyllis Ann" ARDF tactics that would be performed (despite the Top Secret security classification of the program)!]*

Each airplane was stripped of its Classified equipment in order to accommodate the added fuel tanks and fuel weight. But we still had to maintain the Top Secret classification on the aircraft during transit, and were directed to land only (*except in an emergency*) at US military bases where we could arrange for armed Security Police sentries to guard the aircraft around the clock, while they were on the field. This is when I began to suspect that it was the equipment, rather than the mission, that was at the heart of the security classification, but failed to explain why the ferry mission required ground Security Sentries on the empty aircraft, where ever we landed. (A possible cover story for the aircraft?)

We soon discovered in the first week at Sanders, that their people were still backlogged on the delivery of six aircraft ahead of ours. While at Grenier Field on TDY for several weeks awaiting final completion of my aircraft's modification and flight-testing, I volunteered to participate in the ARDF system flight-calibration test on a preceding RC-47. This proved to be a very interesting and difficult proposition, but provided me an opportunity to get better acquainted with the ARDF equipment and tactics that we would use in south Vietnam.

The difficulty was that the RC-47 calibration test had to be flown at night, at 8 to 10,000 feet, in a Military Restricted Area about 35 miles east of the New Hampshire shoreline, in the vicinity of a small off shore island in the Atlantic. The island was instrumented with a 50-foot tower which had a radio transmitter antenna at its summit, co-located with a white high intensity rapidly flashing beacon strobe-light. The test aircraft to be calibrated had a heat-seeking (Infra-red) Sidewinder missile-sensor, gyroscopically mounted in the navigator's sextant dome on the top of the fuselage. The test tower was also equipped with a DME (Distance Measuring Equipment) transmitter, which could be interrogated continuously from our RC-47 equipment. The pilot was required to fly in a near-constant 10-mile radius around the island tower, compensating for wind drift, at night with no visual horizon, no autopilot, and maintaining a near wings-level, *uncoordinated, flat, skidding turn of less than 10 degrees of bank!*

This was done by keeping the wings near-level while maintaining opposite-aileron to the turn direction and using rudder and differential power to maintain the skidding uncoordinated turn in the opposite, desired direction. The calibration was completed after making many aircraft system adjustments, while flying continuous flat-turns and aligning the bearing from the heat seeker and the signal-bearing pointer on the aircraft radio systems until the onboard technicians achieved an acceptable degree of agreement. These missions typically lasted for a minimum of six hours on-station plus nearly an hour each, to and from the island location and Grenier Field. This particular flight had a total duration of slightly over nine hours.

This flat turn procedure was extremely unnatural, fatiguing, and uncomfortable to fly, and when the pilot finally broke off to return to base, his own internal gyros in the middle ear were so skewed that it was almost impossible for him to fly a straight course for a coordinated precision radar, or electronic ILS final approach back at the field.

Several weeks before my calibration flight, one of the RC-47s ran into trouble with the non-standard valving on the ferry tanks and ended up running one of the auxiliary tanks dry. The resulting air in the lines caused first one then the other engine to alternately sputter and quit while the crew was trying to restart the engines, manage the emergency and navigate home over the pitch-black off-shore waters. This near disaster incident lead to some revisions to the ferry tank plumbing and valving, and heightened fuel management procedures for all of the ferry aircraft aircrews.

Operational Mission Description — The Sander's mission equipment included several operator consoles with CRT display screens (like a round TV screen), and an expanded navigator station, all located in the aft passenger cabin, along with some sophisticated radio receivers, and in-flight tape recorders. Also included were a set of three over/under pairs of whip antennas that were mounted in a triangular "phased array" pattern with two paired antennas above and below the wings, outboard of the engines, and another pair just behind the cockpit on the forward fuselage, forming the apex of the array on the aircraft. With this (sophisticated, for its time) antenna system, the aircraft could take highly accurate bearings on any selected radio frequency that was transmitting within its range. The frequency spectrum was displayed on the CRT display, and the operator could home in on any frequency spike of frequency interest. The target-of-interest frequency could quickly be selected by merely cranking an over-lay reference cursor-line, which could be dialed left or right by the console operator. One of the two RMI bearing pointers would point in the direction of the tuned-in transmitter. (The other pointer was used for pilot radio navigation, when available). This allowed the Navigator and Pilot to triangulate the signal location by turning the aircraft to put the bearing pointer on the wingtip and then flying a horizontal orbit around an enemy transmitter while other "back-end" crewmembers were identifying, listening-to, deciphering and recording the enemy message traffic.

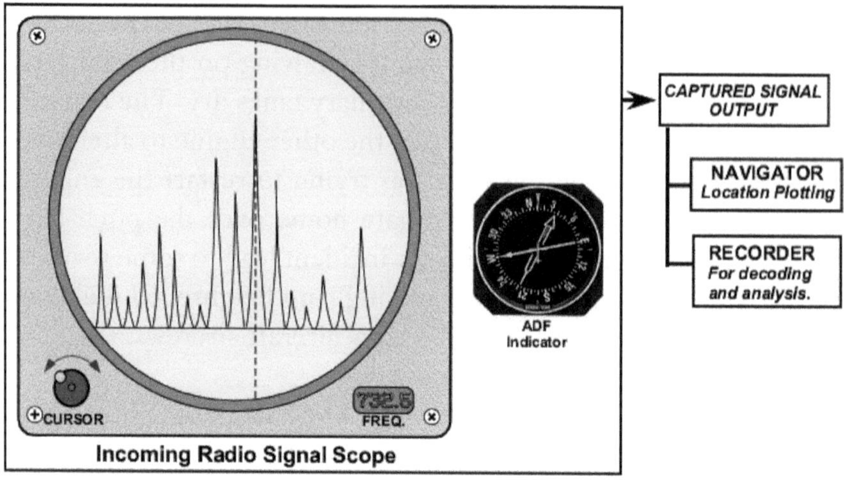

Incoming Radio Signal Scope

With the sophisticated navigational equipment of the EC-47 Phyllis Ann aircraft, the crew could be constantly aware of its exact position over the ground (within the accuracy of the current state-of-the-art maps) and the navigator could then translate the triangulation plots from the ARDF mission equipment into an enemy transmitter site location within about 5 to 10 meters (~12 to 25 feet) of accuracy.

The tactic for accomplishing enemy transmitter triangulation is graphically shown below. Once a target radio frequency had been detected, the pilot would turn the aircraft to place the Bearing pointer on a wingtip plus-or-minus 10° and then fly straight until the needle had moved aft by 10°, or more, while the Navigator plotted the aircraft heading and position. This established the first two LOPs (line-of-position) to the target. The pilot would then turn the aircraft in the direction of the target, again putting the bearing-pointer on the wingtip to establish another cut and a third LOP. This process was repeated until enough LOPs had been recorded to arrive at a series of LOP crossings to define a most-probable center point as the target (transmitter) location.

It did not matter how close, or far, the EC-47 was from the

target, as long as the transmitter remained in radio range, and continued transmitting. However the further away the target was, the longer it would take to get the desired 10° bearing changes.

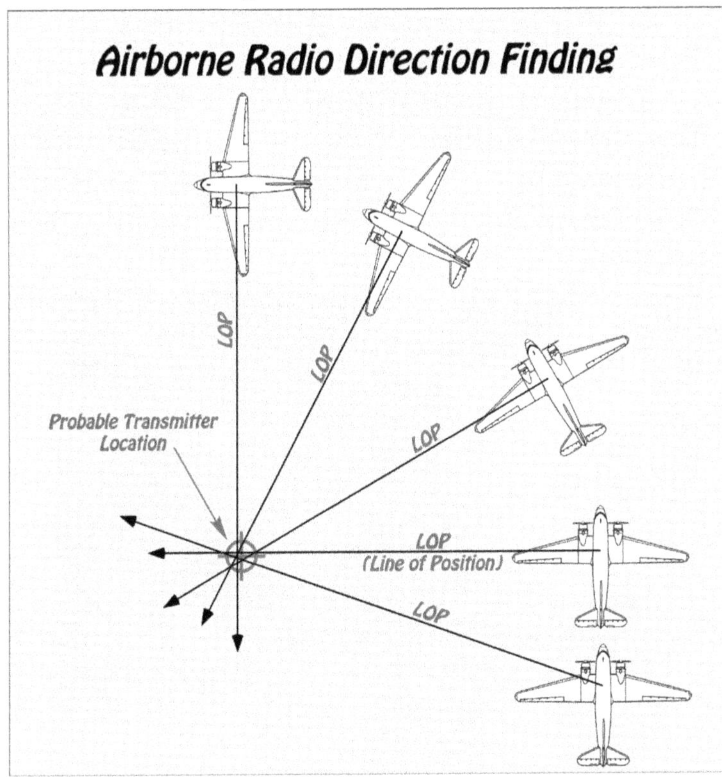

ARDF; Line of Position Bearing Relative to EC-47 Position

In at least one extreme case, we personally tracked the same transmitter over three days to confirm the position was approaching from over 100 miles <u>off-shore</u>, which eventually was proven to be an enemy transport ship. This vessel was then intercepted, run ashore, and captured by the US Navy. It proved to be loaded with enormous quantities of arms and ammunition, which was confiscated and the vessel destroyed.

Ferry Flight to Vietnam — My ferry crew consisted Maj. Chuck F, Aircraft Commander, myself – as First Officer, 1st Lt. Dave D,

Copilot, 1st Lt. John H, Navigator, and SSgt. Jim C, Flight Mech. Maj. Chuck F had several thousand hours flying experience in the C-47 from Korea and claimed to also have flown with Air America (CIA) during the earlier ramp-up of the Vietnam War. Lt. Dave D had about 1,000 hours experience flying the Grumman SA-15 Albatross amphibian, a twin-engined Air Sea Rescue aircraft. Lt. John H was graduated from Navigator training less than a year prior to this assignment. And Sgt Jim C had many hours as a C-47 airframe and engine mechanic with considerable flying time as a flight mechanic.

Ferry Crew (l to r) — SSgt. Jim C, 1st Lt. John H, Maj. Chuck F (in mask), Capt. Miller, and 1st Lt. Dave D – (taking photo)

The most direct ferry route would have been to cross the U.S. to San Francisco (Travis AFB) CA and then proceed to Hickam AFB, (Honolulu) HA and then on west to Midway Island. However the flight distance to Hawaii from San Francisco was nearly 2,100 nm, which was well beyond our range, even with the extra 800 gallons of fuel aboard. So our only suitable choice was to fly the route shown below on the map.

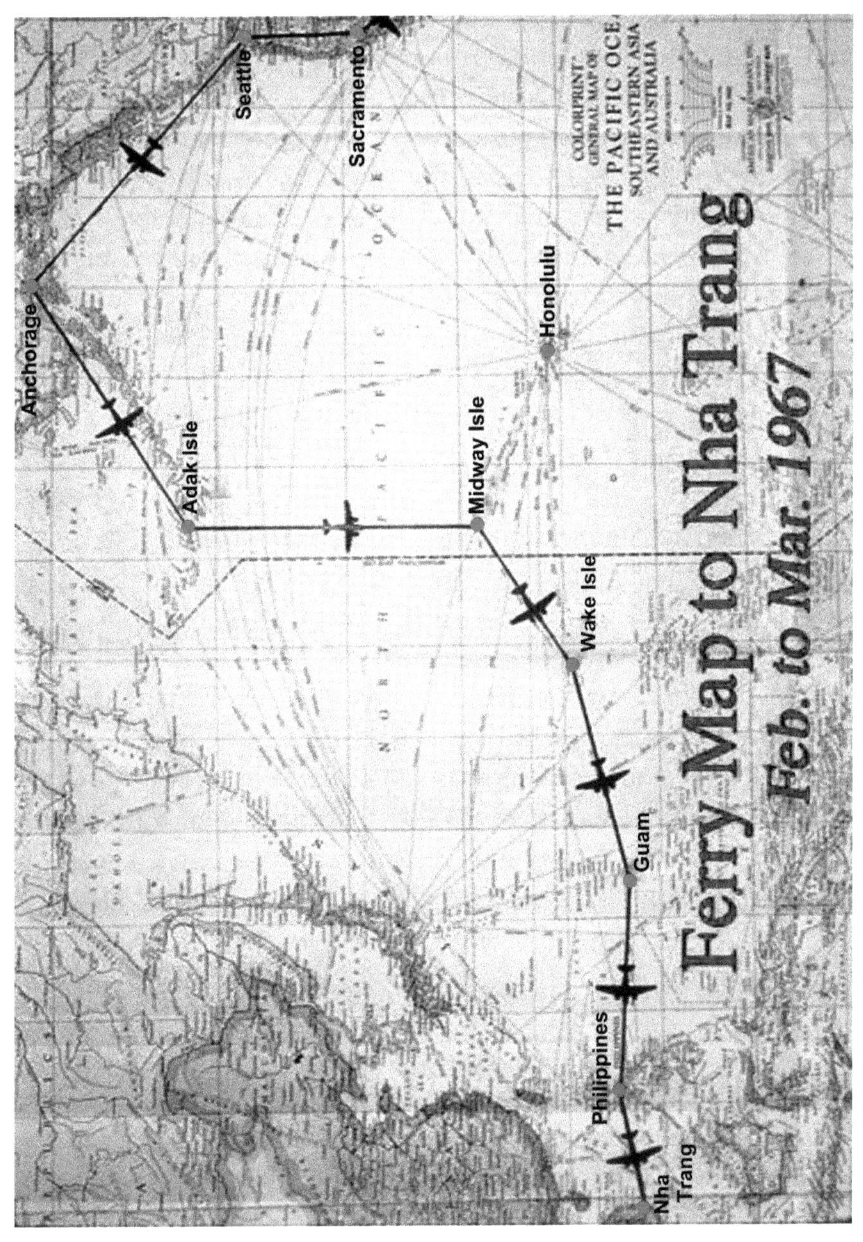
Ferry Map to Nha Trang
Feb. to Mar. 1967
Anchorage
Seattle
Sacramento
Adak Isle
Midway Isle
Honolulu
Wake Isle
Guam
Philippines
Nha Trang
THE PACIFIC OCE
SOUTHEASTERN ASIA
AND AUSTRALIA

Our aircraft was finally ready and we departed Grenier Field on **19 Feb '67** flying across the US to the west coast (in four hops, through Rantoul, **IL**, then Tucson, AZ, then to Sacramento, **CA** and Seattle, WA with all stops being at USAF Air Bases), then to Alaska. Our 12-month Vietnam tour began at the time we departed from McChord AFB, Seattle, WA. From there we proceeded to Elmendorf, AFB, Anchorage, AK, then island hopped to Adak Island (near the southwest end of the Aleutian Island chain), then south to Midway, Wake, and westerly to Guam, the Philippines, and into south Vietnam. ***Beyond Seattle, WA, we were flying in arctic weather conditions, until arriving at Adak Island, and 800 miles beyond (about halfway) to Midway Island.***

Of the 45 total Phyllis Ann aircraft, fifteen aircraft each were flown respectively into Saigon (360th TEWS — Tactical Electronic Warfare Squadron), Nha Trang (361st TEWS) and Pleiku (362nd TEWS), as each unit was filled to full manning. Initially our tentative assigned final destination of aircraft and crew was to be Pleiku.

In-Flight Fire Emergency Enroute to Adak – Our first bit of excitement on the trip occurred after we departed Elmendorf AFB, (Anchorage, AK) for Adak Island (AK), a US Naval Air Station of WWII vintage near the western end of the Aleutian Island chain. The weather on departure from Elmendorf was typical for February with sub-zero temperatures, scattered-to-broken clouds with bases at about 3,000 ft and tops about 7,000 ft. We had filed IFR (instrument flight rules) at 8,000 ft. and were initially on top in clear sunny skies with a broken-to-solid undercast below our altitude. The mission had a flight plan duration of slightly over nine hours against a prevailing headwind and a planned arrival after dark in the short arctic days of late February. Arrival weather was forecast to also be typical arctic island conditions with ceilings and visibility near IFR minimums (500 foot ceilings and visibility of 1/2 mile) in blowing snow and winter sea fog. The runway at Adak was near sea level in a valley surrounded by low mountainous foothills, to elevations of about 1500 feet, which when combined with variable ocean winds caused turbulence, cross winds and difficult precision radar approaches.

Over the Aleutian Island Chain at Dusk

US Navy Air Station Adak Island, Feb '67

It was my leg to fly the left seat. About five hours out of Elmendorf, I was hand-flying (no auto-pilot in these aircraft), when I detected an odor resembling burning cellophane. I asked my acting co-pilot, Maj. Chuck F, who had been smoking, if he had inadvertently set some cigarette pack materials on fire in his ashtray. He checked and replied, "No". I turned and glanced over my right shoulder into the aft of the aircraft to discover the aft portion of the cabin rapidly filling with acrid white smoke. Out of the corner of my eye, a red light caught my attention in the center of the electrical service panel, which was on the secondary bulkhead just behind the cockpit emergency exit door. This was about 24 inches behind the main bulkhead in front of which I was seated. A closer look revealed that this light was labeled "A.C. Inverter Failure".

With what seemed in retrospect like an impossible contortion, I managed to reach around my seat back and associated bulkhead, and flipped the A.C. Main Inverter switch to "Off". With that action, I suddenly found myself with all the gyro instruments showing "Off Flags", my electrical compass system disabled, all navigation equipment off-line, and all but our limited range primary UHF transceiver disabled. As described in the "The Million Dollar Gooney Bird — Project Phyllis Ann" section above, the EC-47 was an all-electric instrumented aircraft — all the vacuum systems and gyros had been deleted and replaced with much more sophisticated (for that aircraft), A.C. electrically powered equipment (which were powered by the failed inverter).

In the meantime, our Flight Mechanic, SSgt. Jim C, and Lt. Dave D had been sleeping in the front of the cabin, while the Navigator, Lt. John H was engrossed in his nav charts, further forward. With the thickening smoke, Sgt. C donned a smoke mask and hustled aft to the latrine in the tail where the inverters were located, with fire extinguisher in hand. The fire was quickly extinguished with the inverter turned off, but it took over 30 minutes for the smoke to clear completely so he could make an initial assessment of fire and wiring damage. The source of the fire proved to be the D.C. motor on the main inverter, which had apparently overheated and burst into flames, even though it was still successfully driving its integrated A.C. alternator. Adding to our concern, however, was the fact that the system design engineers had equipped the aircraft with an "Alternate Inverter" of matching size and specification as the "Main Inverter", but had mounted it immediately above the Main Inverter and had used a common electrical bus (wiring) forward to the Electrical Service Panel, behind the cockpit. This raised the potential that the Alternate Inverter, the bus control relay and/or the common bus cable might have been damaged by the flames and high temperatures caused by the fire in the below-mounted Main Inverter.

For the next half-hour, we were obligated to maintain heading and attitude with "needle, ball, and airspeed" aided by the oil-filled magnetic "whiskey compass" and outside visual reference, while contemplating our possible options. We had already passed the "point of no return" fuel state for returning to Elmendorf AFB in Alaska.

The thought of having to make a "no-gyro" approach into Adak's hilly terrain at night, in IFR minimum conditions and in turbulence didn't sound too inviting, but the thought of possibly ditching into the Bering Sea in the middle of February with limited arctic survival equipment and no radio contact was even less enticing to contemplate. Time of survival in the water, even with arctic clothing, in those conditions was less than 30-minutes! Even attempting a crash landing on the barren and volcanic Aleutian Islands, was even a worse option.

[Where's that Guardian Angel, when really needed? Found Him/Her.]

After the seeming interminable half-hour passed and the damage assessment was completed, Sgt. Jim C suggested that we attempt to activate the Alternate Inverter to see if it would pick up the load. Fortunately, after extinguishing the inverter fire, we found no collateral damage to the electrical busses and were able to restore normal operations using the Alternate inverter. While it was happening, this was probably the most intense hour in flight of my year involved with Vietnam operations. The landing was accomplished without further incident, but added a 9-day delay on Adak awaiting replacement parts. This delay provided the crew time to enjoy some arctic exploration of this historic WWII battle field, and also tour an active nuclear submarine that was in port. Also, thanks to a DoD grade school teacher assigned to the island, we had a guided visit to an Alaskan king crab processing boat that was catching, cleaning and deep-flash-freezing crabmeat and legs for shipment to the states and other foreign ports.

Dead Reckoning "in the Soup" Over the North Pacific — Our sophisticated navigational equipment left much to be desired, so far. We had established on the six previous legs that the new compass system was highly accurate; that was a plus. But the Doppler navigation system proved to have some bugs, and was plagued with navigational inaccuracy and varying drift on the long over-water legs. Or was it errors in the accuracy of the available maps, or our lack of experience with this new technology? The LORAN-C was inoperative (due to lack of 3-phase electrical power from the inverter). This left us with three remaining systems of navigational back-up devices to aid the Navigator with his dead reckoning (DR), which was based solely on the accuracy of the forecast winds over the route. The first, and primary aid was the hand-aimed sextant mounted in the overhead dome of the cabin, which required visual sighting of celestial bodies (sun, moon, or celestial constellations) for calculation of position. The second was "pressure pattern" navigation, which made use of the gyro stabilized drift meter, which required visual conditions to see the surface below the aircraft, which could verify the amount and strength of any drift occurring along the way. The final tool was the ADF radio (low- frequency airborne direction finding equipment). This was notoriously inaccurate (over land) until you got within about 100 miles, or so, of the broadcast AM station or beacon, and was virtually useless if there were electrical storms in the area — something fairly common in the mid-Pacific tropics.

Our Command Headquarters was pressuring us to depart ASAP from Adak and continue our journey to Vietnam where the Phyllis Ann aircraft were urgently needed. It took 6-days to receive a replacement inverter from the supply Depot (McClellan AFB, CA), while related repairs were already underway, awaiting the replacement inverter, and were completed overnight, once received. We prepared for and attempted to launch each day for 2-more days, but were prevented by the very poor weather conditions at Adak with ice-fog and solid ceilings, which created a very dangerous departure condition. Finally out of frustration, Maj. Chuck F decided to launch on the third day (Mar 5th 1967) over my protests, because should we have to abort anytime after take-off, there were no alternates closer than 1,000 miles (back at Anchorage, AK), the closest base where the weather was suitable for an emergency landing. That would be an extremely adverse situation if we lost an engine or had another fire. (During the subsequent marginal take-off, we held our breaths as the right engine oil pressure gauge began to fluctuate mildly during Take-Off Power, but finally settled down after passing about 5,000 feet altitude – with No Place to Abort to, had it not stablized!)

Once airborne, we were unable to get out of the arctic weather system for more than 6-hours, either above or below the clouds, in order to get any positive navigation fixes. Our route was from Adak straight south for 1,420 n.m. (nautical miles) to a tiny tropical rock in the middle of the Pacific called, "Sand" Island, on Midway Atoll. This would be a true challenge for our newly graduated navigator, Lt. John H and was the longest leg of our journey (1,422 n.m.) to South Vietnam.

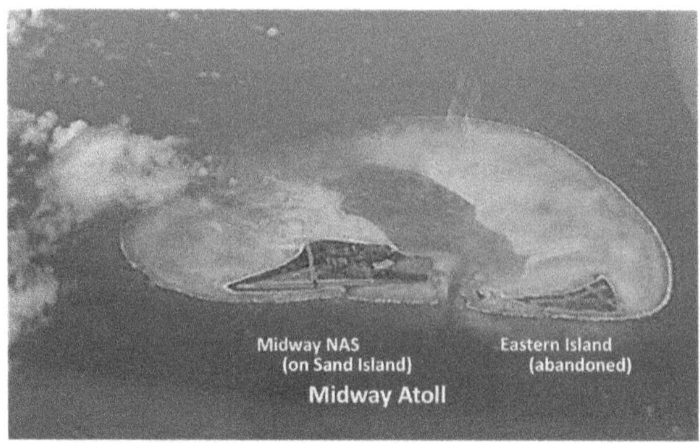

Tropical Midway Atoll (Sand Island) Found – Fortunately, each of us three pilots were highly experienced in overwater flying and Maj. Chuck F gave our Navigator, Lt. John H one of the best pieces of overwater dead reckoning advice. He said, "Whatever you do, DO NOT navigate <u>if by dead-reckoning alone</u> directly to Midway, but rather aim for a point abeam of Midway, but about 50 n.m. up-wind (west) of the destination. That way — if we never get a positive ADF or radar pick-up — when your DR estimated time enroute (ETE) runs out and should there be no land in sight, you will at least have a good idea which way to turn to try and find the island".

The flight took about twelve hours, of which over eight hours were "in the soup". But again we obviously had a "Guarding Angel" watching over us and we were able to pick up the Midway ADF beacon over 450 miles out — though at that range it was varying plus or minus 10 degrees off of the nose. But it finally became more stable as we became closer. By the time we reached Midway, the weather had turned to routine tropical VFR conditions with scattered-to-broken clouds ranging up to about 6000 ft. Boy was that little rock in the middle of a huge ocean a welcome sight! But with a scattered cloud cover, the shadows on the sea below made it almost impossible to identify the island until we were within less than 25-miles of it.

We spent two days at Midway waiting for adverse headwinds to die off. It was a small island — so small that one could walk around the entire perimeter of about 4-miles, in a couple hours. It housed maybe 300 Navy personnel who maintained and operated the airfield, the seaport and the communications facilities there. It had two main attractions.

Midway Island, WWII Debris (note Radial Engine) in Surf.

First, Midway had been a major decisive battle site with the Japanese invaders during World War II, shortly after the Pearl Harbor attack. And now, twenty-six years later, it was still strewn with the wreckage and debris from the battle. Military truck axles, wrecked aircraft engines and fuselages, and other identifiable derelict vehicles and parts were still lying in the surf just off the runway, where they had been bulldozed during the conflict. Beaches still had fortifications, pillboxes, and naval cannon emplacements scattered around the perimeter. There was the hulk of a grounded transport ship rusting on the reef at the north point of Eastern Island. It was like stepping back into history and hearing the sounds of the attacks, and the fighting. The "presence" of history felt surrealistic. And the base itself was marked with many Naval monuments — artillery pieces, white-painted anchors, and memorial plaques and markers.

Secondly, 85% of the world's population of Lysan Albatross (also known commonly as Gooney Birds, like our airplane is known) numbering 1.5 million, 1/3rd of which nest exclusively on Sand Island of the Midway Atoll. With their nests and hatchling chicks covering every bare surface of the island at a density of about one nest, huge egg, or molting chick for every 5-foot radius on the ground, it sounded (and smelled) like we were in a huge bird cage. The incubation cycle is 65 days long over fall and early winter, and the mature birds remain at sea for 3 to 5- years between mating cycles. The Lysan Albatross resembles the appearance of the common seagull, but is a giant version of that with a typical wing-span up to 6-feet, or more. The few chicks remaining in the nest when we were there were about the size of a 2-pound chicken, and the unhatched eggs were about five inches long, by three and a half inches in diameter.

Nest with Egg; Chicks in Background

"Gooney Bird" Mating Dance

Because of their long-life span (up to 40 years) and their time spent at sea between mating cycles, they are far more proficient at landing at sea, making them the most comical, and clumsy when they return to the land after so long at sea. When they swoop down to land on the island, they flare out above the touchdown point and hit sand instead of water, causing them to tumble head over heels for two or three somersaults before coming to an awkward full-stop on-shore landing. When they get ready to fly again, they head into the wind and run to get up speed while flapping their wings. When they sense that they have reached sufficient speed they retract their "landing gear" webbed feet and soar away. If the lift isn't sufficient, down come the feet and they run a little further, for more speed. If that fails, they either try for more acceleration, or do another crash-landing somersault. What a riot! They are far more graceful than a soaring eagle, once in flight.

Next Stop, Wake Island —We permanently stowed all of our arctic flying gear upon arriving at Midway, and it was time to start acclimating to the tropics where we would be flying for the next 12-months. We departed Midway on March 7th, 1967 on the next leg, which was 1,030 nm west-southwest to another Pacific atoll, Wake Island. As seen in the picture below, Wake Island was formed from the long-extinct semi-submerged caldera of a mid-Pacific volcano, at the surface resembling a wish-bone. It had a 9,800-foot runway – probably the roughest runway I've ever experienced, almost like a giant washboard surface – on its northwestern rim, which appears to be about 20% of the total land above sea level. The total length, from the eastern tip of the northern leg, counter clockwise through the neck of the wishbone to the western tip of the southern leg, the island is approximately 8-miles in circumference. So if one could walk the outer coral beach around the outside perimeter (excluding the beach around the inner tidal lagoon, and the submerged reef at the eastern end), it would be about twice as far as walking around the perimeter of Midway Island. But it represents approximately one-half the exposed land mass.

Wake Island and Atoll

There is a small inlet, separating the small arrowhead shaped island, named Peale Island, right of the hook in the photo and opposite the runway, which forms a really interesting tidal flow during the daily ebb and flow of tides from the tidal lagoon. Peale Island, is connected to the larger main island by a narrow bridge, and during WWII had contained the Officer's Club and the officer's quarters and was the FAA personnel housing areas, in 1967.

The stop at Wake was an opportunity to provide a little tropical rest and relaxation. We spent our arrival afternoon at the beach on the lagoon at the Officer's Club. I went snorkeling and got caught in the current under the bridge as the tide came up and forced the flow of water from the lagoon out to the Pacific. (The tidal lagoon is the pale blue in the center in the above photo; Pacific surrounding the caldera). Looking closely (below) you can see the jagged rusted pilings from the prior bridge that was bombed out during the war, or possibly just corroded away by the salt water tidal flows, over the years since. I was concerned that I could be dragged across and torn to shreds, by some of those that were submerged. Instinctively, or from some earlier lesson learned, I decided to concentrate on navigating wide around the pilings and just allowing the 5-mile per hour current to carry me forward until the channel widened, and the currents abated. Then I could swim perpendicular to the flow and come aground on the lower-current channel shore.

The Bridge Between Wake and Peale Island

The hooked peninsula facing the lagoon was fortified by a rocky beach and low concrete seawall at its crest. This peninsula had housed the enlisted barracks area, which had been heavily bombed during the war, and the only remnants were parts of the barracks' foundations, poured concrete entry stairs, broken porcelain commodes, toilet seats and dense jungle that had reclaimed the remains. Dave (our third pilot) and I toured down this beach and then crossed to the opposite side only to find the area posted with signs declaring it "Off-Limits - Potential Unexploded Ordinance!"

Fortified Peninsula Beach

We had left the Continental US on this ferry flight only 17 days earlier, and I had already been kept safe by my Guardian Angel at least four times (the inflight fire, the fool-hardy no-departure-alternate take-off out of Adak, the rip-tide snorkeling current sweeping me out into the Pacific, and wandering through an area of unexploded ordinance)!

Three Days Later, On to Guam — We set out on Mar. 10th 1967, our third longest flight, 1334 nm to Guam (Anderson AFB), which was the main Pacific B-52D staging base to Vietnam. (There was a second main B-52 staging base on the other side of Vietnam in Thailand). We saw probably 30 of these huge bombers capable of each carrying one hundred and four, 500-pound bombs, combined internally in the dual bomb bays and externally mounted under the wings. We felt like we were getting much closer to the battlefields at this stop. We were there only one full day, and were given a tour of the B-52 weapons build-up and storage area where the 500-pound bombs were assembled with their fused noses and tail fins, and stacked on pallets like cordwood.

One of Several B-52D Parking Ramps on Guam

One Day's Supply of B-52D, 500-Pound Bombs

Clark AFB, the Philippines — Our final stop before Vietnam was now only 700 nm away. Clark was a fascinating view of the tropics, with palm trees and lush foliage, flowers growing everywhere, warm moist climate, and a highly talented native population. The shops on and immediately off the base were stuffed with tourist items including gorgeous and sometimes humorous woodcarvings in monkeypod wood (statuettes, engraved plaques of all kinds, religious art work, giant forks & spoons, wicker furniture, folding screens, etc.), each unique one-of-a-kind art. The Filipinos were also very talented artist of musical mimickery. Most of them were fluent in English, but spoke with their own unique accent.

Yet the tiniest young female singer, while playing an electric guitar nearly longer than she was tall, could belt out songs made famous by Barbra Striesand, or Connie Francis, making one wonder where that depth and volume of voice was coming from, while perfectly matching the original artists vocal range and American accent. The Officer's Club dining room featured a full 20-piece orchestra and formal service rivaling New York's finest restaurants all at prices well under $10 per meal. The Filipinos also had a real knack for taking WWII scrap automobiles and jeeps and renovating them into amazing vehicles of transportation. Nothing was ever wasted and could be recycled over and over again. This was like an R&R (rest and recuperation) site, on our last day before entering the combat zone.

Clark Base Operations 1967

The ramp at Clark was a microcosm of a combat Air Base during wartime and was filled with dozens of fighter aircraft on one side and a variety of helicopters and small jet transports on the other. We were really feeling now like we were approaching the combat zone of South Vietnam, and would soon be surrounded by the vestiges of the front lines.

F-100 Fighters Being Readied for Battle at Clark AFB

At this time (Mar.13, 1967), while on lay-over at Clark, we still had not received the formal notification as to which of the three EC-47 Squadrons was to be our destination. On 9 Mar '67, one of the 361st TEWS aircraft (at Nha Trang) had gone missing (call sign "TIDE 86"). On 11 Mar '67, the morning before we departed Guam, it was located on the rocky coast 20 miles north of Nha Trang, and identified as being shot down by enemy ground fire, with all hands lost. This was the first EC-47 lost to enemy action in Southeast Asia. (For further info, on this loss, search the Internet for ***EC-47, Tide 86***).

Arrival Destination: Nha Trang AFB —

We were notified upon arrival at Clark Air Base of our reassignment diversion to Nha Trang as a replacement aircraft for TIDE 86. We arrived at Nha Trang on **14 Mar '67.**

Our late afternoon brought us into Nha Trang heading northwest into the haze of the setting sun. So we entered a left visual traffic pattern that took us around to the opposite direction, landing on Runway 12 (south easterly) for better visibility. Picture below shows our final approach view of Nha Trang Airbase, with the city of Nha Trang to the left (north) of the runway, and the US military facilities to the right (south) of the runway. Hon Tré Island is seen in the bay on the ocean side and left of the extended Runway 12 departure course.

Nha Trang AB Landing Rwy 12 (Southeast toward Pacific)

Ferry Flight Recap —The total trip had covered:

12,953 statute miles, in...

11-flying days (averaging 1,178 statute miles per flight-day), (24 calendar-days including crew rest, weather and maintenance delays), accumulating...

83.9 logged hours in flight, and averaging a commendable...

154 mph ground speed!

First Impressions of the Combat Zone – A quick review of the Map of Vietnam below shows the general picture of South East Asia (SEA) with Nha Trang AB shown at the orange arrow at the "knee" of the peninsula (just about 15 miles north of Cam Rahn Bay Air Base. The adjacent statistics will identify some details as to size, weather, and location. Saigon (later called "Ho Chi Minh City") is about as far south of Nha Trang (at the mouth of the Mekong River Delta), as the DMZ (Demilitarized

Zone Border, north of Nha Trang), which marks the separation between North and South Vietnam.

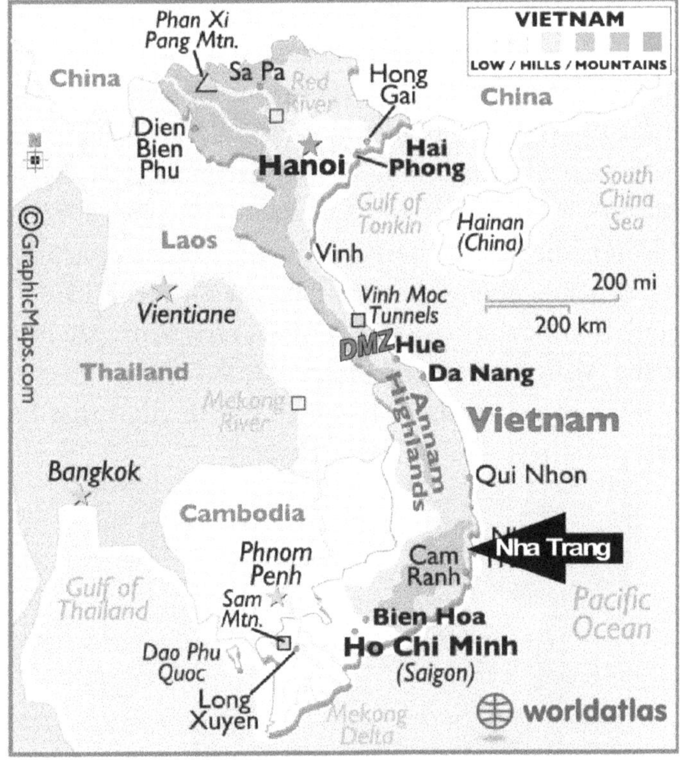

Map of Vietnam (1967)

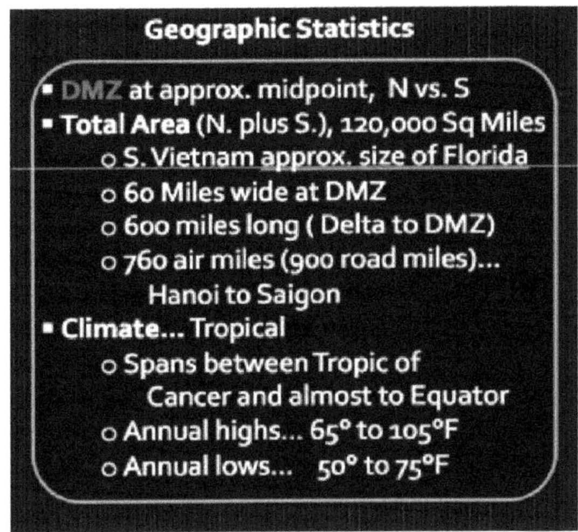

Nha Trang Air Base Facilities – During my one-year tour at Nha Trang Air Base, I found the base security to be very adequate. The Air Base belonged to the ARVN (Army of the Republic of Vietnam), but had been in co-use by them and various units of the US Military. The USAF had renovated the air base and provided most of the infrastructure and buildings on the US real estate (southern half; south-side of the runway). Nha Trang AB was the Vietnam Headquarters location for the US Army 5th Special Forces Airborne Group (the Green Berets), the 14th Air Commando Wing, and many other smaller units including my own (the 361st TEWS). The population of the Base was so great that probably more than 50% of the Military officers and senior NCOs lived in town in rented rooms or as groups that rented entire villas that belonged to our ARVN allies.

Nha Trang Tower behind EC-47 on Ramp

Nha Trang City was often called the "Riviera of Vietnam" and the "Viet Cong R&R Center". I chose to live on base in the aircrew BOQ (Bachelor Officers Quarters). This offered a major convenience of security and close proximity to my working location, as well as a having "some of the comforts of home". The Men's Officer Quarters, were cinder block and concrete, two-story construction with linoleum floors. The windows were unglazed (with tropical & humid climate), but were equipped with permanent screens and exterior bamboo sunshades. Each floor had seven open bays with plywood panels dividing them into 2-man cubicles with a central shower and latrine facility capable of use by up to 6-occupants at a time. I initially shared a small 8' by 8' cubicle with one double bunk, one desk & chair, and two 6' wall lockers. With some earned seniority, after about 3-months, I moved to a corner 8' by 10' foot "penthouse" cubicle which had two separate cots, two desks and chairs and two 6' wall lockers. Each cubicle, which-ever size had a central ceiling fan to provide air circulation. We slept under mosquito netting, when needed, and enjoyed Vietnamese maid service (for about $2 per week, per person, 2-maids per floor housing 7-cubicles, and 14 men to each floor). The maids kept the cubicles, latrines and showers clean, provided laundry services and kept our shoes/boots shined. There was a bunker-shelter next door for protection during enemy mortar attacks. Pretty rudimentary and basic, but much more substantial and modern than the ground troops were provided!

My Officer's Quarters

Bunker Next Door (originally sandbags and tent-top)

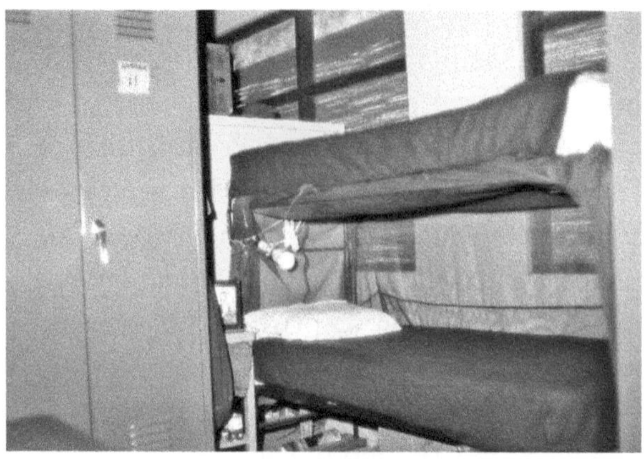

Initial Cubicle (First 3-months)

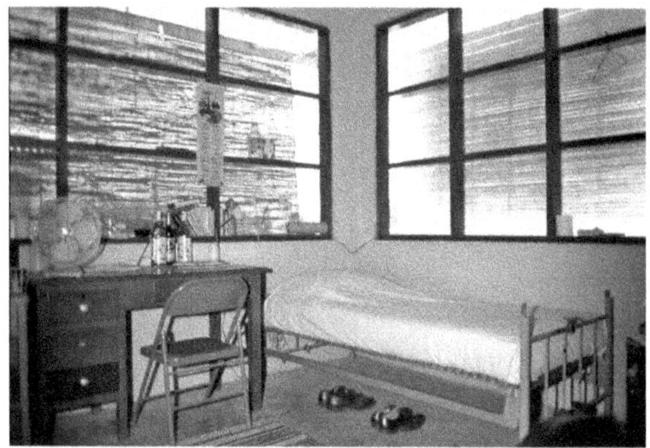

"Penthouse" Cubicle (for 2), After More Seniority

Over the course of the year, a new air-conditioned, motel-like two-story, 64-room wooden framed, facility was built, providing individual private rooms. But being of less-sturdy wooden construction, this was not as secure during mortar attacks. It typically was reserved for more senior officers, and by then, we had a large population of Lt. Colonels on-base. I was nearly half way through my tour when it was built. So I opted to stay where I was already secure and established.

New (Fall '67) Air Conditioned BOQ (Wood Frame)

The US side of Nha Trang AFB was also upgraded with ongoing infrastructure additions during my tour. These consisted of a new non-denominational Base Chapel, a 200-seat capacity covered Outdoor Theater, a Base Exchange shopping complex including, main store, limited-commissary (grocery), and cafeteria. Also provided were a Quick-stop beverage & snack store, a liquor store, barbershop, Laundromat, audio tape club equipped with 20-dual tape-recorder stations and a massive library of master tapes and air-conditioned both Officer's, and Enlisted's Clubs. It also hosted a local Armed Forces Radio station that broadcast from 6 AM to midnight daily. And, of course, being right on the beach provided ample off-duty recreation including a mobile (bus) snack bar ("Roach Coach"), when the weather permitted beach activity.

New Chapel

"Starlite Theater" (Under Construction)

Base Exchange

BX Cafeteria

Stereo Tape Club

Officer's Club

Beach "Roach Coach"

The VNAF, (South) Vietnamese AF aircraft, consisted mostly of Huey chopper gunbirds and A-1E single-engine fighter bombers of late-WWII US Navy vintage. These heavily armored attack aircraft where also heavily used as rescue aircraft for downed aviators. These were operated from the north side of the field, while the south side of the field was all US Forces, which represented 80% or more of the aircraft numbers and activity. There were very minimal on-base living quarters for the ARVN personnel.

Hazardous Operations in Vietnam — I gained many unique insights, and recorded many detailed anecdotes, and took many hundreds of 35 mm slides and photographs, during this first direct combat tour of my career. Many of these form a substantial part of these memoirs. We typically flew two-days on and one-day, or sometimes two-days off. Our scheduled mission times began anytime around the clock. My combat mission operations, largely consisted of regular 6.5 to 7.5 hour missions, spent mostly with long hours of random race-track orbits at a maximum altitude of about 10,000 ft, (restricted because of lack of pressurization and no supplemental oxygen). Depending on the area for the mission, that meant we were orbiting at altitudes <u>above the ground</u> of anywhere between 1,000 and 9,000 ft., over both mountains and low lands – at times, well within small arms range, but I new of very little true danger, or combat-anxiety, as long as we used caution.

One unique contributor to our sense of security was that the US had virtually total "air superiority" over South Vietnam. And the AC-47 Gunbirds (armed with three right side firing 6,000 rounds-per-minute (each) Gatling 7.62 mm rotary guns, looked axactly like our EC-47 airplane from the ground). Our air crews, being connected to the military intelligence gathering operation, received daily intelligence briefings on significant combat activities, before every mission. Although there were occasional enemy thrusts from MIGs off Hainan Island and Hanoi, I never heard of any that actually crossed the DMZ, or launched any attacks on aircraft or ground targets in the South. So there was virtually no fear of being attacked by enemy aircraft. However, the tensions of operating in the combat zone were always present in the atmosphere and was balanced by a heightened sense of humor by everyone involved. It was a regular occurrence in the Officer's Club bar after a day of combat operations, to greet the very unpopular Base Commander with a rousing cheer from inside when he entered, "Say hello to the Base Commander ... ***'Hello A**Hole'***", followed by a second chorus, "Say hello to the A**Hole ... ***'Hello Colonel B...'*** "! But, other experiences involved several other forms of life-threatening danger unique to the combat environment in South Vietnam, and the **Rules of Engagement** (**ROE**) by which we were constrained which politically originated <u>in the US</u>, and were ridiculous to our common-sense defense – <u>and winning the war</u>!

Examples of Rules of Engagement — There were many different ROE for the numerous different combatant groups of warriors. Some that specifically affected my mission are provided here.

1. "Friendlies" were not permitted to initiate strikes against enemies <u>unless fired upon first</u>. Even if we had solid evidence of their intent to cause us harm, or death.
2. Artillery and/or airstrikes were not permitted against enemy ground forces unless approved in advance, in detail, by local native chiefs for approval. (And we never had any assurance that these chiefs were not enemies or collaborators themselves). These approvals required that before any attacks US Forces would use air-dropped leaflets and/or "PsyOps" (psychological warfare operations) airborne-speaker broadcasts, notifying the enemy that, at a designated time the area would be bombarded, and that all non-combatants should vacate the area. (You know who departed and who were chained or confined and left behind, so the enemy could claim we where creating atrocities against innocents)?

3. Our aircraft were unarmed and vulnerable aircraft to ground fire, or more sophisticated anti aircraft weapons. However all aircrew members were issued either personal side-arms (pistols or revolvers) or long arms (M-16 rifles) depending on crew position and accessibility. However, these weapons were padlocked, unloaded in metal lockers anchored on the aircraft. And they could not be loaded except at sand filled barrels on the outside of the perimeter of the parking ramps (some ½ mile or more away from the aircraft for safety). This placed an additional and unacceptable mission time burden on the aircrew between crew briefing and crew arrival at the aircraft for this added procedure. When formal complaints were made to our seniors, we were informed that these weapons were no good except during ground evasion, and we wouldn't want to "piss off the enemy" by shooting at them. "So their only value was as trade and barter for assistance in gaining escape". So not being loaded was acceptable. *This and similar directives came from the Base Commander.*
4. With the high population of officers and senior enlisted living in town, there was a high volume of traffic traveling to and from the base around the clock every day. This travel was done using personal bicycles and motorcycles, walking, hired taxies and Vespa-scooter taxis, etc. As the war activities heightened as TET approached (the Chinese New Year), directives were handed down from senior base officials that no off-duty small arms would be permitted to be carried off base (for fear of accidental encounters with "civilian citizens"). When this was strongly disputed, this ROE was modified that "only the senior officer or NCO in any given residence would be permitted to carry". This was unenforceable because this distinction could not be readily verified; but carried the threat of courts-martial if violators were caught without meeting the criteria. It also failed to identify how any other endangered personnel could obtain

personal protection in the potential combat zone. *What total idiocy!*

Mid-Air Collisions with Friendly Aircraft —The flying weather in South Vietnam was in the inter-tropical conversion (ITZ) zone and had cyclic weather variations each 24-hour day, where over the course of a seven hour flight, we could see the morning haze turn into small powder-puff clouds at about 3,000' by noon, and then would gradually grow vertically as the temperatures continued to climb to become towering cumulous clouds by mid-afternoon, reaching upwards of 18 to 20,000 feet. These towering thunderstorms, lacking horizontal wind movements, would rain down directly through themselves with the intensity of a waterfall and slowly dissipate back to clear skies. These would look so intense on radar that one feared they would tear an airplane completely apart, but because they had no horizontal wind shear, they also had little turbulence, nor lightning and very little energy (compared to typical central US storms). At times the rainfall was so intense we would have to close the carburetor scoop (heat) doors on the top of the engine cowlings for fear of water literally drowning the engines.

Early morning new cloud formations

Mid-day towering cumulous clouds building to the left (N).

It was not the rain and turbulence of these clouds that created concern. It was that missions were flown under lack of state-side-type of IFR (Instrument Flight) Radar Traffic Control. We flew under what was called "tactical VFR" taking advantage of informal radar flight following as long as we had a radar transponder that could relay our aircraft direction, speed and altitude to the ground radar station. But many aircraft, with which we shared the sky didn't have, or didn't use their transponders! Of course we used standard altitude separation practices, flying even altitudes when flying westerly directions (4,000', 6,000', 8,000' and 10,000') and odd altitudes when flying easterly directions (5, 7, and 9,000'). But that was still potentially hazardous when flying north and south up and down the coast, of the VN-peninsula. It was not an uncommon occurrence to pop in or out of clouds like those shown in the left upper corner of the photo above and see a sight like this, passing at the same altitude and opposite direction!

A heavy A-1E "Sandy" fighter and pilot rescue plane that weighed more than an EC-47!

Potential Collision With Tactical Fighters — An equally dangerous experience involved sharing the airspace with a flight of four USAF, F-100s fighters flying formation from orbit at about 12,000' and dropping down in trail formation with about a half-mile separation, conducting an air strike with a low-altitude Forward Air Controller (FAC, O-2 "spotter" aircraft) targeting on ground targets. At the end of the ground attack each F-100 aircraft followed the previous one "coming back up onto their perch", with "Lead" coming at us head-on climbing right over our head with about 500' vertical separation and 2, 3, and 4 passing just under our belly, with their eyeballs locked on their leader. *We prayed they had good peripheral vision!*

F-100 SuperSabre coming through our altitude and passing overhead; eyes looking elsewhere!

At the time I fully recognized that Lead was likely watching over his shoulder at the FAC's smoke marker, while his followers were visually locked onto Lead is they rejoined the tight trail formation in the climb. We just had to hope and pray that these tactical aircraft pilots had their heads and eyes on continuous swivels to avoid other aircraft in the area.

Potential Aircraft Landing Crash Averted — Upon initial arrival for duty at the 361st TEWS, I found that this squadron had been operational for about six months. The pilot manning intentionally was such that there were about twice the number of crews as there were aircraft, with most Aircraft Commanders as Majors (plus a small number of Captains), and some junior Captains and 1st Lieutenants serving as co-pilots to the more senior and experienced pilots. I was initially relegated to the position of co-pilot, as expected, until I could gain more experience in the theater – despite my 2000 hours of C-47 experience and present experience flying the aircraft.

USAF policy was that combat tours would be of 12-months duration, so after six months, those Squadron pilots that were on-site at my initial arrival were now starting to depart for new assignments back home and being replaced by new-comers. However, by mid-1967 the war was reaching a peak level of troops and the incoming pilot replacements (in transport-type aircraft) were more rank heavy, and the Squadron ended up with incoming pilots who were aging Lt. Colonels with Korean War era C-47 experience, or recalled Reservists from desk jobs.

Even though I now had all the mission experience and credentials for an Aircraft Commander position, my full Colonel Squadron Commander felt he could not justify officially designating me, a Captain, as an aircraft commander with a Lt. Col. as co-pilot. Such a gap in rank and the related inversion of command authority just didn't bode well in the military traditions. So I was taken aside by the CO and told that in acknowledgement for my experience he was assigning me as co-pilot to one of the more "worrisome new aircraft commanders". (Gee, thanks a lot!). My new AC was a senior (51 year old) Major, who was a Korean War recall who had accumulated over 10,000 hours of DC-3 and C-47 time over a combined career in the Air Force and in airline service. His weakness however was that he was recalled after a several year absence from the cockpit, and he was about "120 pounds ringing wet", because his primary caloric intake was in the form of gin and vodka! In fact, I observed him on more than 50% of his missions to be flying with bad hangovers, and even with alcoholic tremors (DTs). I reported this to the Commander, but he stated that if he grounded him, we would be shorthanded.

One mid-afternoon, at the end of a seven hour reconnaissance mission, we were on final approach to Nha Trang AB in VFR conditions. Tower had cleared us to land and advised us that there was an Army Caribou (a high-wing twin-engine cargo aircraft of similar size as the C-47, but with short takeoff and landing – STOL capabilities), on the roll-out about two-thirds of the way down the 6,800 foot runway.

DHC-4 Caribou – Vietnam Era, STOL Transport

Old "Maj. Joe A" was used to airline-type operations and was making a normal power-on final approach on a standard airline 3-degree glide path. The Army bird didn't seem too concerned (or even aware) of our landing clearance and was making a very leisurely exit from the active runway. After we touched down — at about 70 knots, tail still in the air, and speed gradually decreasing — Maj. Joe A observed our rapid overtake of the pokey Caribou and commented, "Well I guess I better get on the brakes and slow this bird down". Based on my previous O'Hare experience, I expected him to get on the "binders" with the tail still in the air, but instead, the next thing I knew he was trying to "put the tail on the ground before braking" by applying back stick pressure!

Now understand, when an aircraft is still about 20 knots above the stall speed and you apply back stick pressure, the tail certainly goes down, but with flying airspeed the main gear had no intention of staying on the ground, and we became airborne again! Then Maj. Joe A realized the throttles were still cracked open about 3/8ths of an inch, and pulled them to idle. Instinctively, when a proficient pilot bounces a "gooney bird" on landing, the normal recovery is to just relax backpressure on the controls, bringing the pitch back to level and waiting for the airplane to settle in as airspeed decays — and that is what I was expecting Maj. Joe A to do. But the next thing I realized was that he was sucking the control column back into his gut. I saw the airspeed was decaying rapidly below 60 knots, the nose was headed toward 10 degrees nose-up and approaching 7 degrees off runway centerline heading, and the airplane was climbing past 20 feet.

My almost immediate reaction was 'literally' that we were going to crash as the airspeed and lift rapidly decayed, and that I had better take the airplane away from this precarious attitude. I grabbed the control wheel with both hands and stiff-armed the yoke toward the instrument panel. The aircraft flew what seemed like a zero-G parabola and the aircraft slammed to the ground with the nose-down pitch so steep that I was sure that we would grind off the prop tips.

As can be seen from the above illustration, this C-47 has landed in an extreme nose-down position. The upper set of blue lines shows the tail is up approximately 2.82° from level. The lower triangle shows the angle between the bottom of the tires and the prop tips, at which further down-pitch (an additional 12.5°, for a total of 15.32°) the prop tips would contact the ground. In other words, contacting the ground with a pitch of anything greater than about 15° nose-down from horizontal would have caused the prop tips to grind into the runway, causing damage to the props, potential sudden stoppage of the engines, and probable loss of control of the aircraft!

At this point I was "walking" the rudder pedals from stop to stop trying to keep the aircraft on the runway as we violently zigzagged back toward the runway heading. Whew, that was a close call! Our landing was so violent that the Tower queried us to see if we need crash-recovery assistance, but I reported that we were OK. As we subsequently parked, shut down the aircraft, and deplaned, Maj. Joe A and I were still in a state of near shock, but before leaving my cockpit seat, I took the time to write the aircraft up in the maintenance logs for a hard bounce landing inspection.

The next day, the Squadron CO approached us in the orderly room and asked Maj. Joe A about the hard bounce landing. He replied, "Oh, I just had a bit of a bounce and was going for the "full-stall, three-pointer", but ole' Chuck got excited and pushed the nose over. Why do you ask? Was there anything wrong with the airplane?" The CO replied, "No, but Maintenance spent 350 man-hours doing a landing gear inspection!" The CO then called me into his office and quizzed me in detail about the circumstances. He asked why, if I was so concerned, hadn't I just applied max power and done a go-around. I answered his question by describing my power-on stall-induced snap roll experience, on a test flight at altitude (out of O'Hare Airport) a couple years before, and explaining that I had no desire to repeat that experience, particularly so close to the ground! No further comment was forthcoming from the CO, other than "Well Done, Captain"!

Bombed by a B-52 — Another incident we encountered was a random B-52D flying at 35,000' almost overhead. When unable to drop on his primary target, he decided to drop his load of one hundred-four 500-pound bombs, on a "target of opportunity". His bomb-drop fell almost through our flight path without him knowing we were there! He was so high that I couldn't even see him above! And at 10,000 feet in a slow, top-camouflaged aircraft, he certainly could not see us. I was alerted only when the string of concussions started buffeting my aircraft and could be seen about half a mile off the left side as they exploded at a rate of about one per second for nearly two minutes!

B-52D salvoing all One hundred eight, 500 pound bombs over Laos

Either he had failed to notify his Airborne Command and Control Coordinator (ABCCC) C-130 aircraft, or the ABCCC had forgotten my check-in with him 30 minutes earlier for radar-flight-following, and any weapons notifications in our immediate area!

Fired Upon a by US Naval Cruiser— On another occasion, I was flying south to my base "feet wet" about a <u>half mile off-shore</u> at 8,000 ft. and spotted a big boat headed north that was about <u>three-quarters of a mile off-shore</u>. I had been using radar flight following from "Water Boy", a USAF GCI (Ground Control Intercept) radar sight at Chu Lai, on the coast. He had responded when asked, that there was no Naval artillery from off-shore on my flight path. As I passed abeam the ship, I rolled into a shallow left bank to get a better look down it him, only to see his three, 8-inch guns fire almost directly at me. After taking evasive action I noted that his shells were impacting about two miles on-shore, which meant they went right through my altitude before passing over the top of the ballistic arc and falling back to ground!

I immediately radioed Water Boy and reported the incident, providing him with range and bearing from his TACAN site as to the point of impact. As I proceeded down the coast I heard another aircraft call to Water Boy asking for Naval artillery advisories. Again Water Boy reported there were none. On the common frequency we both were using, I asked him why he had not relayed my advisory of the danger zone. His reply was that my report was not received through intelligence channels and therefore was not considered authenticated!

USS Cruiser, St. Paul in Vietnam in 1967

US Army Artillery Fire — Another fairly frequent occurrence we encountered was US Army artillery fire that could fire within our working area and up through our altitude. The nature of our mission operation was that we would fly randomly over our directed working zone, with random orbits watching for enemy radio transmissions. When we found a strong or particularly familiar radio activity of interest, we would reposition our aircraft and fly 10- to 15-mile radius patterns around the transmitter with our sophisticated equipment to determine its precise location, while our on-board Security Service crew were recording the transmissions for further analysis of content. Often there would be friendly ground Army artillery forces that might desire to attack those same forces. So as we entered the areas of known friendly "fire support bases", we would check in with them for firing advisories and to let them know we were working in the area overhead. Frequently they would identify that they were located at a position, like "three clicks" (kilometers) southwest of "point Romeo", or some such, which used Army special map grids to which we were not privy (they didn't want to broadcast sensitive locations that the enemy might also hear, which would make them vulnerable). And they also would include such information as "firing ordinance to 5,000 feet elevation, to an area north at 8 clicks" (the target location relative to them). If we were flying at 10,000' ***above sea level***, and they were firing from a location that we were uncertain of, it was critical that we know both their precise location and terrain elevation to determine whether their 5,000' ordinance maximum was above their terrain (which might be as high as 6 to 7,000' above sea level), in order to determine if it would penetrate through our altitude. In the year I was there, we never resolved a good answer to this dilemma!

Based upon the priority assigned to our mission targets, occasionally we would have to request they cease firing while we were working the area to avoid being hit. But we understood that this could increase their vulnerability, or the vulnerability of the troops they were trying to support. And we did hear occasional intelligence reports about friendly aircraft that had been hit, or even shot down, with major injuries and/or fatalities. So this was not just an unrealistic concern we faced.

Other aircraft in my squadron weren't always so lucky. One aircraft with its entire crew was lost to enemy fire the day before we arrived (as previously mentioned). Another, a month after my departure at tours-end, was hit in daytime by unknown anti-aircraft fire, but it was able to struggle to an abandoned jungle airstrip before crash-landing, and all crewmembers were rescued. (BREW 41 details on www.ec47.com/Brew41). Numerous other EC-47s came home with small arms bullet holes in the wings, tail or fuselage, but no injuries.

Enemy Gunboat Machine Gun Attack — After flying a 7.5-hour evening mission, I was returning after dark to Nha Trang. Making my return from the northern highlands area "feet-wet" (staying offshore to avoid any potential ground fire) I made my visual approach over the Bay of Nha Trang. The alignment of Runway 30 (300° Magnetic heading) the runway approach took me to the left, but very close to Hon Tré Island, a small mountain rock at about 1500 feet peak elevation. I was flying a normal glide path (dotted line) with my landing lights and red-green wingtip lights ON, and my aircraft descending through about 500 feet at about the location of the first boat in the photo below. Suddenly I saw two arcs of .50-caliber machine gun tracers coming up at about a 45° elevation from the bay below the aircraft, one from either side of the nose. The tracers crossed my flight path, and were about 50 feet or less ahead of the aircraft. I immediately pulled up at max-power and cut off all external lights. We then immediately notified the tower of the attack. The Tower notified the appropriate Naval agencies and we were informed the next day that US Navy gunboats had intercepted and captured two Viet Cong vessels.

Runway 30 Approach to Nha Trang AB

Captured VC Gunboats

Anti-Aircraft Artillery Incident — I am sure that my EC-47 aircraft may have come under enemy fire without my awareness. But on only one other occasion (than the tracer-fire observed above) was I ever near-positive that my aircraft and crew was a target. Ever since my arrival at the 361st TEWS in March of '67, due to the loss the prior week of one of the EC-47s, all of our reconnaissance missions were directed to proceed to-and-from to our working orbit areas by a "feet-wet" route. When we were working the furthest away from "home" – along the DMZ – this reduced our "mission area" time by as much as one-hour each way, from our primary area. On one after-dark mission near the DMZ, as we were flying random orbit race-track patterns looking for enemy radio signals, I observed a couple bright flashes (like flash bulbs) that appeared to be on the horizon (meaning at or altitude), but at a sufficient distance that no sound nor concussion was heard or felt. We initially gave that area a wide zone of avoidance, but each time we came back near the same place, we again observed the flashes. After a couple observations, we located a radio transmission that took us further away for a couple hours. I kept an eye at that general area and saw no more flashes.

After completing the transmitter locations in that newer area, we had indications that there might be transmissions of interest in the earlier zone. Again I observed the mystery flashes several times as we approached the working area. I felt that there was nothing to be gained by pushing our luck, so we moved on to fresh territory and finished the mission without incident. The next day we checked our observations with the Intelligence organization, and confirmed that there were other reports of enemy 77mm anti-aircraft artillery in the vicinity of our observed flashes. But if so, it definitely was being fired at the sound of the aircraft, not at a visual or radar return from the aircraft.

Mortar Attacks On Nha Trang Air Base —For the first half of 1967, there were no significant overt enemy attacks against the base, except an occasional attempted perimeter incursion. However, the range of jungle-covered, low mountains south of the field became more and more infested with enemy combatants as time went on. In August we began to come under mortar barrage from the VC exactly once a month, all most to the date, and always at about fifteen minutes after midnight, as though "Charlie" was waiting for the Armed Forces Radio and TV station to sign-off the air before initiating the attack. For the most part, "Charlie's" aim was lousy, and very little damage, was done other than to our morale. Although one night he succeeded in making a direct hit on a "black" special mission C-130 on the ramp, reducing it to smoldering ashes. And several times we found shrapnel damage and unexploded dud mortar rounds in the revetments with our parked EC-47s.

EC-130 Before

EC-130 After Being Hit by Mortar

Nha Trang was protected by several batteries of 105 mm Howitzers that were integrated with one of the first in-country counter-mortar radar systems. With this system, the Howitzers could return very accurate and deadly fire on a mortar tube within a reported one minute of the first round hitting the ground. As a result "Charlie" soon learned that all he could get off would be about three rounds per tube before the tube was obliterated with 105 mm counter-fire. So we seldom got more than about 30 mortar rounds (from a barrage out of maybe 10 mortar tubes). So within 30 minutes of the initiation of an attack, we would generally receive the "all-clear" and we could return from the concrete and sandbag security bunkers to our barracks for the rest of the night (and the next 30 days).

"Hitting the Silk" — As the end of 1967 drew near, it became widely known by Intelligence that the jungle-covered low mountain just to the south of Nha Trang was infested with VC. That was where most of the nighttime mortar attacks originated, as well as from Hon Tré Island in the bay alongside of the final approach to the northwest-bound-runway. As hostilities escalated, the "friendlies" decided it might be prudent to keep the mountainside illuminated at night to help the friendly patrols and to force "Charlie" (as the VC forces were nicknamed) to keep their heads down.

Trying to sleep under the constant yet random report of the friendly Howitzers and mortars firing magnesium parachute flares all night became quite disruptive, but it was a small price to pay for the extra security from mortar attack.

It was amazing to look up into the mountainside in the morning to see it polka-dotted with white-silk or nylon parachute canopies from the flares of the previous night. It was equally fascinating to notice that by mid-day the majority of the parachute silk had disappeared.

Obviously, some enterprising Howitzer commander realized that Charlie was enjoying the spoils of hundreds and thousands of yards, of free nylon or silk parachute material each day and decided to put an end to these donations to the enemy. At first light, this Howitzer commander had ordered his men to "zero in" on selected canopies lying in the treetops and to monitor them continuously with binoculars. When the canopy was seen to disappear, there was a fire command given and a 105 mm shell followed the canopy into the treetops.

After a few days of this counter-offensive action, Charlie lost interest in salvaging parachute flare canopies for tent making, clothing and resale!

Friendly Night-time Artillery Fire — During the TET invasion of Feb 1968, however, the hostilities were getting a lot closer to home and the city of Nha Trang was attacked and partially overrun by VC and NVA. The tension on base was thick enough to cut with a knife and many of the military that had lived in town were now back, staying on base, in temporary housing.

True to the pattern, but about 2:00 AM (as I recall), the sound of incoming rounds was heard followed by the warning sirens and perimeter small arms fire. We all headed, in our skivvies and un-armed, for the bunkers located between the barracks and listened as the barrage continued and became more intense. Unlike our previous experience, the incoming rounds did not stop after the first several minutes, but continued unabated for well over 30 minutes. Speculation became rampant that the base must be under threat of being overrun and that we could all be sitting ducks in the bunkers, in our skivvies, with no firearms. The sound of the incoming rounds was getting closer and ever more frightening.

Then, still in the midst of the sound of incoming shells, a runner arrived at our bunker proclaiming that it was "all clear", and "only a false alarm". It seems that apparently without full coordination, the US Navy had a "friendly" US Naval vessel in the bay, with its 8-inch guns, which was shelling enemy positions overhead, around the far perimeter of the base and that is what we were experiencing. ***[Do you suppose it was the USS Cruiser St. Paul harassing me again?]***

Pollution & Bio–Hazards in Vietnam — Another hazard of concern was the high levels of environmental pollution that came with living in Vietnam for a year. Living on the base at Nha Trang (as previously mentioned), and we were constantly enveloped in an extreme level of noise – from continuous operation of numerous 1,000 HP portable diesel generators for Base electrical power; from round-the-clock take-off and landing noise and maintenance run-up checks of the hundreds of local and transient aircraft; from the regular but sporadic 105 mm Howitzers firing night and day with parachute flares at night, and counter-mortar radar suppression fire day and night.

Being surrounded by contaminated water from the polluted rivers and unhealthy ground water, our potable water on-base was laced with more chlorine than your average swimming pool, which also created a health concern. To improve the taste, this made it crucial to chill the water to near freezing and then mix it with either orange Tang, or Crystal Light ice tea mix to make the taste bearable. (It is now widely known that high dosages of chlorine in drinking water is an active carcinogen, and Crystal Light is sweetened with Aspartame, a toxic derivative of formaldehyde, which is also a carcinogen in large doses). But that's all we had, short of beer and alcoholic beverages, which didn't mix well with flying nearly every-day. And worst of all health threats, was the potential of daily exposure to Agent Orange (Dioxin) defoliant, and its long-term health issues (cancer, heart disease, neurological disorders, birth defects, etc.), which was widely sprayed for jungle suppression from low flying C-123 aircraft that were based out of Nha Trang and other bases. Fifteen years after retirement from the Air Force, I became personally aware of the health impacts of these biohazards on my health, with the diagnosis of heart ischemia and Atrial Fibrillation attributable to Agent Orange and a future lifetime of VA disability.

NOTE: *Since much of the Vietnam War data has been declassified in 1995, it has been subsequently published that the EC-47 mission contributed more than 80% of intelligence and targeting information for all fighter air strikes, B-52 missions, and naval artillery in South Vietnam during the war. (See <www.EC47.com> website).*

R & R to Singapore — During January 1968 – my eleventh month in Vietnam – I had the opportunity to take a one-week R & R (Rest and Relaxation) trip to Singapore. I proceeded by Huey helicopter with my B-4 suitcase bag of civilian clothing and necessities for the trip, to Cam Rahn Bay AFB (about 10 miles south of Nha Trang on the coast beyond the low mountains separating the two bases), to await transport the next day for Singapore. Transportation was in the form of commercial airliners chartered by the DoD, and mine was a commercial stretched DC-8 with seating for 225 passenger, plus aircrew. On the flight I determined that there were about 180 young enlisted "warriors", mostly Army and Marine ground combat troops (referred to affectionately as "grunts" and "jar-heads") and the remainder were officers and senior NCOs from Army, Navy, Marines and Air Force. This trip was the first real opportunity that I had to mingle with the ground soldiers that were doing battle in the swamps, jungles and mountains of South Vietnam.

Upon arrival, we were all briefed about numerous activities by the Singapore R & R Center staff that were available for the service members optional participation. We were then transported to various hotels and motels in the city for our lodgings. One of the first available activities the next day was a guided tour of Singapore, which included a special "family-style" Chinese dinner at one of the finer restaurants. At the restaurant, we found ourselves in a large dining room, which had 6-large round tables, each accommodating 10 to 12 guests. In the center of each table was a four-foot diameter "Lazy Susan" rotating tray that they loaded up with a dozen or more large bowls and serving dishes with various types of Chinese food, from which we could pick and chose to our own liking.

During the meal, we heard stories from each of the service members of their experiences in combat. The ground troops were mostly draftees with an average age of maybe 20 to 21 years. The officers present were probably anywhere from their late 20's to mid 30's in age. It was fascinating to hear of the stories of the young "grunts", telling of living in the jungles with only the clothes they had on their backs and their weapons; and being on patrols away from base for weeks or even a month at a time. Tales of their sleeping in the jungle, while being ever-on-guard for snipers and ambushes, of having to bathe in rivers and streams with their clothes on in order to get clean laundry, and of foraging for food (snakes, bugs, fish and jungle animals – rodents, monkeys, and such) when their field rations ran low while waiting for the Huey choppers to come to them about once a week with replenishments of food and ammo. These "kids" had come from the good ole' USA almost right from high school, where the most hostile environment they had experienced was from swaggering street gangs or aggression on the football fields, to a place surrounded by face-to-face combat with the Viet Cong blowing away their new friends and comrades with Claymore mines, AK-47 machine guns and hand grenades, or booby-traps with punji stakes coated in human feces. They were surrounded by fear, death, horrendous living conditions, and gruesome bloody injuries.

This exposure to the horrors of war was amply demonstrated, by happenstance, after our meal was ended and we were departing the restaurant. As the 40 or 50 of us exited the restaurant, heading back to the buses for the continuation of our tour, we were suddenly aware of several series of close by small-arms automatic-weapons fire that lasted for several minutes. On hearing these bursts of firing, the "grunts" were instinctively mentally transported back to the battle sites, and hit the ground and rolled for cover under vehicles parked at the urban street curb. Although, all were unarmed and in summer civilian clothing, we were all conspicuous in Singapore as tourists and US Military personnel, by our clothing, our hair cuts and youthful physical stature. Shortly after hitting the ground, the sound of young children laughing was heard, and as the "grunts" came out from shelter — some with eyes as big as saucers — they realized that this was the time of the Chinese New Year, TET, and the firing was actually 20-packs of fire crackers lit off by Chinese pre-teen youngsters who were now laughing at their anticipated reaction from the troops. This was my first broad recognition of what "combat fatigue" or PTSD

(Post Traumatic Stress Disorder) really looked like – that these young combat soldiers had their lives forever changed by the very real experience of the horrors of combat, death and serious maiming from the wartime battles that they had encountered and had been psychologically immersed into at such young and immature stages in their lives! They had come here out of largely non-violent and safe environments of their short immature youth into a world of danger, anger, and instinctual need for survival awareness that would take many months and years – if ever – to fully overcome!

Staying In Touch with Family — Keeping in touch with my wife and less than two-year old daughter would be my major daily priority when I had time between my 7 to 8-hour flying missions that occurred essentially in flying two days on and then one day off, continuously every month that I was in-country. Pat & I started off with hand-written letters (remember there were no personal or laptop computers or Internet, nor FaceTime or Skype streaming live video, then). But Southeast Asia was a "super-bargain basement" of the world for Japanese and Korean electronics in the '60s.

I soon discovered a great bargain in the BX, of small briefcase-size audio tape-recorders for about $25 that used 3-inch reel-to-reel recording tape. I bought one for myself and ordered a second one for delivery to the family in Chicago. The 3-inch tapes could provide either 30 minutes or an hour of audio, depending on the type of tape purchased and the speed of the tape machines, and came in a compact reusable plastic mailing box. Once in use, they provided an almost realistic two-way "apparent live" (but actually only a one-way) conversation capability that was so natural you felt almost like you were talking across the table (rather than across the world) to your spouse or family, and could really stay connected so much better and more realistically than with the written word. Once mailed, in either direction, it took about 4 to 5 days each way from Vietnam to Chicago, or back.

***And the REST OF THE STORY*:** It took a while to get past the usual "brain freeze" of trying to talk to an impersonal microphone and compose at the same time, but after a few trials I learned to make a list of topics to refer to and then got more comfortable talking in a casual conversational tone on the tape, for the duration of the time. Then on a tape I received from Pat, she mentioned that she was having problems with the car not starting, and thought it was the battery. Not being her usual responsibility, and not too familiar with those mechanical things, she was going to talk to our next-door friends for assistance. In my immediate return tape, I told her not to worry, but to take the car into Sears, because the car had a Sears battery with a 5-year warranty, and they would do what was necessary, at little or no cost. After several days with no mention of the battery, a tape arrived and she mentioned that the neighbor had put a jumper on it and charged it, but it didn't seem to be very strong. I worried a bit wondering why she hadn't taken it to Sears, as I had suggested. Then a couple more days went by and she said she decided she had better go and buy a new battery. So I sent another immediate tape reply and strongly insisted she take it to Sears and not waste the warranty and the added $35 cost of an outright new purchase. About 10-days subsequent to my initial comment on the problem, I received a tape and she told me she had received my tape about the Sears warranty and had taken the car in after another jump-start and it was all taken care of at little expense. It was only then that we both figured out that there was a real 10-day lag time between receiving a tape, sending a response back and then getting a return.

On the up-side, a real wonder proved itself at the end of my tour. As I got more proficient with taping in a comfortable relaxed fashion, I decided I would dedicate a portion of each tape by talking directly to my little Caryn (age 13 months when I departed). I would switch to "baby talk" tone and ask her questions, and tell her things that she might like, and even leave short breaks for her to answer my questions or comments.

Pat had a 5 by 7 photo framed, which was taken of me in uniform shortly before my departure, and she kept it on the dresser in Caryn's room as a reminder. When she was going to play a tape she would send Caryn to get the framed photo "of Daddy", and tell her that's who was talking to her on the tape. So that became a regular ritual every couple days when "Daddy" would talk to her and Mommy from the machine next to the photo.

At the end of my year's tour I arrived on a commercial flight at Chicago O'Hare Airport at about 6 AM after over 20 hours of travel and delays, plus a overnight stay in Seattle airport's USO Veteran's Lounge. Pat had left Caryn overnight at the neighbor's house so she wouldn't have to deal with getting her up and dressed so early. It was nearly 8 AM by the time we arrived home and Pat was going to get Caryn (now 2-years old) from next door.

Pat suggested I go hide on the far side of Caryn's dresser, and she would send Caryn in to get "Daddy's" photo, for a homecoming surprise. Caryn was all smiles from ear to ear, when she came in and discovered me hiding beside the dresser. There was no shyness, nor timidity, and she followed me around holding my hand for the next two days or more, even when I had to go to the bathroom! What a wonderful homecoming, and a blessing realized from those tape recorders. Boy this new technology was really something!

Capt. Chuck Miller, "Daddy" – 1966

Caryn – Age 22 mo.

Vietnam Accomplishments — While, at Nha Trang, I served also as the Sqdn Flight Safety Officer, and was also charged with performing some ground and flight instruction, and also maintenance check flights. After arrival in Vietnam, I flew another 1,000 hours in-country in the EC-47.

Following my Vietnam assignment, the Military Personnel Center, MPC, offered me follow-on assignments, flying the Gooney bird at my choice of Wheelus AFB, Libya, or Hurlburt AFB, FL. I replied that, though I loved flying the Gooney Bird, with nearly 3,000 C-47 hours logged, I felt it was time for me to put my all-jet pilot training, combined with combat experience, and high-level security classification into further use. So I declined these offered assignments.

CHAPTER 5

SAC KC-135Q for the SR-71 (1968 –'73)

After declining the several C-47 assignments proposed by the Air Force Personnel Center, I requested a SAC assignment in tankers, on the west coast. I had heard from a fellow squadron member at Nha Trang about the SR-71 operation at Beale AFB, CA, and was properly qualified to seek that assignment.

How, and why? By 1968, the Strategic Air Command was beginning to lose experienced Aircraft Commanders (ACs) to Vietnam and with my Top Secret compartmentalized security clearance already in-hand (which typically requires six to twelve months to obtain), and the SR-71 operation – unknown to me at this time – just barely underway, I was accepted by SAC Personnel and assigned to the 903rd AREFS, Beale, for support of that operation, even though I lacked experience in flying heavy jet transports.

The KC-135A (Background) — The KC-135A was the first all-jet powered tanker in the world, designed and built by the Boeing Military Aircraft Co, in Wichita, Kansas, and on production contracts from 1955 through 1964; the first (of over 700, plus 20 for sale to the French AF) were delivered in 1956 and became operational in June 1957. A total of 820 -135s were manufactured of all series, of which 732 were in the "A" model tanker configuration. These original tankers were powered by four Pratt & Whitney J57-43 or -59 axial-flow turbojet (non-fan) engines, which were augmented with water-injection take-off to obtain a full 13,750 pounds thrust (per engine) during operations above 65° F and take-off (pressure altitudes) of up to 10,000 feet. The 88 remainder (originally designated "C-135B" non-tanker models) were produced with P&W TF-33 low-bypass turbofan engines of 17,000 to 18,000 pounds thrust (no water augmentation required).

The KC-135A tanker (Boeing designated as B-717) was the forerunner to the original Boeing 707-720 commercial airliner, which was largely built on the USAF -135 tooling (which preceded the Commercial 707). The tanker version was structurally much stronger, through the use of special materials (needed by the heavier weight of its primary cargo – fuel – and it had no passenger seats or side windows; 97% of its fuel tankage was either internal to the wings, or in the belly below the cargo floor (where commercial airliners have their baggage holds). It also had one small fuel tank on the upper deck aft of the fuselage aft-pressure-bulkhead (in the tail), to help with center-of-gravity balance when heavily loaded to capacity and rapidly transferring fuel to a receiver). And of course it had all the special equipment for refueling large aircraft including the "flying boom", the expanded fuel-panel tank controls and gauges in the cockpit, and other equipment, plumbing, valves, and pumps for the basic refueling mission requirements.

KC-135A Flyover, Castle AFB, Summer 1968

The KC-135A Pilot Transition Course — First Impressions

Contrasted with the C-47 aircraft I had been flying for 6-years, the KC-135A (and KC-135Q) from their original, late-1950s entry into service, were probably ten-times more complex in design and operation. The original KC-135 tankers were equipped with under-powered (yet the newest-state-of-the-art of the mid-1950s), non-fan, water-augmented straight turbojet (Pratt & Whitney J-57 series) engines of still unproven reliability (at their introduction); a maximum takeoff gross weight of 301,600 pounds (12 times heavier than the C-47); a fuel payload of up to 200,000 pounds – reduced respectively by any cargo and passengers carried (nominally ~169,000 pounds of fuel – nearly 32 times more fuel weight than the C-47), virtually all of which could be either offloaded to receiver(s), or could be consumed by the KC-135 engines. The KC-135A had an operational altitude of up to approximately 41,000 ft above sea level (~ 4-times higher than the C-47); and Mach .86 max speed (~585 MPH at 30,000'), approximately 4.3 times faster than the C-47 (Mach 0.2, 150 MPH at 10,000 ft). The KC-135 had 6-fuel tanks spread across its 35° swept-back wings, and 3-more tanks in the fuselage in the belly under the floor, plus an additional tank above the floor in the aft fuselage under the tail, all of which had to be carefully managed to keep the aircraft center-of-gravity within safe flight limits, especially during rapid fuel offloads to inflight receiver(s), and during the slow flight of take-offs and landings. Unlike the C-47, this was definitely NOT a "seat of the pants" flying aircraft.

Take-off and landing data for the KC-135 had to be computed from many pages of performance charts in the Pilot's Manual to account for multiple environmental considerations (field pressure altitude; ambient runway temperature; available runway length; runway up or down slope; terrain around the airport; prevalent winds – head, tail, or crosswind components, and gusts; – aircraft gross weight, fuel distribution – center of gravity of fuel dispersal; and wing flap configuration. Also in each initial take-off calculation was the determination of need to use water augmentation for the initial take-off (125 seconds worth, one-time per take-off using demineralized water), and many other considerations including single and multiple engine failure speeds and the resulting added drag of required rudder deflection to maintain controlled engine-out flight direction. Similarly, every approach and landing required updated aircraft weight computation to determine stall speed, landing speed, approach speed, and speed in various landing gear and flap configurations, during an approach. These computations could vary in time to compute from 10 minutes to over 30. There were no computers available onboard to speed up these chart calculations.

The KC-135 aircraft flight controls were largely unboosted, direct cable and pulley physical connections between the pedals and control wheel to the aerodynamic flight controls. Only the rudder had a hydraulic boost, to help with engine failure conditions, but if the right-side hydraulic system failed (driven by the right two engines) then that boost would not be available. So the aircraft was very heavy and sometimes difficult to handle. Compared to the C-47, the take-off and landing speeds were 90 to 100 knots faster in the KC-135, and that meant that critical geographic references came up and sailed past in about one-tenth of the time, than on the slower C-47 flight-path.

All of these conditions meant that things could happen very quickly, and the pilot had to remain "at least five-minutes ahead of the aircraft", particularly during maneuvering and take-offs and landings with precious little time to think and analyze what was happening when transitioning between taxiing to flight, and back to landing. *(No time for a cup of coffee on final approach between the start of descent on glide-path and touch-down, as on the C-47).*

Another consideration was the myriad number of complex interacting systems with hundreds of circuit breakers, switches, dials and gauges in the cockpit, numerous fuel tanks with both considerations of fuel quantity, and variation in center of gravity as fuel was transferred to receivers, adjusted for emergency feed and/or dumping, or setting up for landing, and the various sensors used for quick determinations of critical limits (elevator trim setting displayed crude C.G. info in flight, etc). And the aircraft did not have a flight engineer to handle many of these systems operation or inflight calculations, etc. The Boom Operator (when not doing A/R) could assist with some of these chores, but he did not have a cockpit workstation and separate duplicate controls or displays typical of Flight Engineers stations. So most of these responsibilities had to be handled by the AC and Copilot. *The level, currency, and proficiency of training were the most critical aspect of handling all the various operations encountered.*

My experience in the Strategic Air Command (SAC), did not come about in the traditional way. Most pilots flying in SAC during the Cold War, made their entry as a young recent graduate from Under-graduate Pilot Training (UPT). They then received three months of formal transition training in the designated aircraft they were to fly, at a SAC Transition Training base like Castle AFB in Merced CA, graduating as a "minimally qualified" copilot before proceeding to their assigned base, where they would fly as a copilot for a several years – until typically attaining 2,000 logged flight hours – in the right seat with lots of OJT (on-the-job-training) before being recommended for upgrade training to the duties and responsibilities of the left seat, as Aircraft Commander (AC).

In my case, I was assigned to SAC six years after completing UPT, and had already accumulated nearly 3,000 logged (post-graduation) pilot hours, and completed five years flying the WW II vintage C-47 configured as a Navigation Trainer (TC-47), plus a one-year combat tour in Vietnam flying the same C-47 type, but in a Top Secret mission configuration with totally modernized systems and instruments, in the electronic reconnaissance version (the EC-47).

My SAC experienced began with the typical three-month transition training at Castle AFB in the summer of 1968, but in the crew position of Aircraft Commander. The training was focused on saturation learning of the highly complex aircraft operations and systems, simulator training – primarily for Emergency procedures and operations, combined with systems and cockpit instrumentation familiarization, and some rudimentary instrument flight procedures and approaches, plus emergency condition simulations.

In that time-frame, flight simulators were pretty crude, each one occupying a railroad car with a room-sized very slow tube-type computer, and an interior cockpit mock-up with an instructor console behind the pilot's seats. It had no motion simulation, nor any visual outside references to assist with pitch, bank, or runway environment like today's full motion and visual simulators. It was all based upon flight-instrument readings with a small input of audible engine sounds with tire touch-down noises (and occasional simulated crashing sounds).

After five or six weeks of extensive classroom and rudimentary simulator training we were finally assigned to an Instructor Crew consisting of an Instructor Pilot (IP), Instructor Navigator (IN), and Instructor Boom Operator (IBO), plus three student transition pilots and one or two student navigators and a student boom operator. Each day during the flight-line portion, consisted of a couple hours of mission planning followed by a 4 to 6 hour flight session including a refueling of some type of receiver (bomber, transport, or fighters) and then procedures of in-flight maneuvers at altitude (approaches to stalls, slow flight, steep turns to 45° bank, practice of recovering from unusual attitudes in clouds and Dutch Roll recovery, etc.), navigation, and then numerous instrument approaches for each student pilot combined with touch-and-go landings, simulated engine failure procedures and in-flight emergencies, and some flight handling emergencies with simulated loss of hydraulics or electrical systems. Upon satisfactory completion of the 3-month training, I was certified as a KC-135 Aircraft Commander ... but under SAC regulations, I was not qualified to fly the copilot seat and perform those duties without being under the supervision of an Instructor Pilot!

While still in training at Castle AFB, my family and I took several weekends to drive to Beale AFB, Marysville, and Yuba City, looking for housing (less than a two-hour drive, away). We eventually found a great buy on a builder's 3-year old custom 3-bedroom ranch home (built for himself), which would be available at my transfer date to Beale AFB. We negotiated an offer, which the builder accepted and started the paperwork for purchase.

Upon completion of the 90-day course at Castle, I proceeded with my family (Pat, and Caryn, then age 2-1/2) from the 3-month training to my new duty assignment and home base of the SR-71 Blackbird, outside of Marysville/Yuba City, CA and about 30 miles north of Sacramento (a 30-minute drive to the base). Upon reporting into the 903rd Aerial Refueling Squadron (AREFS), I was assigned as copilot on an Instructor Crew (Capt. Neal S – Instructor Pilot, Capt. Dick B –Instructor Nav, and TSgt Angie C - IBO) which meant I could fly in either pilot seat under instructor supervision, until I became proficient in the unique tactics and procedures of refueling the SR-71 and other types of receivers. This also provided time for learning all the other nuances of SAC procedures from the co-pilot's (and AC's perspective and responsibilities), until such time as a crew became available for my assignment. This arrangement lasted for approximately six months before the opportunity arose to get my own crew, during which time I flew an average of 2 to 3 times a week while at home base, and went on temporary duty (TDY) three times for 6-weeks each to Kadena AFB, Okinawa, where I was familiarized with Operational SAC procedures in South East Asia and the SR-71 (and bombers and fighters) in operational missions over Vietnam.

KC-135Q Differences from a KC-135A? — The KC-135Q was the same as the KC-135A, except for modifications to the fuel tanks plumbing to isolate the SR-71 special fuel. It also had added special secure (encrypted) radios for communications between tanker and receiver, and unique electronic navigation systems to assist with the unique SR-71 refueling rendezvous procedures.

In other words, the "Q" model was basically a unique SR-71 modification from the KC-135A configuration, which was applied to 56 of the total 732 KC-135"A" fleet. Thirty of these 56 (all of 1958 production dates) were designated as "Full-Qs" and initially were exclusively assigned and operated by the 903rd AREF Squadron, for the SR-71 (and other experimental or advanced aircraft receivers requiring special exotic fuels). By the early 1970s, the successful SR-71 had become more global in nature and required more special tankers based in wider operational locations. These were provided initially by an additional 26 (1959 and 1960 A-model assets that were converted and designated "partial-Qs"), because their configuration did not have some of the unique Q-model electronics, but had only the fuel-systems modifications, which provided fuel isolation in various tanks for the special SR-71 fuel.

The SR-71 special fuel (initially "PF-1", and then JP-7) could be isolated in the KC-135s fuel tanks, from those tanks carrying JP-4 (used for the tanker engines). The standard JP-4 jet fuel was carried in the inboard and outboard wing tanks, and the small gravity-fed tanks internal to the outer wing tips. The SR-71's special fuel was carried in the forward, center, aft body and upper-body tail tanks (all were below the floor in the fuselage, except the "upper-body tank", also known as the "upper-deck tank", which was above the floor line). All of the "Partial–Qs" over the next several years eventually received the unavailable avionics equipment and became fully modified Q-models.

Bits of SR-71 Fuel Details (For the Technically Inclined)— The KC-135 engines could burn the highly expensive SR-71 fuel, and frequently had to, because the tanker had to take off as much as four or five hours before the SR-71, in order to be in-place down-track when the supersonic SR-71 arrived for its next refueling. However, if the tanker needed to burn the SR-71 fuel for operation, the tanker was unable to air-start the engine on JP-7, because that required a rocket oxidant fluid, unavailable for the tanker engines. So the tanker engines had to be already operating on JP-4 before switching to PF-1 or JP-7 (SR-71 fuel).

Another restriction on the tanker, was that the only fuel the tanker could dump (i.e. pump-out through the boom, to lighten load in an emergency), was that which was in the fuselage body tanks. That meant that the SR-71 fuel was the default fuel that would be dumped first in those tanker emergencies. If this happened, and the Q-model electrical isolation valve separating the two fuels, had to be opened to dump additional JP-4, then the tanker fuel tanks and systems would have to be purged and flushed before it could again be used for SR-71 operations. (This same restriction applied on occasions when the KC-135Q carried a normal load of only JP-4 load for missions not involving the SR-71), which was not uncommon, for Vietnam operations.

Similarly, the SR-71 needed its special fuel for two reasons. First, it provided a coolant to the over-heated titanium airframe structure during Mach 3+ supersonic flight. And secondly, because of the high super-sonic airframe heat, if contaminants to his special fuel – like JP-4, or even water – existed, the fuel would explode from the elevated supersonic temperature.

There were rare occasions when the SR-71 might be forced to use JP-4, such as if it had been forced to land away from home base in an emergency, or weather diversion, and JP-7 was not available there. Or if certain maintenance operations had to be performed at a "non-provisioned" base, and certain fasteners which had been opened for maintenance and would require special heat treating again before super-sonic flight could be accomplished. In such rare but infrequent situations, the SR-71 could be fueled with JP-4 to get home, but would have to remain sub-sonic and at lower altitudes (and therefore be significantly more range limited) and would require a complete purging of the SR-71 engines and fuel systems, before returning to normal "high and fast" operations.

SR-71A Supersonic Blackbird

A Brief History of the SR-71– The Top Secret SR-71 was an "ahead-of-its-time" creation of Kelley Johnson's Lockheed Skunk Works. It was the ultimate offspring of the CIA's single-seat A-12 "Oxcart program" aircraft for a similar mission, conceived in 1957. which first flew in Apr. 1962 and was retired in 1968. The first five (of 18) A-12s were under-powered, using a pair of P&W J75 engines of 17,000 lbs thrust, each plus afterburners, while awaiting final development of more advanced engines. The A-12 mission proved to be too complex to achieve efficient capability with the pilot doing ALL the work. The next variant of the single-seat A-12 was born in the early '60s for the USAF, as a fighter/ interceptor two-seat version designated as the YF-12, "a prototype". This variant was determined to be a great performer, but a poor interceptor because of its requirement to be refueled at altitude immediately after take-off, before being flown in the primary intercept role, and would have faced a long and very expensive period to develop the still required fire control systems and armaments to deal with supersonic intercepts. All of the surviving YF-12s were ultimately modified to the SR-71 configuration. From this rapid development; the SR-71 was the ultimate product for strategic high altitude and supersonic reconnaissance for the USAF. The SR-71 first flew in Dec 1964 and entered USAF service in 1966. Its first "operational" mission was over Vietnam out of Okinawa, Japan, in March of 1968, (less than five months before my arrival in Aug. '68 at Beale).

During the transformation to the SR-71 platform, the experimental P&W J-58 engine, which produced 20,500 lbs thrust (dry) with added after-burners bringing the total thrust per engine to 34,500 lbs., became proven and was included in the conversion (from A-12 and YF-12 platforms). The J58 provided another "ahead-of-its-time creation" by introducing a hybrid turbo-fan/ ramjet design, allowing the engines to be operated in high altitude and speed environments in a "hybrid ramjet" mode.

Once topped off to full tanks (immediately following take-off, and at about 30,000 feet), the aircraft could then climb to its maximum altitude and maximum speed with an unrefueled range of approximately 2,900 miles. The SR-71 became the highest flying and fastest operational man-piloted air-breathing aircraft in the world with an Official record altitude of 85,069 feet above sea-level, and Mach 3.3 (approx 2,200 mph), limited only by the maximum temperature of the engine inlet near 950°F, and the weight and altitude of the aircraft. The substantial majority (over 95%, by some accounts) of the airframe structure and skin was made from Titanium, which primary source was from the Soviet Union (without their knowledge of its use), and which the processes of manufacture of Titanium had to be developed in the US along with the rest of the SR-71 technology!

The SR-71 was defunded by Congress in 1989, based upon operational cost considerations. This had long been debated because many of its functions could be provided by satellite imagery and intelligence. However, the SR-71 still had the advantage of flexibilty not held by orbital satellites who's path could readily be calculated and anticipated by enemy resources. Several SR-71s were kept in operational storage for continued special operations through 1996, and one flown by NASA until Oct, 1999. The SR-71 fleet accumulated over 17,300 fleet sorties (missions or flights), at an average cost of operation of ~$38,000 per flight hour in Fiscal Year 1980 dollars (which does not include support costs, nor tanker mission support). *The record speed and altitude record is still held by the SR-71, even 19-years after its 1999 total retirement from flight, and 46 years since I last flew support for its operations.* There are numerous unclassified books and articles published and available that detail all of the many additional unique characteristics and capabilities of this phenomenal aircraft.

{To view "Tour of the SR-71" check this link, recently released https://www.youtube.com/watch?v=F4KD5u-xkik&t=62s.}

{NOTE: 398- KC-135 tankers plus 50 other special mission C-135 aircraft of the original 800 US military produced, still remain in USAF operations at the date of this writing, with an airframe life still existing for usage through 2040!]

SR-71 Aerial Refueling (A/R) – During my initial six months, I learned that refueling the SR -71 was unique from all other SAC refueling techniques and procedures. This was created by several unique characteristics of the SR-71 which had less than an hour of fuel on board from take-off to landing (<u>if no aerial refueling could be accomplished;</u> typically accomplished at approximately 25,000 feet). The SR-71 family required a special type of fuel (originally PF-1, and finally reformulated as JP-7), because of the extreme heat of Mach 3.3+ flight. This special fuel was carried only in the tanker's fuselage or body tanks and required isolation from the tanker's wing tanks), creating the necessity of splitting offloads from two or more tankers and taking typically about 80,000 pounds from the tanker(s). The flight profile of flying the tanker (at refueling's end) was at the KC-135's max speed, while the SR-71 was almost at stall speed. The mission required very unique communications and unique rendezvous procedures for the faster SR-71 to join the much slower tanker formation. There was also a very unique mission crew attitude about refueling the SR-71 – due to the uniqueness and cost of the aircraft, specifically ***"No SR-71 tanker crew ever wanted to be in the same hemisphere, if the SR-71 was lost due to a failed inflight refueling"!***

The Complexities of SR-71 Aerial Refueling — Aerial or Inflight Refueling is a highly skilled and choreographed "ballet" between tanker and receiver aircraft. Each different type of USAF tanker (KC-135 turbo, or fan-jet powered; KC-10 fan-jet jumbo; or KC-130 turbo-prop) has different flight capabilities and characteristics. And each type receiver, be it a relatively small fighter, an intermediate size cargo aircraft, a jumbo transport, or a large bomber, requires different considerations, tactics, airspeeds and altitudes to accomplish. Also, depending on receiver size, a refueling top-off to full tanks may involve a large capacity of fuel flow (through a centerline boom) or a much diminished fuel transfer through multiple hose and drogue refueling systems. For these reasons, a particular pairing of tanker and receiver types are generally the first consideration of tasking, so that the best-match of tanker with the receiver's fuel transfer needs and flight-matching capabilities. At the timing of my initial SR-71 operations, the KC-135Q was the only tanker configured to accomplish the SR-71 mission. *[Five years later a small number of jumbo KC-10s were upgraded to support special SR-71 missions].*

Focusing on the KC-135 tanker, it was designed to refuel primarily the B-52 and other large sub-sonic receivers, which required several tens-of-thousands of pounds of fuel at fairly high flow rates, and therefore used the telescoping boom, where fuel transfers rates can be as high as 10,000 to 12,000 pounds of fuel per minute (into largely empty receiver tanks). Smaller fighters (some boom receptacle equipped, some probe equipped and some either/or) may only require transfer rates of 1,500 to 4,000 pounds per minute *(jet fuel averages about 6.5 pounds per gallon, for you mathematicians).*

With the boom equipped aircraft, the receivers typically join the tanker for refueling and fly up to the appropriate position under and behind the tanker, using visual markers, lights, and/or reference points on the tanker to establish the correct position, and then fly steady formation in that position while the boom operator—using the boom "ruddevators", within its operational envelope – to fly the boom up, down, right, left – until aligned with the receptacle on the receiver. The boom operator then telescopes the boom into the latches in the receptacle housing for a "contact". Once "contact" is made, the tanker pumps can be activated to transfer the fuel. In other words the receiver flies into close formation and the tanker boom operator executes the connection to the receiver.

With hose and drogue aircraft (smaller fighter-type aircraft having lesser fuel transfer requirements), the tanker becomes the steady platform and the receivers actively control the approach to the drogue, the physical connection to the hose, and then maintain a mid-position on the extension of the hose to keep it tensioned and neither at the outer-limit of its length, nor the inner limit of the "hose reel" to keep the hose tensioned. The pressure sensors in the hose allow the tanker pumps to operate only when selected and engaged, and uses fuel pressure in the hose to keep the drogue latches engaged tightly on the receiver's probe.

A second consideration in the "ballet of aerial refueling", is the aerodynamic interaction of the different aircraft. When two aircraft get as close together as required for refueling, there is an interaction between the two aircraft. If for example the relatively smaller KC-135 is approached from behind and below by a C-5 jumbo transport, the bow wave from the C-5's nose will tend to push the KC-135's horizontal tail-plane (elevator) up, thus forcing the nose down and into a gentle descent. The tanker pilot has to compensate by gently applying back (up) pressure on the elevators. When using the hose drogue configuration, the hose pod is typically mounted at or near the tanker wingtips, so that two fighter receivers can be fueled simultaneously to support fighter formations of 2, 4, or more receivers in a group (or "flights"). At operating speed, the tanker's swept wings generate an airflow vortex trailing the wingtips. The vortex airflow swirls off the bottom of the wingtips in an upward (toward the top of the wing) and trailing direction. If the receiver flies up too high while maneuvering behind the drogue, he can get caught in the vortex and flipped over, inward toward the tanker's fuselage. Similarly, if two airplanes get close enough together (wings overlapped), the funnel of air between the two wings will create a suction that draws the wings together, which could create a catastrophic mid-air collision.

A final "ballet" consideration, is that during refueling, the tanker is quickly transferring fuel offload of anywhere from under 5,000 pounds to as much as 120,000 pounds (depending on receiver type). This is causing center-of-gravity changes that require delicate balancing of which tanks are losing the offload and keeping everything within safe balance. Meanwhile the receiver is experiencing a rapid increase in weight requiring more power, smoothly applied to maintain balance and also causing the need to increase flight speed to avoid slowing near to their stall speed, as they get heavier. This is where the ballet partnership becomes as important as the name implies. The tanker pilot is always in front (in the leadership position), and therefore he establishes the margins that must be maintained during the "dance". If he fails to gently increase speed as the receiver becomes heavier, he may precipitate the receivers inability to maintain sufficient lift and speed to stay in "Contact".

When inflight refueling the tri-sonic SR-71 with a sub-sonic KC-135 an environment exists at the end of the refueling track, where the tanker is flying at its maximum aerodynamic speed, and the receiver is nearly at its minimum speed just above stall. (More about this in the subjects to follow).

Now that you have a feel for the complexity, you may feel that this activity is highly dangerous, if not totally impossible to perform. Not so. It is highly precise, and highly disciplined flying, but it is analogous to riding a bicycle. Once you have trained and mastered the feel and perception of it, it is done without thinking about how and what to do next. During the join-up after a rendezvous the relative speed difference at closure to "contact" the speed differential is less than one or two knots. The basic skill of flying close formation is taught to every pilot in Pilot Training. The only difference I found in flying the 300,000 pound KC-135 in close formation (20 feet separation during maneuvering and banking flight) is that the weight of the aircraft creates momentum that has to be compensated for by early detection of movement and smooth application of power and flight control corrections. And the further apart the aircraft are, the more difficult it is to perceive minor changes and variations.

An Example of an Early Experience – During one of my first TDY deployments to Okinawa, I experienced my first formation operation from the pilot's seat. We had made a three-ship tanker formation departure from a refueling stop and my aircraft was in the number two position. Taking off with a one-minute interval between start of roll, generates about a two-mile separation at lift-off. Climbing at the same speed means that we would never close to normal trail position (one mile). The first (lead) aircraft maintains a 275-knot (Indicated) air speed in his climb, so I increased my speed during climb to about 290 knots. But that faster speed also created more lift and allowed me to climb faster so I ended up being several hundred feet above the leader, even though I started at more than 1000 feet below him when I first became airborne. We were in visual conditions the entire time. In addition, I had a radarscope on the edge of the throttle console that was almost at my right knee, so I could see a calibrated blip showing his distance precisely (and relative direction from me). But at two miles separation, the relative movement appears to be very slow. By the time we moved to within ½ mile, the rate of closure at a 20 knot overtake speed became conspicuously more rapid.

At about a mile separation, my navigator – using his own radarscope – began cautioning me that I had too much overtake-speed. I replied, "I have him visually and on my scope", and reduced power while increasing my climb rate further to bleed off the speed. But I still continued to rapidly close, from my momentum. When I finally slowed to a more reasonable speed, I found myself leaning way forward trying to keep my leader in sight under my nose and over a thousand feet below us. I had to swing right to keep him in sight as I slowed further, allowing him to catch up to me and I could descend and get behind him again. This was a great lesson on the affect of momentum.

Typical SR-71 Operational Refueling Mission — To better understand my later mission description, it will be helpful to understand the overall mission scenario, as diagramed 2-pages below. I will focus on the Blue (more typical, longer mission) scenario. Scanning briefly around the mission path, beginning at the left end labeled "*BASE*", and moving around the BLUE line clockwise, you will notice that THREE planned aerial refuelings ("*REFUEL*", "25,000 FT") are shown as 150 nautical miles (approximate) in length. for the SR-71 after take-off until returning back to "*BASE*". (The standard SR-71 refueling altitude is at 25,000', optimum mating altitude for refueling for both tanker and

SR-71 types of aircraft, regardless of whether the SR–71 rendezvous approach track is “Low and slow” or “Hot and fast”).

You will note the label “T 0:00”, at the far left of the diagram, which is the Take-off reference time for the SR-71. Following clockwise around the graphic blue line, you will observe that there are three level plateaus at 25,000 feet, which are the refueling “brackets” for the SR-71 refueling. The initial (#1) refueling beginning at T 0:30 and ending at T 0:50 (all times and distances, approximate). The tanker cell takes off first, 30 minutes before the SR-71 (T minus 0:30) to be in place for this refueling followed later by the SR-71 take-off. This initial refueling could be performed by a single tanker, however, every SR-71 operational mission always utilized an additional spare tanker in the event of any abort or system malfunction. (This first refueling occurs at the arrival of the SR-71 at 25,000 feet and top of initial climb and is described as a “low and slow” approach by the SR-71, and is the easiest and most typical style of receiver rendezvous).

After completion of refueling (at T 0:50) the SR-71 climbs to cruise altitude (78,000 ft then cruise climbs to 80,000 feet +) over the next 2,200 miles, then begins a “high and fast” descent again to 25,000 feet to rendezvous with the second (#2) tanker 3-ship cell at T 1:40. Making allowance for headwinds and other variables, this means the #2 tanker cell, combined with the fact that the tankers cruise at about one- forth the speed of the SR-71, provides a timeline where the middle (#2) refueling tanker cell must take-off from *BASE* approximately two hours prior to the SR-71 take off. And the leading (#3) refueling tanker cell must take off about T minus 3:30 from *BASE*, before the SR–71 takes off. (In other words, the #3 tanker cell takes off first, since it has the furthest to go; then about an hour and 30 min. later the #2 cell launches; then about an another hour and 30 min. later the first tanker cell for the #1 refueling takes off. Finally after all tanker three cells have launched, the SR-71 launches 30 min. after the the launch of the #1 cell for his top-off at the top of his initial climb-out to 25,000 feet). Each refueling track is approximately 150 nautical miles along the mission course for completion, with the SR-71 descending "high and fast" for the second and third rendezvous. Due to the longer flying times of the second and third refueling tanker cells, they must necessarily burn some of the SR-71 JP-7 fuel enroute, and thus require a "split offload" to the SR-71 in their respective refuelings.

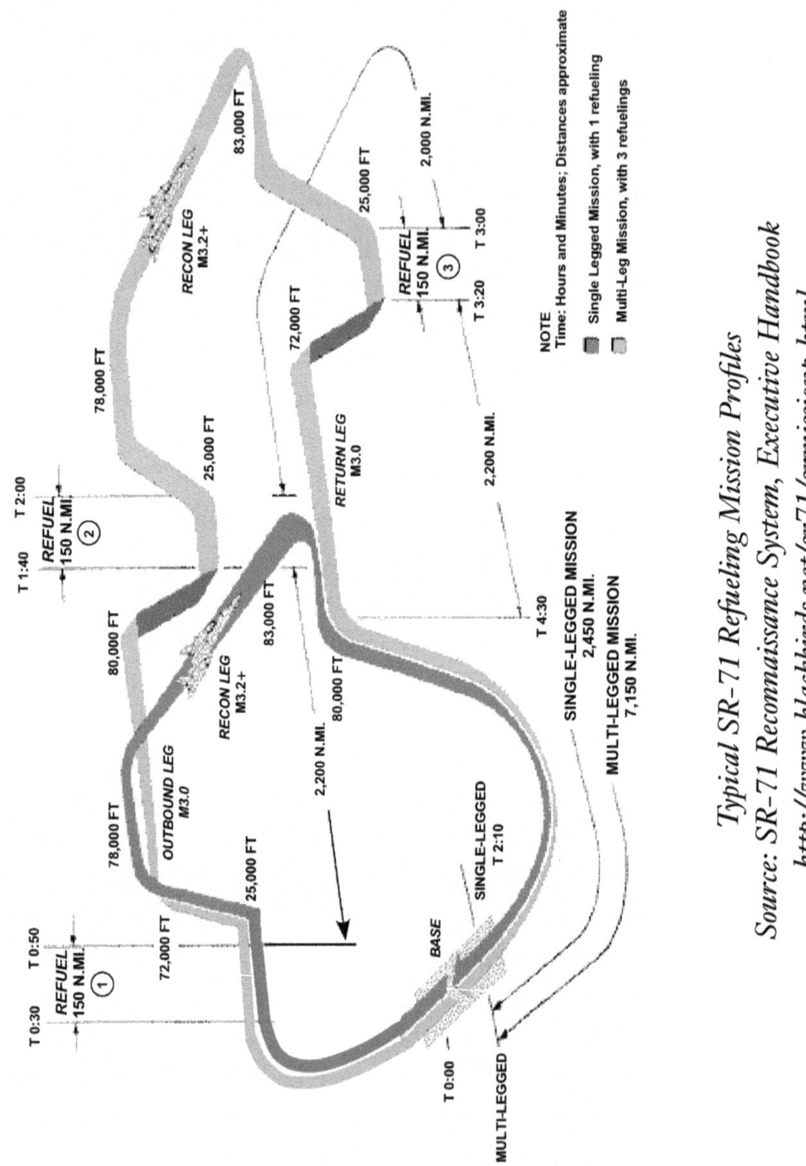

Typical SR-71 Refueling Mission Profiles
Source: SR-71 Reconnaissance System, Executive Handbook
http://www.blackbirds.net/sr71/srmissionp.html

The "high and fast" refueling rendezvous is much more complex than the initial refueling, because the SR-71 has no speed brakes, which means he must accurately compute his supersonic descent profile taking into account the winds aloft in the descent, and any thermal inversions that will affect his descent rate and speed, and ensure that he does not arrive ahead of the tankers. He can always accelerate and catch up if too far behind, but he cannot slow quickly enough if he ends out in front, nor is the job simplified by reversing course and circling around the tanker before approaching for fuel.

Once the SR-71 tops-off after the #2 refueling, he again accelerates as before climbing as shown to about 78,000 feet and Mach 3.2 for his target reconnaissance over the target area, climbing to 83,000' over the "hot zone", as he burns off some of his fuel weight. At this extreme thin-air altitude and tri-sonic speed, the maximum-bank turn radius is about 150 nm requiring about a 45 degree bank and 300 nm arc to reverse course. Consider, if he makes this turn parallel to and over the 60-mile long DMZ, his radar and photo sensors could see as far north as Hanoi, and if it is instead made over Hanoi he could see well into China, and most of Laos). After completing his "hot run", he will then meet the final (#3) tanker formation after a "high & fast" descent rendezvous over less hostile territory (for Vietnam this would put him typically over, or approaching Thailand) for his final refueling to home *BASE*. After the third refueling, the SR-71 returns "high & fast" to Kadena, and the third tanker cell of three lands in Thailand to refuel and then returns to *BASE* (Kadena AFB, Okinawa).

You can see from this complex mission plan, it required 2 +3 +3 tankers (8 total) for the primary mission. But for safety there was a 9th tanker orbiting an area over the Pacific about 100 nm southwest of Okinawa from about an hour after the SR-71 departed Kadena for the duration of time the SR-71 was airborne until he was safely on the ground again. If any irregularity should occur, this air spare could join up with, or meet the SR-71 inbound, in the event the SR had to descend to lower altitude and need a top-off. That makes 9 airborne tankers. And finally, there was a tanker at the take-off end of the runway with engines running for the entire interval from before the first tanker cell launched until the second and third cells had launched, in order to drop into the formations as they took off in the event of an abort – making a total of 10 tankers to support one SR-71 sortie from Kadena AFB to Vietnam and return!

Split-offload A/R Procedure — I will next "zoom-in" further to the "split–offload procedure for further clarity. In normal bomber or fighter formation refueling, the tanker formations maintain 500-feet vertical and 1-mile lateral separation between tankers (and 5-miles between adjacent cells, when multiple concurrent cells are being used). Due to the nature of the speed and performance differences between the subsonic tankers and the tri-sonic SR-71, the tactics and procedures had to be modified for success, and efficiency.

While waiting in a holding orbit for the SR-71 to rendezvous with the tanker cell, the tankers fly a "racetrack" oval orbit at "maximum endurance speed" to conserve fuel (250 knots indicated airspeed), at 27,000 ft, msl ("mean-sea-level"). During the orbit, awaiting the arrival of the receiver, the lead tanker commands the 2nd and 3rd tanker in the cell of move into the echelon positions off his right wing (typically flown at about 40° aft, about two hundred feet laterally apart, and fifty feet vertically lower for each respective tanker (to provide safe separation).

The rendezvous planned orbit "anchor point" is called the Aerial Refueling Initial Point (ARIP), a preplanned navigational map point, which is also the same navigation point that the Receiver (SR-71) navigates toward. The lead tanker navigator directs the tanker pilot as to the heading the pilot should fly down track from the ARIP to compensate for wind drift and maintain course down the refueling track. Based upon the navigators inbound plot of the receiver, he would call the pilot when to initiate a rapid roll into a 30° left bank turn and reverse course back toward the incoming receiver, but offset about half a mile from the receiver's inbound course to the ARIP.

Depending upon when the receiver was calculated to arrive at the ARIP, the tanker might have to make several orbits of about 3 to 5 minutes in each direction. Once in positive radar or other distance-measuring-equipment between tanker and receiver, the navigator would calculate when the receiver would reach the appropriate point (separation distance from lead tanker and inbound SR-71) to direct the final course-reversal of the tanker formation, so as to cross the ARIP wings-level on the outbound refueling track, as the receiver approached the tanker from behind, while flying level remaining at the orbit altitude (lead tanker, for example at 27,000', and the receiver inbound level at the bottom of his descent at 25,000' on essentially the same heading and inbound behind the lead tanker with an indicated closure rate slowing to match the tanker's speed. Typically (but not always), the tankers and the SR-71 each had visual contact on each other as the tanker initiated his final left course reversal to turn in front of the SR-71. As the tanker cell performs the final turn to cross the ARIP ahead of the inbound receiver, the number two (and number three) tankers close to tight right echelon, near-wingtip-to-wingtip formation (about 10 to 15 feet between wingtips and 50-feet vertical stack-down, respectively).

Final Turn (Photographed from #2 tanker)

As the tanker formation rolls wings level on the outbound refueling track and the boom operator has visual contact out the rear facing boom-pod window (or during the final turn if positive visual contact was made and separation distance was confirmed), a command is made by the lead tanker pilot, to the tanker cell, to "Descend and Accel", at which time the tanker leader would advance power and initiate a 500-ft. per min. gradual descent of 1,000' (to 26,000' for lead tanker). This maneuver brought the lead tanker aircraft to 1,000 feet above the receiver altitude and stabilized airspeed (of 275 Knots indicated). Once the receiver, is inbound to the tanker at 25,000' he proceeds inbound visually (or by instrument reference) to 1/2 mile in trail of the lead tanker, until cleared by light signal, radio contact or boom signal (a slight up and down oscillation, like a head nod of the boom), which tells the receiver he is cleared to move forward to "Contact" the boom. (Typically this was a continuous slow and controlled climbing closure with little or no pause required at 1/2 –mile).

Receiver's View of the Boom Envelope Check
(Note: Receiver Pilot's Alignment Markings on belly)

Since the boom receptacle is about 8-feet aft of the SR-71's rear cockpit, the SR pilot could not see the contact, but would follow the refueling director lights on the belly of the tanker to find the proper position from which the boom operator could fly and extend the boom to the "contact-made" position. At that point the lights inside both aircraft cockpits would show "contact made" and the tanker copilot or pilot could flip the fuel transfer pumps – ON, and monitor the transfer to the SR, and the transfer from the tanker's appropriate tanks, while maintaining a safe tanker center of gravity on the tanker.

Closing to Contact

Contact Made

Once the boom nozzle arrives within 4-inches proximity of the receptacle, inductive electrical coupling occurred and we had secure boom intercom contact between the two aircraft crews. This permitted secure conversation, without fear of radio interception by enemy forces. Once in contact we could negotiate banks and smooth turns up to 30° bank. Also once we made stable contact, the tanker pilot would initiate a smooth and gradual power increase and accelerate slowly from 275 knots (indicated) to 325 knots, achieving this speed at the same time as completing about one-half the desired offload. At this point the lead tanker discontinued off-load and cleared the SR-71 to "disconnect" and to transition to #2 by sliding back and to his right to the precontact position on the second tanker.

At the transition to #2 tanker, this tanker would be tucked in very close and in an almost abeam position, on Lead's right wing. In this position, the SR-71 pilot could see the #2 tanker in his peripheral vision, out of the very restrictive side view of his cockpit. With coordination between the boom operator and SR pilot, the SR-71 would disconnect, move aft about 20-feet and then slide directly over to the "pre-contact" position on #2. Meanwhile the former tanker lead would transfer lead position responsibilities to the second tanker by radio or hand signal. Once visual contact was made of the SR by the former lead tanker, the former lead would advance power and gently climb 500 feet, then slide back behind the formation, cross over and descend from behind and rejoin on the new leader's right wing (if only two in the cell in position to resume offloading, in the event the new lead tanker had any malfunctions) or onto the right echelon position of the former #3 tanker, in order to retain formation continuity to destination after completing the refuelings.

In the instance that the original tanker leader failed to accelerate to the 325 knot airspeed in a timely manner, with the SR-71 becoming heavier, the SR would have to go into afterburner on one or both engines to keep from stalling or falling off the boom. If he had to go into both afterburners, he would burn fuel faster than we could transfer it to him resulting in failure to refuel to top-off. [Our maximum transfer rate to a large capacity aircraft such as the SR-71 was 12,000 pounds per minute (approx, 1,845 gallons per min)!]

Once the change-over to the second tanker was completed, the second tanker would thus become the new "Cell Leader". The formation would continue to gradually accelerate to the tanker's Vmo (Velocity of Max Operating Mach number, or 0.86 M, approximately 585 MPH no-wind ground speed based upon 26,000' flight altitude).

At full tanks on the receiver and arriving at the end of the refueling track, the SR-71 would be close to stall speed from the total fuel transfer of as much as 100,000 pounds, and would have to dive after disconnect for about 4,000' to get back to normal angle of attack and climb speed on afterburner. He would then climb while accelerating to supersonic flight to his high altitude cruise level, where his fuel consumption was at its lowest, most efficient rate of the entire mission profile.

KC-135Q Refueling SR-71
(Note location of boom receptacle behind aft cockpit)
http://www.habu.org/credited/landis_SR-71A_968_Refueling_01.jpg

My SAC career progressed rapidly after I gained my first crew. First, however, I made a name for myself (good or bad) on my first AC operational mission at Okinawa.

Upgrade to Squadron Aircraft Commander— I had completed all the required training and check rides finally and had the opportunity to depart the "supervised flying" nest and assume the duties as Aircraft Commander. The operation at Beale supporting the SR-71 had the characteristic that each and every week, two qualified integrated-crews would be deployed on a single tanker to Kadena AFB, Okinawa (Japanese Island), for a 6-week rotation of temporary duty (TDY). Arriving some 15-total flight-hours later at Kadena, another pair of crews, on station there for the past 6-weeks, would depart and redeploy back to Beale AFB, CA. A tanker force of 12- to 15- tankers and extra crews were maintained at Kadena, year round, along with the assignment of three SR-71s, (or more) and appropriate number of crews. *[Tasking orders to meet potential operational missions over Southeast Asia, and the western hemisphere for the SR-71, originated from the office of the Secretary of the Air Force (SecAF)].* On this occasion, a few days before the upcoming deployment, the tanker Aircraft Commander of one of the two designated crews to deploy, suffered a fractured vertebra on a tobogganing accident in the Lake Tahoe, NV area. I was offered the temporary assignment and jumped at it despite the short planning to get my affairs in order for the long absence from home. At this point, I was a 31-year old Captain. The injured Aircraft Commander was Maj. Walt N, his Copilot was Major Ben M, who was a former B-52 Navigator that had just completed a year of Undergraduate Pilot Training to become a pilot and had been reassigned to KC-135Q tankers and the 903rd squadron about 3 or 4 months earlier. The crew Navigator was a well-seasoned Lt. Col., Ed R, and the Boom Operator was a well-seasoned T/Sgt. Dave D. I obviously would have a number of special issues to deal with as the junior ranking officer and Aircraft/Aircrew Commander, on my initial assigned command.

Yikes! My First Operational SR-71 Mission, as AC — My crew and I were informed on arrival, that on all future SR-71 operational missions involving multiple separate tanker formations (cells) and schedules, all SR-71 related runway communications at Kadena would be virtually "radio silent" or without use of mission identifiable individual call-signs. This was a new procedure from any of my prior TDY operations at Kadena. [It was known that there were foreign agents on the island outside of the Air Base that were monitoring and relaying all observed movements of the SR-71 and its supporting aircraft. As well as Russian trawlers in the adjacent waters]. To implement this new tactic, rather than each formation cell leader radioing the tower for formation taxi clearance, take-off clearance, etc., we were briefed that we would move autonomously based upon Tower generic broadcast. To accomplish this, the Tanker staff at OL-8 had placed a qualified tanker Aircraft Commander in the tower with all the tanker performance manuals and details of the tanker tail numbers, individual call signs, and operational schedules for each launch on the field to coordinate with the Tower controllers of needed info for them to broadcast at designated times. For example, at the designated time the tower would broadcast what seemed to be a routine Runway status to everyone who might be on the Tower frequency, which identified the active runway number, the altimeter setting, the prevailing temperature and winds, etc. The tanker cell planning to launch in the next several minutes also understood this was permission to taxi to the designated runway and fine-tune their Take-off performance calculations to that latest info, but would not acknowledge, or request further clearance information.

The take-off performance calculations were sufficiently complex for the under-powered and heavy weight KC-135Q aircraft, that to do the calculations from scratch would take an experienced copilot and Aircraft Commander up to 30 minutes to complete. However having done a preliminary data sheet (based on forecast weather), it could easily be updated within about 10 minutes. All KC-135Qs were within about 5,000 pounds of the same empty weight, so as long as the fuel load was consistent between them there would not be much variance in each tanker's performance.

The day started out with a weather briefing for the mission

route and an intelligence briefing and other significant variable details. Each tanker crew, briefed two-hours before their planned aircraft take-off time. The SR-71's 2-man crew and their alternates had a different series of preparations and time-lines, so they mission-briefed separately from the tanker crews.

On this mission, I drew the earliest potential taxi time. I was assigned the duty of "hot spare" sitting on the sidelines at the take-off end of the runway with engines running, ready to instantaneously fall in at the end of any tanker cell that had a failure, or aborted departure, so each cell could launch on time (one-minute interval between each aircraft in a 2- or 3- ship formation "cell". As an additional duty, prior to preflighting, starting engines and taxing to the end of the runway sideline (referred to as the "hammerhead" of the departure runway), my crew, also had to preflight the "unmanned spare" tanker right up to the point of an "alert start" of the engines – ready to taxi away with all instruments set and take-off performance cards completed – and leave it "cocked", so that if any aircrew needed it they could rush to the aircraft and be off and into the stream of aircraft with minimum delay. Having completed that task, my crew then proceeded to our assigned aircraft and repeated the exercise up to engine start, and then started engines in preparation to taxi at the designated schedule time. In my capacity as "hot spare" I could end up flying with the first, second, or third tanker formation cell, if required. If nothing went wrong, I could end up sitting with at least one engine running for up to 7 hours, just in case we should be called upon to launch.

As I sat in my aircraft in the parking area of the ramp, after preflighting two aircraft and starting my engines for an on-time taxi, we heard the Tower broadcast the active runway details and current temp, winds and weather. At that time, Kadena had only one runway long enough for heavy B-52 and heavy KC-135 operations – 12,100 feet long by 200 feet wide; Runway 05R/23L. On this mission the tower designated that Runway 05R was the chosen runway (taking off to the northeast at a heading of 055°), which had an uphill slope such that the departure end was 65 feet higher than the start position. Taking off from the opposite end, which was Runway 23L (taking off to the southwest at a heading of 235°), the runway descended almost to sea level, the same 65 feet, ending up almost immediately over water. The weather at Kadena was tropical, so even in mid-morning the temperature was in the mid-80s and we were fueled to full gross weight, so we had to calculate to a precise degree to determine if we had sufficient wind to get off within the runway length available.

When I heard the Tower call the active Runway, temp and winds, I immediately had major concerns. The "active" for the first launch was designated as Runway 05R which started at 63' of elevation and went uphill to the far end to 128', with the flight path continuing over a ridge before dropping again to the sea on the far side of the island. The winds were being given as a direct crosswind of 20 knots with gusts varying to 35 knots and variable up to 20° plus-or-minus from the direct cross wind. This meant that we had as much probability of having a 20° quartering tailwind, as we did a 20° quartering headwind – and would be going on an uphill slope for 12,100 feet that would also extend our potential ground roll before we would reach flying speed. This was intuitively obvious the worst choice scenario, which could potentially leave us at or below safe flying speed when we reached the departure end of the runway pavement – even if all four engines were performing at full rated thrust!

View Kadena AFB Rwy 23L, downhill toward the bay

I asked my copilot, Maj. M, to quickly confirm that we had sufficient runway available under that worst-case scenario (the quartering tailwind at 55 knots including gusts). He calculated the numbers and said "No". I quickly weighed the seriousness of this situation and decided that safety would over-ride the need to maintain "radio silence", so I punched my transmit button on the control wheel and discretely, without using my call sign said, "Tower, Say again Active Runway and winds". His immediate response was to call out the original info, "Active 05R, temp 85°, Winds 140° at 20 Knots, gusting 120° to 160° variable to 55 Knots". I completed my taxi to the hammerhead and while waiting for the first formation cell of tankers to arrive (about 15 minutes later). I recalculated the numbers, along with Maj M, and verified that with the uphill runway (05R) the critical field length computed at 12,800 feet, and if the downhill runway (23L) was used, the Critical Field length worse case scenario calculated at 11,600 feet. With only **12,100 feet available**, it was a "no brainer" which runway was the only acceptable choice, and it was **NOT 05R** (if the given conditions remained the same)! And then I prayed to myself that the first formation leader (a senior Standardization/Evaluation Check Pilot Instructor) would challenge the Tower to change the assigned runway direction to the downhill slope, or that the conditions would improve at the final weather call. (His was the #3 three-ship formation that would take-off, and be furthest down track, before the SR-71 launched about 4-1/2 hours later).

Again just prior to the first tanker cell take-off, the Tower broadcast the same conditions, which was the first cell's clearance for take-off. Still having great apprehension from my years of doing flight safety work and being aware that accidents happen, not from a single event, but from a sequence of weak links that suddenly cascade into a catastrophe, I was torn to intercede and break radio silence again. Being also aware that it was a long time before the SR-71 departure, I again broke radio silence with a discrete call to the take-off leader on the interplane frequency and said, obscurely, "Check your critical Field Length!" I got no response as the flight of three tankers proceeded to take off position and then departed. I sat there horrified as the formation leader took off and then sunk below the crest of the hill, out of sight, followed 60 seconds later by number two, who also descended out of sight, then number three.

After an interminable two-plus hours went by to launch the #2 refueling cell. The same scenario repeated itself – no change was made to the reported wind condition or active runway in use. In the meantime my copilot and I did several recalculations to recheck every computation and chart selection for correctness, while I logged the "Rwy 05R, or Rwy 23L comparison" table of every computation using both runways. I asked our Navigator (Lt. Col. R) his opinion of the circumstance, and he agreed with mine. I knew that I was going to be standing before the Operations Officer, or Commander later, for my actions and I needed to know if I was on solid ground and my Lt. Col. navigator would be covering my back, while I was the least experienced of all the tanker pilots in the unit. Despite my discrete warnings to the second 3-ship cell, being led by a newly upgraded young Instructor Pilot (Capt Denny B), neither the Tower's information had changed, nor the resultant scary take-off. A few moments after the second cell launched, I heard a weak transmission, "Two, this lead. Did you make it"?

I asked out loud, but to no one in particular in my cockpit, "What the hell was the tanker AC Supervisor doing in the Tower?" This was part of his duties to ensure the operation was being conducted safely according to the book performance data"! What was the OL-8 "Supervisor of Flying", SOF (Lt. Col. Bob B), who also was the OL-8 Tanker Operations Officer (number two in command), doing during all of this? He was watching and listening on his aircraft-radio-equipped Staff pickup truck – which I assumed was somewhere sitting beside the runway. He was a senior long-time pilot with this operation!

Now we had nearly another two hours until the final two-ship tanker cell would take off to do the SR-71 refueling immediately after their take-off and climb to 27,000 feet. I kept praying to myself that the winds would either slacken, or that for sure I would not have to pull into the slot and take-off after another tanker aborted (or crashed!).

Finally the two-ship formation taxied out with the same weather call or slightly more variable wind speed, and again they barely made it airborne. Then the SR-71 taxied out and took an excessive amount of time, but finally launched followed by the airborne local spare tanker, which would orbit south west until the SR-71 was safely back on the ground after the mission. At this point, after all primary aircraft had launched, I had made up my mind and I called the tower and informed them that, "If needed, I required taxi permission to the opposite end of the runway. They asked me why. I told them that, if I would have to be launched, I would not accept the current runway under these circumstances because, based on the runway conditions, the uphill runway had insufficient critical field length to make a safe take-off. I was pleased to get that transmission on the Tower tapes. After a several minute pause, the tower granted my request, and I taxied to the opposite end and then, about an hour later, was released back to my ramp parking spot.

The grizzly old SOF, Lt. Col. B, met me in the squadron operations area when I came back into the building and proceeded to "chew my backside" for breaking radio silence. He wanted to know what my beef was.

Being well prepared, I pulled out the page of two-column computations that my copilot and I had worked over so very many times and showed him what the books showed. He retorted that he was out there observing and the winds weren't as variable nor as strong as the Tower had called them! I replied that this made no difference – that if an aircraft (or several) had run-off the runway, or crashed, it would be what the tower tapes reported, not the un-instrumented SOF vehicle, nor any witness observing the accident had testified, but that the pilot at the controls would have "bought the blame" for not properly calculating the takeoff performance and had been responsible first and foremost for the accident(s), the loss or damage to the aircraft and the loss of any and all lives!

I saw Col B later at the bar in the O'Club, and he apologized for the "wire-brushing" he had given me, and informed me that the weather had continued to worsen as the day progressed and that the SR-71 and the tankers had aborted their return flights and were forced to land at an alternate base (CCK air base in Taipei, Republic of China) to wait out the typhoon system that had moved through the region. This had depleted our tanker force and any potential to fly further missions until all aircraft had been recovered to Kadena and all the crews had received sufficient crew rest – at least a 3-day stand down to reconstitute the SR-71 mission capability, and a compromise of Classified Security in forcing the SR-71 to land at a Chinese base, when officially it had been denied that it was being flown in Southeast Asia.

Further Details —

After the crews had finally returned to Kadena with their aircraft, I had the opportunity to participate in a debriefing of the situation, as I had observed it, with the other formation pilots. I asked why no one had recalculated the numbers. To me it didn't even take the formal recalculation to realize that the use of the uphill-sloped runway, especially when confronted with gusting quartering tailwinds, was a very risky operation, which doing the several recalculations only further confirmed. I asked the second cell to further explain the radio call to his number-two asking "if he made it". He admitted that in the cockpit there was confusion because he had a new, minimally experienced copilot. He felt confident that his copilot was already recalculating the take-off data when asked to refine the take-off critical field length quickly under the stress, but his recalculations were still incomplete when time to launch arrived.

In the process of this distraction, while doing his pre-takeoff checklist this low-experienced copilot had inadvertently failed to complete a critical item, which was to turn all the fuel boost pumps to ON before take-off to ensure adequate fuel flow at full power. The Flight Manual states that, "There is typically sufficient gravity feed to supply adequate full power from full fuel tanks, but that there is a possibility of fuel flow disruption from a rough runway, therefore it is essential to have both pumps in each tank operating for safety during take-off to assure full power fuel flow". Further, there is a yellow light on the fuel panel (this panel located between the vertical instrument panel and the center throttle quadrant, which is angled at about a 30-40° angle from the horizontal. From the pilot seat, the landing gear handle in the Gear Down position obscures this yellow low fuel pressure manifold light from the pilots vision. The piloting AC told the group that he had his hands full keeping the airplane from running off the side of the runway in the crosswind and that when he finally reached rotation speed and lift off he was almost off the edge, from the cross winds. When he called for "Gear-Up", he suddenly saw the yellow low fuel pressure light and almost had heart failure (even though the engines were putting out full rated power)!

In my opinion, these crews had become so accustomed to doing everything as unique with the SR-71 and without concern for understanding and strict adherence to technical requirements, that their complacency in the routine was heading them towards a potential major accident. Five supervisor-rated pilots with above-average experience had all failed to catch this potentially critical error and they were offended and embarrassed because a new guy had caught the oversight on four separate takeoff sequences involving nine aircraft, not to mention the oblivious Control Tower supervisory tanker pilot, and in ill-prepared SOF. In hind-sight, I realized I should have filed an Operational Hazard Report (OHR) with the Flight Safety Office to maximize the learning from this highly serious deviation from safe practices. But with the high level security rating of this mission, I was not sure that this would not create more issues. I'd call it, "Christening by fire"! This was certainly a mission that I would never forget!

Adding to My Family — In Oct '69 during this early time period at Beale, Pat and I adopted our second daughter in Sacramento, at the age of 10 months. She had been born with physical disabilities in her feet and had to undergo two rounds of surgery before being placed with us for adoption. Being in the Air Force meant we had the financial stability and means to care for her special physical needs, but we had a long wait before we could bring her into our family.

SAC Duty Progression — Over the next several years I progressed rapidly to positions of ever higher responsibility, but these often created extreme challenges for an outsider to SAC. After my "christening experience" on my first Okinawa tour as an aircraft commander, I was soon elevated to Senior Crew Status. Several of my experiences are worthy of recapping in order to appreciate the levels of initiative and responsibilities that I encountered.

SAC Check Flight Failure — As I gained KC-135 experience in SAC, I had the opportunity to observe and participate in crew and individual crewmember periodic-scheduled and "no-notice" flight proficiency tests, accomplished by a Stan-Eval (Standardization & Evaluation) instructor(s). These occurred several times a year (some pre-scheduled, and others as No-Notice surprises). They were a very thorough evaluation of the crew and their individual and collective knowledge of every facet of their job. It began with an on-the-ground individual page check of the crewmember's personal 1200 to 1500 page Flight Manual, to verify that every supplemental revision had been received and posted to their three-ring book binder; an outdated Manual was an automatic check *Failure!* This Flight Manual currency check was followed by both a verbal test by reciting from memory selected Emergency Procedure checklists, verbal questions about general understanding of various systems operation, a lengthy open-book test on pertinent operating regulations and safety practices, generally a full flight planning session including calculations of all the take-off and landing performance data (all based upon forecast weather conditions). This was graded for accuracy, and grounds for a "Failure", if excessively in error. And then a following flight that was quietly observed and graded on knowledge, actual flight parameters during approaches and landings for staying within very tight limits of airspeed, rate of climb and descent, maintaining of designated headings, proper crew coordination and completion of checklists, and about every other facet you could imagine.

During the flight, the Evaluator sat in the cockpit jump seat and made copious notes without comment. If one asked for an opinion or a comment during the flight, the Stan-Eval Instructor/Evaluator would insist that he could make no comment or critique until after the flight, and after he had run his notes and numbers through the grading criteria to get a detailed objective decision.

The entire process of a check ride typically was spread over a two-day period of ground and inflight observations and tests, before the crew, or individual crewmember received a "debriefing", a detailed score, and a determination of whether he had failed, passed minimally or passed with high grades. The flight phase was typically about five to six hours duration, and included all phases of a normal mission – Aircraft preflight; Engine start and systems checks; Taxi-out; Take-off and climb to high altitude; Rendezvous with receiver aircraft and completion of a safe and successful aerial refueling; Then flying an hour or longer navigation and cross country segment, followed by doing high altitude flight maneuvers (steep turns, approaches to stalls, Dutch Roll simulation and recovery, simulated emergency depressurization and descent from high altitude to 10,000' altitude, simulated engine failure procedures with power reduced on one or more engines at altitude; Tripping off one or more of the electrical generators and discussing the implications and restoration of this fault, etc. Any failure, or significant sub-performance dictated that the crew (or individual member) would require additional training with an instructor, on supervised operations until he (or the crew) was up to "SAC Standards".

If an Aircraft Commander failed a check ride he would have to face the Wing Commander, Deputy Commander of Operations and Squadron Commander (all either Colonels or Lt. Colonels) and hear of his failures publicly detailed to the panel (like a Grand Jury) and hear his corrective action(s), required, if any. In SAC, there was a saying, ***"To err is human; To forgive is divine; Neither of which is SAC policy"!*** A related SAC training cliché was, ***"You either have, or will, suffer a failed Check Ride. It's not if; it is when".***

As you can surmise, these procedures were very thorough and served a terrifically important role in the safe and effective completion of the SAC military mission and air discipline. But they were also flawed in their implementation. The Stan-Eval process was specifically NOT intended to be primarily a "learning process", but rather became a critiquing process, meant to show up the individual or crewmember deficiencies – to be not as skilled an airman as the Stan-Eval instructor held himself to be. Many Evaluators became elitist, and often-demanded proficiencies from the crew that the evaluators, themselves could often not achieve. (They spent so much time observing, that they didn't actually do enough physical hands-on flying to remain proficient and current). And their evaluation reports had the potential of severely degrading the tested member's career and promotion potential (not to mention their Flight Pay) and self-confidence in their ability to perform.

Upon entering SAC, I had over 3,000 flight hours logged, for which a few hundred was in the capacity of Instructor Pilot. But I had never seen anything since Pilot Training like this ego trip that I found among many SAC Stan-Eval instructors. And my prior experience, (though not in heavy, and high performance complex jets) combined with my scholastic training as an aeronautical engineer, had generated a strong basis of common sense and intense curiosity about ***WHY?*** things were done. And when I asked the questions, and received an answer, ***"Because that's the way SAC has always done it"***, nearly always generated my pushback for more info, until people realized that they could not buffalo me into accepting their lack of understanding or insight – or worse, their lack of personal responsibility! The instructor that was my crew AC for the six months after I first arrived did a great job of providing lots of information and OJT. But when it came to his ability to teach me how to perform specific flying techniques, he knew how to do it himself, but couldn't relate muscle memory perceptions or analyze what I was doing incorrectly, to help me learn how to correct my deficiencies.

For example, I had an awful time mastering how to land the airplane consistently every time. The KC-135 had a unique aerodynamic attitude necessary to make a proper landing. Unlike the other aircraft I had flown, you did not fly the tanker down a shallow glide path to ground proximity and then "flare out" in the descent and hold the nose off until the main gear touched down. Every landing was a surprise for me. The aircraft stood higher because of its physical size than any other aircraft I had ever flown. When on the ground, the seat of my pants was over 15 feet (a story and a half) above the pavement. If a flared out, as in the C-47, the nose was at three degrees or so above the horizon, which added several more feet from the ground when the main gear touched down. And when I was struggling with getting to the touchdown point, my instructor-AC was riding the controls with me. And I never knew what I was feeling – the aircraft forces, or his pushing and pulling on the flight controls. And then he would try and give me confidence by slapping me on the back and telling me how good the landing was, when I KNEW it was just guess work and the "luck of the draw" for me.

I got to the point that when ever I was flying with him and I sensed him on the controls pushing and pulling against me, that I finally would either reach across the cockpit and give him a mild karate chop across his wrists to "get off the controls", or I would just let go of the control wheel and raise my hands and say, "If you must fly it, then I'll get off the controls and let you do the landing". Finally he got the message!

When the time came around for me to get my first annual flight check, needless to say, I was a nervous wreck facing the ordeal. I had a miserable ride, and I was so tense that I lost my attention span on things I usually had no problems with. I felt my flying was sloppy (though not unsafe, just NOT precise), and I failed to remain well ahead of the aircraft due to the overload of artificial distractions. On this check-ride, after flying half dozen instrument landing approaches by the end of the flight, I knew it wasn't going well. Upon taxiing in and shutting down, I asked the Stan-Eval check pilot, "How did I do, overall?" His reply was the standard, "I can't say, until I run the numbers through my matrix". I would not have been surprised, if he told me on the spot that I had failed the ride. In fact I expected that answer.

The next day he called me in and told me that I had in fact failed the check ride. But then he proceeded to overlook the most serious and obvious failings that I was aware of, and told me I was more than 10 knots (plus or minus) on the approach speed, and had flown 5 feet above the glide slope on final (instead of on it), and that I had failed to call out passing minimums on crossing the threshold, I was amazed at the niggling items for which he found me "*unqualified*".

When I stood in front of the Commander's "court" the next day, I was totally amazed that several of the Colonels, actually chuckled or giggled at the critique that was offered for why I had failed the ride, as if to say, "Don't worry lad, it was just your turn to fail the SAC check ride"!

It was a week later, to that day, that the Wing Commander called me into his office and told me, "Based upon my observed and reported performance over the past several months, your knowledge of the aircraft and the mission techniques, and your obvious pilot maturity and common sense, I am nominating you to become an Instructor Pilot under local training and check-out, followed by formal training at the SAC Central Flight Instructor Course, within the next two months". *[I completed this course in May 1972].*

The rest of the story —

By the time I had completed the SAC CFIC training and been certified as a SAC Tanker Instructor Pilot, I had realized several important facts. My initial SAC transition training in the KC-135 was so intense and filled to saturation level with information, – like the proverbial "try-

ing to get a drink from a fire hose" – that all I had time and absorption ability to do was to learn how to, analogously "fly down the stripe in the middle of the runway", so to speak. In the month of flight training at CFIC, they taught me to fly the aircraft to the extreme corners of the flight envelope. I knew exactly how, by feel and additional senses (without reference to the flight instruments), how far I could take the airplane before it would depart from safe flying limits. For example, we flew the traffic pattern with cardboard in front of the instrument panel, so I could not see the power instruments, nor the airspeed indicator, or even the attitude indicator — I learned to judge by reference to the physical horizon outside of the cockpit what my altitude was above the runway using visual horizon references on the windscreen, the familiar sound of the engines, and by the fuel flow gauges what my power was; by the trim settings and feel of the back-pressure on the yoke, whether I was approaching the stall.

I was taught to visually (without reference to instruments or altimeter) bring the airplane down to 3-5 feet from the runway and then apply back-pressure and just enough power to fly the full length of a 12,000 foot runway without touching down, by imagining I was flying into and along the inside of a tunnel. Once I mastered that in one pass of the runway, he taught me that to land the airplane perfectly, every time, I just had to use that technique, and once established to hold the pitch constant as I slowly reduced the power for a "squeaker", virtually <u>every time</u>. He taught me, ***"Power controls altitude; Pitch controls speed"!***

Within four months of busting that no-notice check ride, I had become Chief Instructor pilot for the two Beale tanker squadrons (903rd AREFS, and 9th AREFS, the second of which had a fleet of "partial Q", partially modified tankers for SR-71 operations). I attributed this success largely to the experiences I had brought to SAC from my prior non-rigid training exposure based on cultivating the student's confidence, rather than trying to destroy it.

As SAC became more strapped for training manpower at Castle AFB and the need to accelerate the upgrading of pilots elsewhere (due to the loss of pilot assignees to the Vietnam conflict), I was relieved of my designated crew assignment and became head of SAC's 15th Air Force PUP (pilot upgrade program) doing mainly upgrade flight training for expe-

rienced tanker copilots to Aircraft Commanders, and experienced AC's initial upgrades to Instructor status, all at Beale, while still attached to the 903rd. This gave me a break from the long TDY deployments and more time with my newly expanded family.

I had never thought of myself as the world's greatest pilot, but I was surprised at how rewarding I felt when I became a fully trained Instructor. I was truly in my element and I had many "students" tell me that I had really given them a work-out, but they really felt that I had raised the mysteries of how and why to fly the aircraft safely and proficiently.

Special VIP Mission to Korea — I learned in SAC) that "command and control" was a very big issue. With the advent of operations involving nuclear weapons after WWII, SAC's founder, General Curtis LeMay, had implemented tight command and control policies. Proving very effective in the "nuclear" bomber arena, these policies and procedures were quickly carried over into all SAC aircrew operations, whether or not nuclear weapons were involved. As a new-comer to SAC, I was amazed at how this could be so conflicted with SAC's and USAF's other regulations, which identified the Aircraft Commander as the ultimate final responsibility and authority, for the proper and safe operation of his aircraft and crew — despite the "command and control" chain of Command Posts and other senior officers within SAC, which frequently tried to take the final decision from the AC (without incurring responsibility for the results).

I was assigned to SAC in 1968 as a Captain, 11-years after LeMay had departed SAC, and three years after he had retired as Air Force Chief of Staff. Upon arriving in SAC, I had previously accrued several thousand hours of pilot experience and a combat tour in Vietnam. I was not intimidated by prevailing SAC policies, and had become sufficiently well informed of "SAC and USAF regulations" (especially through the SAC Central Flight Instructor course), so I was frequently unwilling to let the "command authority" usurp my <u>defined responsibilities and authority</u>. The following event is an example of one such incident – which almost cost me a hard-earned promotion.

Since the beginning of SR-71 operations at Kadena AFB, Okinawa (in early-1968), a special task force was established there, which was designated "OL-8" (Operating Location Eight), under the detached command of the 9th Strategic Reconnaissance Wing (9th SRW) at Beale AFB, CA (my home base in SAC). The OL-8 tanker unit, to which I was assigned when operating from Okinawa, had been pretty autonomous from SAC in their operations due to the Top Secret and "need-to-know" "Senior Crown" compartmentalized classification with high level tasking of the SR-71 mission. As a tanker aircraft commander in this role, when deployed to Kadena, I reported to the command and control authority of the OL-8 (SR-71) Detachment Commander and was tasked with my crew, through him by the same tasking authority as the SR-71 (usually under direct authority of the Secretary of the Air Force, SecAF). However, by mid-1971, the 376th Strategic Bomb Wing at Kadena had gradually eroded our shield of classified-autonomy and we were periodically tasked to support Arc Light (B-52) bombing missions over Vietnam, when not otherwise committed to OL-8 (SR-71) missions. We also came more and more under the 376th Wing's administrative and operational control, while on TDY (Temporary Duty) at Kadena, AFB, which frequently led to the confusion of determining "who's the boss" to whom the aircrews were responsible.

In the early fall of 1971, during one of my 6-week TDY tours to Kadena, my crew was on a crew rest day (off of the flying schedule), when I received a puzzling phone call in my quarters. It was from the 376th Bomb Wing crew-scheduler advising me that my crew and I had been scheduled by them to fly a priority mission to Korea early the next day. At first I thought they had mistaken me for another "Capt. Miller", since OL-8 crews were unaccustomed to being scheduled by the 376th Wing. They verified that they knew I was assigned to OL-8 and that their mission tasking authorization was correct — I had been selected because I was an instructor pilot (though just newly upgraded, at home base, but not yet having completed the formal SAC Central Flight Instructor Course), but I was the most qualified crew commander/instructor available from the OL-8 for this high priority mission to Korea. (All other OL-8 tanker instructor pilot crews were on the schedule for an SR-71 mission, the next day).

Upon reporting to the pre-mission briefing at the Wing aircrew briefing room (rather than usual OL-8 briefing room) before dawn the next day, my crew and I were informed that we had been tasked for a special mission carrying a "Code 3" (meaning a Senior Congressman or Ambassador-level VIP) passenger or team, from Kadena AFB in Okinawa to Kimpo AB, in Seoul, South Korea. This mission was designated as "highly classified" and the briefing officer could not even identify the Code 3 VIP's identity. (This VIP and team would be brought directly to the aircraft at engine-start time, and we would learn his/their identity then).

As I learned later during this mission, an SR-71 had experienced in-flight engine oil pressure problems, had aborted its mission and diverted to a precautionary landing in South Korea for the second time in less than two weeks. This was especially sensitive because the US State Department and DoD were publicly denying that any SR-71s were operating in Southeast Asia. At the first diversion occasion, the US Ambassador to Korea was placated with a brief coded message explaining the SR arrival, but after the second diversion, the SR-71 parent organization, the 9th Strategic Reconnaissance Wing at Beale AFB, CA, felt it was necessary to provide the Ambassador with a complete briefing on the SR-71 missions and circumstances, so the he could appropriately handle any related high-level reactions or publicity in Korea. The OL-8 Commander, in response to 9th SRW tasking had set up an OL-8 tanker mission to take two staff members (the OL-8 Commander and senior SR-71 pilot, and his SR-71 Reconnaissance Systems Operator, RSO) to Seoul for the Top Secret Ambassador's briefing. This airlift tasking had been almost immediately over-ridden by the 376th Strategic Wing command section, claiming that only the 376th had the command authority to task transport to Korea for such missions.

When the OL-8 Commander discovered he had been over-ridden, the story had it that he picked up his secure phone in the OL-8 Command Post and spoke to his contact either in the Pentagon, or at the 9th SRW Command Post at Beale. Within less than an hour there was reportedly a tasking order from the office of the Chief of Staff of the Air Force informing the 376th Strategic Wing Commander that OL-8 was tasking their tanker and crew for a Top Secret Code-3 VIP transport sortie to Kimpo AB. The VIP party was to be left at Kimpo with later arrangements for their continued travel, and the tanker and crew were to immediately return to Kadena after servicing, if necessary, and re-filing a return flight clearance. *[Probably never before, nor since, had two Lt. Colonels been accorded the VIP status of Code 3 on a flight plan]!*

During my 376th Wing pre-mission briefing, I was told that before landing at Kimpo (due to its short, for SAC, 9,000 ft runway, and forecast blowing snow with 20 knot crosswinds), I would have to radio the 376th Command Post, while still in-flight, via HF radio or VHF-land-line "patch" and obtain "execution authorization" from them for me to land at Kimpo. ***("SAC Command and Control", in action).*** If they deemed the weather and crosswinds too severe, they would divert me to Yakota AFB, in Japan and arrange for a C-47 to make the final delivery of the unidentified "Code 3" party to destination. Since I had experience of over 3000 hours in the C-47 prior to my KC-135 assignment, I knew that if a KC-135 couldn't land at Kimpo due to crosswinds, then a C-47 certainly couldn't either. The 9000 ft "short runway" was not an issue either, because we would be operating with a relatively light fuel load, for this flight of less than 3-hours duration.

Upon arriving at Kimpo for approach, we were still too close to Kadena for effective "HF atmospheric-bounce" communications and the Kimpo Command Post (a non-SAC facility) had no land-line-phone capability to reach Kadena. I was certain my "aircraft commander authority" was sufficient, and made the decision to execute an approach and landing, since local weather conditions were well within acceptable limits and my capabilities, and were not nearly as severe, as initially forecast.

The "nightmare" <u>had only just begun!</u>

To continue the adventure, this mission proved to be one that nearly resulted in my being court-martialed due to series of "non-routine" mission characteristics, and "political" jealousies between the 376th Bomb Wing DCO (Deputy Commander for Operations, a senior Colonel) and the OL-8 Commander, (a senior Lt. Col.).

During my recent EC-47 tour in Vietnam, I had personal experience with **Space Available** travel and appreciated the scarce availability of these resources. I also knew that there were very limited opportunities for authorized military passengers to catch any flights out of a relatively small base like Kimpo, which was primarily a fighter base. So I wanted to help any fellow servicemen that I could with a hop to Kadena where there were many more global Space Available opportunities to be had. And I felt I was well indoctrinated into the "fine nuances of SAC operational regulations" from my recent Instructor upgrade training at Beale AFB.

Upon my arrival at Kimpo, I advised the Base Operations Dispatcher that I had an empty KC-135 "dead-heading" directly to Okinawa in an hour and would be glad to take any "Space-A" passengers that were legally manifested. Upon my return from the weather office and filing my clearance, the Dispatcher informed me that he had "an Army 0-6 (full Col.), <u>his wife</u>, and <u>two teen-age daughters</u> manifested and already on board". I figured, though unusual, if they were legally manifested, they were OK by me. Upon arriving at the aircraft, I gave my passengers the obligatory pre-departure safety briefings and informed them that we had no female facilities on board for the two-plus hour flight. If that was understood and OK with them, we would be off. Again, I was unable to make any pre-launch contact with 376th Wing Command Post for launch authorization, but was within the alternate execution authority of my written orders, so we launched for the routine return flight to Kadena.

According to existing SAC policy, we were always obliged to radio the arrival Command Post (376th Strategic Wing, at Kadena) about 45 minutes prior to landing and advise our arrival maintenance status. At that point, I was faced with two options. I could either taxi to the MAC (Military Airlift Command) side of the runway, shutdown my two left engines and deplane my passengers down the vertical crew ladder (with baggage), then restart the engines with an external power cart, and taxi to the SAC ramp. Or, I could taxi to my regular spot on the classified SAC ramp (our normal parking location), and request a SAC VIP staff car to transport the Army Colonel and his family to the MAC terminal across the field. The latter seemed the most efficient and proper protocol, and I made the obligatory radio call with my staff car request.

Upon landing and taxi-in, I was surprised when my aircraft was met by a jeep "Follow-Me" vehicle, sporting a manned 50-cal machine gun mini-turret. (The Follow-Me jeep was often routine at many overseas bases, but never before had I seen one with manned weapons). It directed me to taxi nose-in to a steel revetment, which I noted was also manned by several prone Security Police on the top of the revetment walls with M-16 automatic weapons aimed at my aircraft. After engine shutdown, the tanker's main cargo door was opened "without incident", boarding stairs were wheeled into place and a white-top staff car pulled up with a SAC Colonel at the wheel. The Army Colonel and his family were promptly greeted and ushered to the staff car, while I was informed to report to the DCO's office (Deputy Commander Operations), immediately upon completing maintenance debriefing!

At the DCO's office, I was first read my Uniform Code of Military Justice rights to private counsel, informed that I had "broken every rule in the book", and that the (DCO) Colonel was contemplating Article 15 Disciplinary Action against me. The DCO explained that my "unexecuted" (meaning, "unauthorized by the 376th Command Post") landing and return flight, followed by my "bizarre request for a staff car for dependent passengers with a Col. escort" was presumed by the SAC Bomb Wing Command Post as a potential covert attempt by me to advise them that I had been sky-jacked! This explained my greeting with the armed "Follow-Me" jeep and the "secured" nose-in revetment shutdown and parking. Since this was not a correct assessment, I was then informed that "*no tanker is ever authorized to carry dependent passengers*", particularly without coordinated approval of the controlling Wing Commander.

I explained to the DCO that the training, which I had just received during Instructor Upgrade, which represented the current interpretation of SAC regulations, was:

The prohibition on carrying dependents applies only within the CONUS (Contiguous United States);

The prohibition against carrying non-mission essential military passengers, or unauthorized civilians outside of CONUS, applies only on refueling or high risk sorties within active combat zones, and/or ...

The restriction against an aircraft commander carrying Space-A VIPs, otherwise authorized under Air Force regulations, applies only in regard to the generating of a special mission for the sole purpose of that VIP's personal travel.

None of these prohibitions applied to the circumstances at hand. Although I effectively explained my actions, I was dismissed from the DCO's office still unsure if court martial charges, or a formal reprimand in my official records would be pressed, and whether or not my recent selection for promotion to Major had just been potentially compromised.

Only through the support of the OL-8 Commander and his relay up his chain of command to Beale (and HQ SAC) was this matter finally decided in my favor, after keeping me on the hot seat for nearly 72 hours. I subsequently learned that the OL-8 Commander was so incensed by the action of the 376th DCO that he was overheard to state, jokingly, "I would love to have an immediate opportunity to deny another senior Army O-6 with enough seniority to have wife and dependents accompanying him in Korea, a ride on a SAC aircraft, based solely on the specific order of this arrogant and clueless DCO"!

[This very significant and high-level mission was of such importance to international military diplomacy, that I was subsequenetly awarded the Armed Forces Expeditionary Medal (Korea).]

Still "soaring with destiny", I received my promotion to Major, effective in April 1972, without further repercussions!

Moments of Stark Terror — It has often been described that FLYING is, "*Hours and hours of pure boredom punctuated by a few moments of stark terror!*" One such incident I encountered seemed quite extraordinary. I was flying in a tanker formation during the summer of 1970, returning from an SR-71 mission over Vietnam. After landing and ground refueling the three aircraft tanker cell, we were flying after dusk in 3-ship spread-formation from U-Tapao AFB in Thailand to Okinawa, over the Pacific. This was a standard SAC tanker enroute flight – using trail formation with about 1-mile longitudinal separation (as monitored on our cockpit radar) and 500-foot vertical altitude separation, so that there was minimal potential that crew distractions or weather issues might cause a potential mid-air collision. The three tankers were all flying on a coordinated common heading and standard cruise speed. I was flying the number two, or middle aircraft in the formation stream. We were cruising at an altitude of about 35,000 feet (above mean sea level, or "msl") and were flying on autopilot using the "Altitude Hold" function. We encountered some scattered clouds at our altitude, which meant we were also getting some light turbulence or "chop", which made the long day somewhat more fatiguing and uncomfortable, and eliminated virtually any opportunity to achieve and maintain visual contact with our formation buddies.

KC-135Q, #2 Enroute to Okinawa from Thailand

The formation leader suggested he would get clearance to climb about 4,000 feet higher to see if we could get out of the clouds and annoying turbulence. I had done this type of formation procedure in the past and had learned, in order to maintain a consistent safe vertical separation in the climb and a relative constant 1-mile in-trail separation, the technique was to initiate the climb on the leader's radio command by advancing throttles to "climb power" and simultaneously switching the autopilot from "Altitude Hold" to "Mach Hold". Since the air becomes thinner as an aircraft climbs to higher altitude, the flight Mach number changes proportionately as the speed of sound decreases at higher altitudes. Thus a constant Mach number in the climb means the True Air Speed (zero-wind equivalent ground speed) and longitudinal separation of all three aircraft will also remain constant through a climb (or descent), using constant Mach number during the altitude change, even though the Mach for each aircraft was slightly different at the start, due to their different altitudes.

After climbing for a couple thousand feet, suddenly my aircraft dumped its nose abruptly into a rapid dive! It took just a few split seconds and not more than a thousand feet, for me to grab the yoke, trip off the autopilot release button and re-establish the climb, as my heart settled back into place. “What the hell just happened?”, I asked out loud on the intercom, asking the same question everyone else on the crew was thinking. I triggered the transmit button on interplane frequency and asked if anything strange had been encountered by the other two aircraft, thinking that maybe I passed through the leader's wake, or had encountered a vertical wind shear, or something. The reply came back that each of the other aircraft had experienced the same pitch down that we had, at virtually the same time. It therefore could not have been from a wake-passage situation, since certainly the lead aircraft had no one in front of him to cause this. Nor was a vertical wind shear, or down draft, likely to have been the cause because they only occur in much higher turbulence than we were experiencing and are not known to be large enough to cover a two to three mile diameter area that could capture and affect all three spread-out aircraft simultaneously. It was definitely an autopilot input that caused the rapid nose-down input.

It didn't take very long to figure what had taken place. It seems while flying in the clouds before starting the climb, we had been picking up some moisture from the clouds in our pitot-static airspeed sensing system. The aircraft, like most all large military dual control aircraft, has two separate pitot-static systems (for redundancy) -- one for the pilot's instruments, and another for the copilot's. Also, since the pilot's airspeed indication system is the primary one, it was equipped with a higher temperature pitot-tube heater (which obviously requires more electrical power to operate), while the copilot's system had some extra equipment connected to its system (including the Autopilot sensors), all of which, as a part of the cockpit redundancy, was powered by a lower power hydraulically driven alternate generator. When the copilot's less well-heated pitot system (which measures the ram air flow through the hollow pitot-tube and establishes “indicated airspeed”) began to freeze over, it sensed a significant “drop in airspeed”, and thus a drop in Mach number calculation in the autopilot, which the autopilot tried to correct by rapidly lowering the nose proportionately to the increase in perceived airspeed/Mach number (i.e. impending aircraft stall due to perceived rapidly decreasing airspeed). All the while, the pilot's well-heated pitot probe continued to show normal airspeed indications.

The part of this incident that seemed most difficult to comprehend, was that when we reported this incident to the maintenance people after landing, we were told that "no-one had ever reported this deficiency before". Since, at that time, the USAF aircraft fleet of 800 planes in the various C-135 and KC-135 mission configurations had been flying for 10 to 12 years, it was unbelievable that we were the first to ever encounter this anomaly (or to report it through channels long and loud enough that the maintainers had ever heard of it before). I reported this incident through Safety on an Operational Hazard Report (OHR), to make sure it received adequate future attention.

I further looked into this later in my career capacity as fleet Weapon System Manager (during a subsequent assignment, during a System Review several years later) and verified that this deficiency had been corrected during the many system updates that took place in the aircraft cockpit and autopilot system's that occurred over the next dozen years.

Safety Incident That "Angered The SAC System" – On a situation that occurred before I became an Instructor, I arrived at my aircraft with my crew for a routine proficiency flight. The early version of the KC-135 which I flew, had straight turbojet (non-fan) engines, which required water injection for take-off when runway temperatures were above 65°F, in order to achieve the full 13,700 pounds of take-off thrust that otherwise would have been lost at the higher temperatures and above sea level field elevations. The aircraft was designed with a 1200-gallon (5,800 pounds-worth) water tank for demineralized water, mounted between the main gear wheel wells inside the belly. This amount of water was pumped during activation to the four engines upon initiating full throttles for take-off and provided approximately 125 seconds of water injection. This amount was a sufficient one-shot use for the aircraft to reach safe level of altitude of about 1,000 feet, or more, and time for gear and flap retraction before water run-out.

During my exterior inspection, upon arrival at the aircraft, I noted that there was a significant amount of water running out of the belly of the aircraft, which I queried Maintenance about. They informed me that they had discovered a small crack at the tank mount on their morning inspection, and had determined only about 1 gallon-per-minute had leaked out during the half hour since discovery and would require about four hours to repair necessitating draining the tank and welding the crack, then testing the fix and reservicing the tank with water – a time that would cause them to have to select an alternate aircraft and still would not allow us to achieve our launch window.

After explaining my elevated safety concern, they proposed that we taxi the aircraft, as-is and that they would top off the tank at the take-off end of the runway just prior to launch to insure we had full service for take-off. I said that I would try to accommodate their request, but would need to get a confidence-measure of how much total water had leaked after taxiing over a mile to the end of the runway, before making a final decision. My engineering training in aircraft structures, raised my concern that the vibration of taxiing, the load of the sloshing water and the much greater vibration of take-off acceleration and the jostle of a two-mile take-off roll could cause the crack to split open like a ripe watermelon, leaving me at worst case with loss of substantial water resulting in power reduction during take-off and potential insufficient runway to safely abort, or to get safely airborne.

Upon reaching the end of the runway, the maintenance crew topped off the water tank, but reported it was "really leaking pretty good now". They informed me that the tank had leaked out about a bit over 15% of its capacity in the time it had taken me to start and taxi to the take-off runway ramp. I informed the crew chief that this was not a good sign and that I would not risk the attempted take-off under these conditions. Their supervisors were informed of my decision and sent for the "Cavalry" to try and persuade me to take the gamble. I was informed that this was a "FSAGA" sortie, which had an elevated requirement to fly, but meant nothing to me. When I asked, they explained that FSAGA meant "First Sortie After Ground Alert". This aircraft had been on SAC Ground Alert for two weeks prior (coupled with a B-52 bomber in the event of a SAC wartime launch, or SAC Alert exercise/inspection). SAC Bomb Wing grading criteria by Higher Headquarters kept maintenance statistics on alert aircraft mission capability, and paid particular attention and held very harsh grading on FSAGA aircraft that aborted the first time after being on alert and scored the Wing as though this had been an abort of a potential real wartime launch.

The "Cavalry", in the form of a 903rd Squadron Lt. Col. pilot who happened to be the SOF (Supervisor of Flying) for the Wing, for the day, arrived to persuade me to play this game. I explained my concern for safety and the potential seriousness should a failure occur, as I speculated – especially since this was not an actual alert, nor wartime situation. The Colonel held fast and tried by intimidation to state that if I was unwilling to fly this aircraft that he would fly it himself (despite the fact he was not properly attired in flight gear, nor fully cognizant of the mission details, much less concerned about the safety of the aircraft, nor my crew). I called his bluff, entered the aircraft on a Red-X status (in the aircraft Maintenance Log), and exited the cockpit. [Note: A Red-X status cannot be signed off without corrective action, or declaration of non-mission essential status of the system or equipment, and high supervisory inspection and status sign-off]. I never heard one word from any source in the way of push-back to my authoritative decision. I was not prepared to put the aircraft and myself and crew at risk for the lack of a proper maintenance decision – ever. Not withstanding, the Wing staff obviously supported upgrading me to Instructor status in the not-too-distant future after this event.

Safety Dispute with My Seniors in Maintenance – This incident felt a bit like insubordination, but it was born from my prior experiences in combat and earlier before-SAC assignments, and is correctly an example of full knowledge of who has decision-making authority and responsibility in flight operations. By this time I had been elevated and certified as an Instructor Pilot in the Squadron. I was on a daytime routine proficiency training mission of about 6 hours duration with my own crew, intended to consist of normal take-off, inflight refueling an SR-71, flying a couple hour navigation leg, and then winding up with about an hour and half of traffic pattern work for both my copilot and myself accomplishing numerous different instrument approaches and touch and go landings. We had very recently received a new Squadron Commander and he had selected our crew and this flight for one of his first crew familiarization rides (one of many), and would be observing the entire crew performance from the cockpit jump seat.

The mission was normal, and went well for the first 3 hours or so, until we returned to base for the approach and landing phase. I was in the left seat and the copilot had the controls for the first portion of the pattern work. When operating in this mode, and touch and go landings were performed on the practice approaches, normal procedure was to leave the gear down in the pattern after T&G landings, to save wear and tear on the mechanisms. After the copilot completed his portion and it was my turn to practice, we arranged clearance to climb back to high altitude (20,000 feet) over the approach fix (VOR, VHF Omni-Directional Range, beacon) for a couple holding patterns followed by an instrument penetration descent (to 1,000 feet pattern altitude) for several instrument approaches and touch & go landings, for my personal proficiency.

After the copilot's final T&G he transferred control to me for my portion of the training (under the observation of the new Squadron CO in the jump seat). I called for "Gear Up" upon commencing my climb to high altitude. The gear started up, but one of the mains failed to fully retract. After recycling the gear, down again, then up while continuing our climb, again the same main gear did not fully retract to the Up & Locked position according to the landing gear lights and a mild but conspicuous airflow vibration from the fuselage. I asked the Boom Operator to go back into the main fuselage where there is a small glass port in the belly, to visually check the main gear status. Sure enough, one was up and locked, but the other was not. Each main gear has a bogey of four large main-gear wheels (about 4-feet in diameter, including the tires) that are in a two-forward and two-aft configuration with the landing gear strut forming a leveling-pivot in the center of the formed rectangle of wheels. Included in the mechanism is an air-charged leveling-strut and numerous leveling sensors and switches that insure the bogey assembly is leveled to a position parallel to the fuselage after becoming airborne, so that the gear strut and bogey can squarely retract into the wheel well, over which the gear door on each side then closes to streamline the opening. The boomer observed that the faulty gear retraction on one side was caused by the fact that the leveling action had not correctly occurred causing the bogey to be cocked and not fit inside the wheel well.

With this fault I knew that, if not jammed, the gear could be placed into the down position and would lock down normally and safely for landing. I therefore requested "Gear Down" and then moments later verified "Three Green, all down and locked" and proceeded to make my instrument penetration from 20,000 feet and approach. I informed the Tower of our difficulty and informed them I would be making a "precautionary" straight ahead, full stop landing on the runway, and requested they contact Maintenance to send a vehicle to install the landing gear lock pins on the runway before I could safely taxi clear of the runway. I also asked my Navigator to notify the Command Post and advise them of our intentions, and to have Crash Rescue notified and standing by at the side of the runway— just in case.

Once the landing was safely accomplished, the blue maintenance van met us on the runway and installed the safety pins. They connected an intercom cable into our external intercom jack and verified they had found the leveling strut depressurized. They informed me that they recommended for me to taxi to the opposite (take-off) end of the runway, after they disconnected their intercom cable, and there they would reinflate and charge the leveling strut, so I could complete my scheduled mission time. My knowledge of the system indicated that it could not be just a single failure, since the system sensor switches on the bogey should have signaled the failure-to-level on the previous take-off, which would prevent the gear handle from being moved out of the down & locked position. This system design feature was intended to insure that the gear never tried to retract when the bogey was not level, because of the potential for it to become jammed in the wheel well during the retraction and cause a gear-up crash landing.

Conversely, the Maintenance crew knew that the SAC Wing Maintenance function would get a Headquarters red mark on their daily scoring for any mission-incompleted because of maintenance deficiency, and that was the pressure they responded to. I stated to them my intention to taxi off of the runway to reopen the landing field, as I sat with 4-engines idling on the active runway, gear-pins installed. But maintenance personnel wanted to get reinforcements from their seniors, before allowing me to move. After several minutes a Colonel from the DCM (Wing Deputy Commander for Maintenance) representative arrived and began ordering me to do as they wished. I refused within my Aircraft Commander authority, and said I was placing the aircraft on a red-cross status in the onboard maintenance logbook with appropriate description. The Colonel continued to argue with me on the intercom cable while my aircraft was still sitting on the runway with all four engines running and the aircraft attached to the maintenance van. Finally, I had had enough debate and told the Colonel respectfully, that he had only two options – He could either disconnect the intercom cable and move the van out from in front of the aircraft, so I could taxi it to the parking spot, or I would shut the aircraft down on the runway and they could tow it to the ramp. I reminded him he did not have the authority to order me (under these circumstances) to take-off in a known unsafe aircraft. He acquiesced and removed the cable and cleared the path for me to taxi.

After taxiing in, and before departing the aircraft, I turned to my new Squadron Commander, with whom I had just had my first face-to-face introduction, and asked him about his reaction to my confrontation with the DCM representative, acknowledging that it could be interpreted as outright insubordination. He patted me on the shoulder and said that was exactly the right call and he could expect no less from one of his Aircraft Commanders, especially a senior squadron crew pilot. But I knew that he felt uncomfortable as a new Commander in the Wing. I heard the next day that the maintenance inspection had discovered two failed sensor switches as well as a blown seal in the leveling strut. I realized that when you must countermand a senior officer, you must have good reason, and you must be sensitive in your assessment of the safety implications of the situation.

An Opportune Training Lesson – As lead instructor in the PUP (Pilot Upgrade Program), I fully identified that my primary mission was to instill good flying and decision-making skills with my upgrading students. I spent many hours with each of many candidates for Aircraft Commander in ground training discussing insights into situations and consequences of emergencies that are seldom ever covered "by the book". In my early SAC days, I had experienced the intensity and saturation learning of KC-135 pilot transition training. With the more recent instructor training at the Central Flight Instructors Course, I had realized vividly how much I had <u>not learned</u> about the total operation of the aircraft following my practical OJT (On the Job Training). From my prior Flight Safety responsibilities, I was a firm believer in the importance having pre-thought (through discussion AND practical exercise), while under a controlled environment, as many details of the consequences of an action or sequence of failures is forming – and preventing – a potential accident. And I knew that unfortunately, when an emergency occurs in-flight, the pilot cannot "hit the pause button" (as in a simulator) and then take the time to analyze and resolve the situation before proceeding. His ONLY safe option is to calmly relate to his training <u>and continue to fly the airplane</u>, while making a timely analysis and resolution to the problem(s) under the real-time pressure of an irreversible ticking clock.

For a candidate to undertake PUP training, he was typically required to have accumulated more than 2,000 hours logged copilot time in this type aircraft, during which time he had gained many basic OJT skills and experience, in addition to his initial qualification training. But this often also included many bad habits without understanding many of the underlying experiences of his "OJT-trainer", nor rationale of the decisions routinely and quickly made by his example.

In the PUP program, each candidate would typically receive a minimum of four-instructional rides, flying from the left seat, with the instructor pilot in the right providing instruction in tactics, procedures, and explanations in each and every facet of a typical mission (from an AC perspective), including heavy weight takeoffs, formation procedures, in-flight refueling, navigational segments, a variety of approach and landing sequences, and handling various simulated failures or emergency procedures. Each of the four missions would be with the same instructor (for continuity of training advancement). These missions would be debriefed after each flight and debriefing notes recorded on paper to document the level of training and advancement.

A following fifth and final ride would be conducted by an instructor – sometimes the same one, but preferably a different one – in order to obtain a different level of tension and an unbiased impression of the candidate's progress. It was conducted in similar fashion to the first four rides, but under different ground rules. This time the instructor would perform solely as a copilot (and observer) and would not offer guidance, nor "decisions" that would coach the student's responses. However, as would be the case with a normal crew, the co-pilot could make recommendations during unusual circumstances, but not offer decisions. In other words, it would be a situational scenario where the left seat candidate would perform and handle all situations as would be expected of a competent Aircraft Commander. If this ride was completed satisfactorily, the candidate's next flight would be with a Stan- Eval Instructor Pilot under similar ground rules as the fifth ride to gain the candidate's AC rating (if satisfactory).

In the scenario next described, I was flying the fifth ride in the PUP syllabus with a very competent copilot candidate, and had encountered a real scenario of real emergency situations for evaluating his performance. This situation WAS NOT a simulation, but an actual "precautionary" emergency.

The mission was scheduled to operate under some very demanding conditions. The aircraft was loaded to maximum take-off weight, and it was a typical 100° day in northern California, making aircraft performance critical. Everything was normal, and as planned, during the preflight checks, engine start, taxi-out, and take-off, with the exception that the candidate kept attempting to validate many of his procedures and thought processes along the way, as typically happened during formal training, by asking "his instructor" if that was the correct way to perform or respond. I kept reminding him, "I was only a basic copilot and would not make or verify decisions for him."

With Beale AFB in the valley on the foothills of the Sierra Mountains, our flight path after take-off was to reverse course, with a left turn, from the runway heading and climb out over the slowly increasing elevation of the foothills. Being loaded to maximum weight, and struggling with the heat, the climb rate after water run-out was about the same as the foothills were climbing beneath us, and we were maintaining about 2,000 feet above the foothills. As we were passing about 4,000 feet, as I scanned the engine instruments, I noticed the oil pressure gauge on the #3 engine (inboard engine on the right side) take a couple slight dips, but all the others were rock steady. I tapped my student on the shoulder, and then calmly tapped the #3 oil pressure gauge to draw it to his attention. He asked me, after a glance, "What should we do"? I played the copilot "indecisive role" and replied, "Just keep it under watch to see if it gets worse".

A few moments later, the oscillations became greater and the back-up low pressure light below the gauge started to flicker. When I saw that he had seen these degenerating signals, I asked him, "What should I do, Boss"? He replied "Call the Command Post?", with a question in his voice. I shook my head in the negative. He responded with even more questioning reply, "Shut down the engine"? I suggested, "We are kind of heavy, and the terrain here is climbing about as fast as we are". He took my hint and replied, "Guess we should dump some fuel?" I replied, "Is that a question, or a command?" He was starting to understand that he WAS expected to act as AC, as I had previously instructed. I offered an opinion, (because competent copilots typically will help that way), "If we shut down a running engine before initiating a fuel dump, we are going to make the situation worse, before it starts getting better". (This made him think. The engine shutdown first would be the normal procedure… if we had not been climb-critical and close to the terrain, but we needed to lighten the load down to maximum landing weight (about 25 to 30% reduction in our current fuel state, so we can achieve a better climb rate). Again he asked if we should call the Command Post. My reply again was, "Negative, the Command Post can't do anything but add distraction, when you already know what needs to be done". I suggested, "You might want me to notify Air Traffic Control of our situation, so they can assist keeping other distractions and traffic out of our way. Then tell him what your intentions are, and any assistance you want from them". "Do you want me to advise Approach that we are declaring an "Emergency", or a "Precautionary Landing? I reminded him we already had clearance enroute above 20,000 feet, so we needed to do what? He correctly responded, "get clearance to the Beale approach holding fix at 20,000 feet and, advising him that we will need to dump fuel and shut down the engine". Then he asked me, "But what about the Command Post"? I said, "Later. We will discuss that once you have the emergency under control, and have no other distractions to deal with".

We dumped about 40,000 pounds of jet fuel (as I recall) pumping it out through the retracted boom on the barren mountain-side as we continued our climb (all of which visually evaporated aloft before reaching the ground). We established an improved climb rate and then, at his call, we performed the engine shut-down checklist, did a few circuits around the holding pattern at 20,000 feet, while getting the aircraft trimmed and stable for the engine out yaw, reviewed what systems (electrical generator, hydraulic pump, rudder boost and auto-pilot rudder yaw-damper) had been lost or compromised, and only then called the Command Post to inform them and to advise what our actions had been, and what we planned to do next (make a 3-engine approach to a full stop landing when down to a safe landing weight, with emergency equipment alerted for our landing). I knew that the CP would, with-out our request, know to notify Tanker Operations of our abort and missed refueling off-load and would coordinate to find another available tanker, if any, without bothering us for details. The 3-engine approach and landing was routine and the aborted flying mission safely completed. I called the Command Post once on the ground and advised we would stop down and discuss the circumstances with them, after the maintenance debriefing and paperwork was completed.

I could tell from my student's concern that he feared Command Post criticism of our delayed calls, based upon his OJT experience that 'the Command Post call "traditionally" was always first'. So we discussed what had happened in more detail after arriving back in the building. I reiterated that the pilot's (AC's) number one responsibility and priority, is *to Fly the aircraft*. His second, is to recognize that by regulation, his is the final and highest authority on, or off the plane, especially when safety is an issue (except in times of actual warfare) – Not the Command Post, nor the Wing Commander, nor even a the Commander of SAC! He expressed the belief, based on his several years of SAC experience, that we were going to get a lot of negative push-back and heat from the

Command Post for not contacting them at the first indication of a problem. That is what the SAC system appears to teach. But that IS NOT what the regulations actually say.

[This is a lesson that I initially learned back in my early days of flying the C-47 – remember the incident, in Chapter 3, when the O'Hare Tower controller "told me to", make the 1st turn off the runway after asking me to make an abnormal high speed approach?]

So I took him down to the Command Post duty Controller who was on the desk during our situation. I told the Controller who we were, and what the situation was in the cockpit, and asked him if there were any repercussions because of how we handled the situation (from the Command Post's perspective). We were both told emphatically that they wished every crew would react that way. The Command Post provides an excellent communications to all Command and Control agencies all the way to the Commander of SAC, if/when necessary, and to any and all technical support agencies up to and including the aircraft or the systems engineering expertise at the original manufacturer's plant (Boeing, or Pratt & Whitney Engines, etc.). But if higher trouble shooting expertise or advice is NOT needed in the AC's judgment, then the Command Post needs only to know what your intentions are and any assistance you might request, so they can make a time stamped record and notify the Chain of Command to the level appropriate to the situation, once the crew has the situation in hand. Unnecessary Command Post intervention can often be a distraction and compound the seriousness of the situation.

My student passed his practice check ride AND learned a very good and lasting lesson from that experience.

My Mission From Hell — When I relate stories like this to others, I usually get one of two reactions. The first is from current or former SAC crewmembers. Their reaction is to offer a story of similar or greater incredibility. The other reaction is from non-SAC people who find the stories so incredible that they believe them to be untrue or overly "embellished". But I assure you this is what actually happened.

By July, 1972, in my capacity as Wing Chief Instructor Pilot, I had not been on a Kadena AFB, Okinawa TDY deployment for nearly 10 months (and no longer had a crew of my own). I was crawling around under the house one day doing some plumbing modifications — just preparing to cut the main water line — when my wife called that I had a phone call from the Command Post. At the time, I was in "crew rest" prior to a scheduled 4-hour local evening training mission for an upgrading copilot.

The call was from the Command Post advising me to pack my bags for a 3 to 4 day trip and report to the flight line for a departure in two hours (about 4 PM). They further informed me that an augmentation crew would complete the flight planning, get the weather briefing, file the clearance, and have the airplane preflighted upon my arrival. My sole reason for being scheduled was to take B/Gen. H, the 14th Air Division Commander, to Kadena AFB, Okinawa to Chair an accident board on an SR-71 that had crashed there on the runway upon landing. This aircraft was lost without crew injury when a strong crosswind gust carried the aircraft off the side of the runway upon landing roll-out.

Wreckage of SR-71 at Kadena, July 1972

SAC Regulations required that anytime a General officer flew at the controls of a SAC airplane, there must be an instructor pilot in the other seat with full access to the controls, and the instructor was the designated "Pilot in Command" regardless of rank. This would be my first experience flying as an Instructor Pilot with a General officer in the pilot's seat. B/Gen. H resembled your stereotypical General's personality, a "high-born southern gentlemen"; a graduate from the exclusive Virginia Military Institute (VMI); a commanding presence, with a fine southern accent. As typical of most pilot-rated Generals, he was known to want as much "cockpit time" as possible. He was a former B-52 pilot and also had previously received a basic "VIP-checkout" in the KC-135, commensurate with his rank and pilot experience.

I arrived at the ramp and went immediately to the aircraft as briefed. All personnel — except the General — were on board and ready for departure. The augmented crew was under the command of Lt. Col. John C who was a 903rd Squadron line pilot, but not instructor rated. I had an additional crew consisting of copilot, navigator and boom operator assigned to me. By SAC regulation, I was the overall crew commander, for Safety reasons. Shortly after I arrived, the white-topped staff car with the General arrived at the aircraft. The temperature on the ramp in California in July was over 100 degrees, and there was no air-conditioning available until after take-off. There was only a small amount of ventilation from the open pilot's and copilot's side-windows prior to take-off. Just as we were about to start engines (with me in the right seat) my temporary boom operator advised me that in the rush of things, no-one had ordered coffee and water for the flight. This created a 20-minute delay in our "steam-oven" cockpit, while the supplies were delivered, and was the first sign that this was not to be a smooth well-coordinated and planned flight.

As we sat there waiting, the General chatted about how he had been up since the wee hours and was extremely tired. He was also not enjoying this hot delay and was fuming at the apparent oversight of the unnamed individuals responsible for the undelivered supplies. Once the supplies arrived and were secured, the engine start was made and B/Gen. H performed an uneventful take-off and departure. As soon as we reached initial cruise altitude for Hickam AFB, Honolulu — our intermediate refueling stop, some 5-plus hours away — the General excused himself to go to the crew rest bunk for a nap, leaving instructions to wake him 45-minutes before landing so he could resume pilot control of the aircraft, for approach and landing. My temporary co-pilot came to the cockpit in the interim to ride the left seat. And so it was done. B/Gen. H returned to the left seat for the approach and landing at Hickam AFB. Upon arrival, after an uneventful landing, the aircraft was met by the anticipated staff car, which whisked the General off to the air-conditioned VIP lounge.

The normal procedure practiced with an augmented (second) crew on board, during Kadena deployer missions, was for the crew flying the first leg to Honolulu to stay with the aircraft and attend to any maintenance requirements and to oversee the refueling of the proper fuel load and center of gravity management. Due to the ambient year-round temperature in Honolulu of 80 to 85 degrees — and the available runway length (12,300 ft, Runway 08) — we were constrained to a maximum take-off weight of 280,000 pounds. This meant that we would be at about 80% of full fuel capacity for this next long (approx. 5000 mile) leg. So, dependant on how much other cargo and personnel were onboard, the total fuel we could depart with was limited and critical. The turn-around time on these servicing operations in Honolulu/Hickam AFB was about an hour and a half (which included reservicing the 5,800 pounds, or approx. 1,000 gallons of demineralized water used for injection into the engines for take-off thrust augmentation in hot climates). While the landing crew took care of these pre-departure details, the members of the augmentation crew (who would be flying the second non-stop leg of about nine hours, the rest of the way into Okinawa) would go into the terminal, cool-off, get some refreshments and a meal and then go to Base Operations for a weather briefing and filing of the flight plan. During this Base Ops stop the departure crew would be briefed on all local conditions including the unique noise abatement departure procedures over Waikiki

Beach and "hotel row". They would then proceed to the aircraft and conduct their through-flight checklist inspections and "Before Start Engine" checklist. Meanwhile, the first crew, having completed their arrival tasks, had an equal time for a terminal cool-off and a meal before returning to the aircraft where they would take passenger seats for departure.

After the five and a half hour flight to Hickam, it had been over 18 hours since I had been to bed. The long day, the tension of the special mission and flying with the General, the heat of the ground delay at Beale and of the ground reservicing at Hickam had all taken a toll on me. I was exhausted. The General had already complained that he was exhausted at the beginning of the prior flight-leg, so I felt certain that my services would not be required and the second crew, according to our established operational routine, would fly the second leg of the mission, unassisted by the General, and without my required presence in the cockpit. So when I returned to the plane after dinner, I informed Lt. Col. John C to plan on continuing through the take-off and departure from Hickam since he and his crew had gotten all the briefings and procedural updates in Operations. *WRONG assumption, on my part!*

I went and strapped into a passenger seat in the passenger/cargo cabin of the aircraft. At the designated engine-start time, the staff car arrived with the General. He climbed the boarding ramp-stairs on the left side of the aircraft and made an immediate left turn toward the cockpit. The next thing I heard from the cockpit was an irritated General saying to Lt. Col. John C in the left seat, "Col., what are you doing in my seat?" The Lt. Col. replied that he was just following my directions as "Pilot in Command". The General then told the Col. to move over to the copilot's seat, so he could have the pilot's seat. The Col. advised the General that he was not "instructor qualified" and therefore could not fill that position. With that, the General headed back toward me and wanted to know why I was not in the cockpit. I explained my assumption and my fatigue. He promptly informed me, "The only reason this damned airplane is going to Kadena is because ***I*** am on it, and by God you are going to get in the right seat **so I can make the take-off**." Against my better judgment, I conceded and did as the General demanded. (As you no doubt realize, a General's "request" is the same as an "order", and as a newly promoted Major, I felt obliged to comply).

Since I had not attended the Hickam Base Ops departure briefing, and it had been over ten months since my last westbound departure from Honolulu, I had forgotten one *not-so-small detail.* The aircraft was at its maximum gross weight for the temperature and runway length available. This required that the take-off be performed as a "static" run-up rather than a more typical "rolling take-off". This meant that rather than taxiing onto the runway, when cleared, and just advancing power as the roll began, it was necessary to "taxi-back" the aircraft to the very end of the runway under-run. The brakes were held on, power was then advanced to take-off setting confirming that the water injection was operating properly on all four engines, and verifying that full thrust had been attained on all engines, before releasing the brakes and starting the take-off roll. This procedure gained an extra 800 feet equivalent of runway availability at take-off thrust for critical maximum weight take-offs.

Due to my oversight, combined with fatigue and all the other distractions, I failed to advise the General of the requirement (briefed at Base Ops – in his and my absence –) to not make a rolling take-off. At this point my **Guardian Angel** came to the rescue, and precipitated an aborted take-off to prevent the inevitable consequence of running out of runway before lift-off speed had been reached, which would probably result in a stall and crash. But this would occur as another apparent event on the "Mission from Hell". Let me further explain:

As the General initiated his rolling take-off, the #3 engine water injection system failed to activate (*we had lost nearly 25% of the take-off thrust on that engine*), and would certainly never get safe take-off speed, before we ran out of runway. In my recently completed SAC Instructor Course, I had been taught that the recommended way to handle abort situations was to call attention of the problem to the "qualified" pilot at the controls, but not to call, "Abort". That is, the secondary pilot was to notify the pilot at the controls of the condition, NOT to make the decision for him. In hindsight, as Pilot in Command, I should have called "Abort". In this tense instance, I called out the failure on interphone and then followed procedure by momentarily retarding #3 throttle and re-advancing it, to see if it might kick in (an often effective remedy). It did not. So I again stated on interphone, "Sir, #3 failed to take water". The General acknowledged my call, but continued with the take-off acceleration. At this point the #3 throttle was all the way forward to the mechanical stop, and the other three were at maximum take-off power setting (on the Exhaust Pressure Ratio, EPR, power instruments), which was maybe an inch back from the forward mechanical stop position. The aircraft was accelerating rapidly past 70 knots (halfway to T.O. speed) and I called the General again and stated firmly, "Negative water on three. Sir!"

He responded (apparently relating to his more familiar B-52 take-off with one of eight engines not getting water injection); he asked "We can still go on three can't we?" I replied, "No Sir. This is an abort condition." Now the General realized he could not continue the take-off and he reached up and grabbed the throttles and pulled them to idle. Unfortunately, he missed the #3 throttle that was pushed ahead of the others. (I had to reach up and pull the #3 throttle to idle). Then he failed to deploy the speed brakes (a lever alongside the throttles that deploys aerodynamic "fences" along the trailing edge of the wings). *This is an "automatic" step to any abort situation!* I had to remind him, "Speed brakes, Sir". Then I had to warn him to start maximum anti-skid wheel braking since the airport procedure was to avoid crossing the intersecting runway, during an aborted take-off, which was 500 feet short of the end of our runway. (*In the early model tankers, only the left seat had anti-skid brakes and if I applied braking from the right seat, while he was braking from the anti-skid system, we surely would have blown the tires*)! *[Hickam AFB shares the primary runway with Honolulu International*

Airport, and the lighter commercial aircraft often took-off and landed on the shorter (9,000 foot) crossing runway]. With this reminder, he jammed on the wheel brakes so aggressively that the anti-skid system started to cycle heavily — a much too aggressive action for such a heavy aircraft on a hot day at nearly 100 knots, by then. The General was very unhappy with himself (and me) because I had found it necessary to remind him three times as to the proper abort requirement and three more times about proper abort procedures which any proficient KC-135 pilot should have known and done instinctively.

In Instructor School, I was taught that, in flying with a General officer, he would recognize that he was not fully current and proficient, and that he would appreciate the instructor's need to stay in command of the flight. Unfortunately, the General had obviously NOT been to this course and didn't appreciate my intercession… a mere Major harping at him about proper procedures!

But the WORST was still not over! At this point, after getting the aircraft almost stopped, I called the tower advising them of the high speed aborted take-off and requested a fire truck to meet us at the turn-off to check for hot brakes, which could start a fire or blow the tires. The civilian fire truck arrived at the aircraft as we approached the last turn-off before reaching the active cross-runway. At a normal SAC base, the fire department would typically check the temperature of the brakes with the aircraft engines running, and then if necessary direct large portable fans onto the wheels to cool them, without engine shutdown. But the civilian crew at Hickam/Honolulu International Airport signaled us to shut down the engines before they would approach, while we were still stopped on the runway. The wheels were hot, but not smoking, so they set up their fans while we cooked in the near 100° cockpit for 15 minutes, on the now closed runway.

Once the brakes were cooled, we had to return the 2-miles back to the other end of the 12.300 ft runway, to the military ramp for maintenance on the #3 engine water system. With all engines shutdown, that meant we would have to be towed back. The tug and tow bar arrived after another 15 minutes delay. In trying to tow this nearly-280,000 pound airplane, an abrupt start of the tug succeeded in snapping the shear pin in the tow bar and they had to disconnect and go back for a replacement tow bar. The delay of the second tow bar and slow tow back to the ramp took nearly another hour while we all sweltered and the General's neatly pressed uniform got soaked with sweat. So far, we had been confined inside the "sauna" for 90-minutes and the General was more than figuratively "hot under the collar". The poor 40 or so passengers in the cabin were nearly fried without any circulation for that long!

When we arrived at the ramp, again the General was whisked away in a staff car while we turned the aircraft over to maintenance for an indefinite standby, during repairs. This type of problem was not uncommon on the early water injected turbojet KC-135s. It was usually caused either by a loose or corroded electrical connector, or a faulty engine-mounted switch. But it would take *some* time to re-service the water and fuel tanks after diagnostic checks, run-up checks and repairs were made. I remained with the aircraft to monitor the progress of activities and to be able to alert everyone quickly once we were set to have another go. The others, including the 40-support passengers, went back to the Base Ops cafeteria to cool off.

The maintenance chief, a very tall Senior Master Sergeant, advised me that they thought they had found the problem (a bad switch) but that he had to start the engines and make a run-up check to verify it was fixed. Then they would top off the water tanks and replenish the fuel used and we would be away within *another hour*.

I went to stay cool on the grass under a palm tree at the edge of the ramp. The Sergeant returned several minutes later. He said, "I have some bad news, Sir. When I went to get into the seat for the engine run-up and attempted to slide the seat aft, the seat adjustment handle broke off in my hand". In total exasperation, I asked him how long it would take to fix. He informed me that a fix would require removing the seat from the cockpit floor in order to gain access to weld the handle-shaft where it had broken. This would be a 3 to 4-hour job, at best. This was clearly unacceptable, as this long a delay, plus the additional hour required to complete the run-up and reservicing would certainly force us to remain overnight due to crew duty-time running out before reaching our destination. Could it get any worse? ***YES, it certainly could — and it did!***

I asked the Sergeant if there were any other options. He replied that the only other option was to put the pilot in the seat, and have the Sergeant adjust the seat one-time to the fixed position, by using vice-grip pliers to release the slide latch under the seat. If we could do this, we could get to our destination and then have the seat repaired at destination while we were in crew rest.

At this point, the General was absent, probably in the VIP Lounge and unavailable for discussions, which would add even more delays. I was looking forward to a very hazardous "Noise Abatement Departure Procedure" out of Honolulu to avoid over-flying Waikiki Beach, and I was too fatigued to cope with the General's over-inflated importance and low KC-135 proficiency. So I took my "Pilot-in-Command" prerogative and decided that Lt. Col. John C would have the seat adjusted to his physical requirements and would make the take-off and final landing. Now this was not just a trivial matter. Seat adjustment was very critical on the KC-135. The fore and aft position, was critical to insure the pilot had exactly the correct position set so that the pilot had full travel on the rudder pedals (in case of the loss of power on one side or the other when taking off), and in the right position that he would have full access to the brake travel in the pivoting rudder pedals if an abort occurred on take-off. Secondly, the seat height had to be at the exactly correct for the individual, so that his view and depth perception were correct for his physical attributes upon landing the aircraft. This temporary adjustment "fix" was made, the water injection system was repaired and the re-servicing completed.

When the General returned to the aircraft and found the Lt. Col. pilot in the seat — again —, we had a replay of the previous discussion. This time, I refused to back down and informed the General that I had made a safety decision and that was that (or so I thought!). We made the departure (take-off) with the General and I both sitting in the aft of the airplane, with him grumbling at me for the next several minutes. After airborne, we both retired to the crew rest bunks and began some much needed sleep. ***More grief to come!***

Five or six hours later, I was awakened by the boom operator and told that Lt. Col. John C needed me in the cockpit, "for a word". I went forward to find that the SAC Command Post at Andersen AFB in Guam had called and advised that a typhoon (hurricane) condition was approaching Okinawa and they recommended that we divert into Guam. I told them to standby advising them that I had a Code 5 (General) on board and he urgently needed to get to Kadena ASAP to preside over the accident board investigation (which was keeping the Kadena primary runway closed until the General's arrival, and the wreckage was removed, pending the investigation). I then used the long-range HF radio to check with Kadena AFB to get their weather conditions and forecast for our arrival time. The sky conditions were forecast to be within acceptable limits and the winds were forecast to be high and gusty, but essentially down the runway. We still had another several hours before arrival time and were another hour before we would be abeam of passing Guam. I called the Andersen AFB Command Post back and told them that we were proceeding to Kadena due to the urgency of our mission and the prevailing weather forecast for our arrival.

About an hour later, as we approached the position abeam of Guam, the Andersen Command Post called us again and reported that Headquarters SAC had now "directed us to divert to and land" at Andersen AFB. The rationale explained was that Kadena was currently running a typhoon evacuation of all large aircraft on the field, and they did not want another one arriving to contend with (not to mention the closure of one of the primary runways due to the SR-71 crash). The Anderson CP advised that they had arranged to send the General on to Kadena on a T-33 (two seat jet trainer) and that we should crew rest at Andersen AFB and return home with no further involvement with the General's travel. At this point I was greatly relieved, but still had to face the ordeal of informing the sleeping General that we were not going to take him to his required destination.

I woke the General to inform him of the multiple communications I had received from the SAC Command Post on Guam. As expected, he wasn't happy with the ordered diversion, but he seemed eager to divorce himself from this "challenge-plagued" deployment. And he was to get his final licks in at the end of the day. At this time we were less than an hour to our diversion destination at Andersen AFB.

KC-135Q at Cruise Altitude

Notwithstanding, that the pilot seat that was no longer adjustable and had been set for Lt. Col. C's physical stature, the General insisted that he would make the approach and landing in Guam. Fortunately, the General and the Lt. Col. were of similar size and I felt obliged not to antagonize the General again, since I was capable of taking control and flying the final landing at Guam from the right seat, if necessary. Upon completion of the uneventful approach and landing, I was relieved to see the staff car whisk the General off to his quarters, with the knowledge that my involvement with him on this mission was over – and he had unwittingly compromised safety more than once!

The next day, after a good night's rest, the General proceeded on to Kadena in a T-33, and we proceeded the return flight to Beale AFB, CA through Honolulu, leaving our other passengers and cargo at Guam. Nothing further was heard from the General, or the on-board SR-71 support team, upon our return home.

***Another example of an angel on my shoulder* keeping me, the General, and all of the passengers and crew safe from harm!**

*[This anecdote was printed in the National Museum of the USAF (NMUSAF) "**Friends Journal**", Fall 2005 Edition.]*

***EPILOG* to my "Mission From Hell"—** Unrelated to this episode, a few months later I was reassigned into a position of more critical need. The 456th Bomb Wing Safety Office (at Beale, my parent location) had received two prior Unsatisfactory Inspector General (IG) no-notice ratings in a row over about a six-month period, and with my Instructing and prior Flying Safety Officer experience, I had been selected by the Wing Commander to take over the Office from the now "fired" Chief of Safety. My path was about to cross with Gen. H, once again, as described below regarding my Safety Office responsibilities, and then shortly thereafter regarding my follow-on HQ USAF reassignment. (Further details to follow).

*A Humorous Navigator Anecdote — [One of the many things I learned **early on was** reinforced in my tour in SAC. In the crew force we learned to cope somewhat by being able to find humor in our circumstances to relieve stress by a laugh at ourselves to retain our sanity. Here is another example of this.]*

While flying during the Cold War on a SAC tanker or bomber aircraft, at least one member of the crew was required to continuously monitor radio contact with the SAC Command Post (call-sign, "Sky King" located at Omaha, Nebraska) in order to respond immediately to any potential nuclear threat, mission changes, or launch messages. The requirement was that on every flight either the crew Navigator, or the Co-Pilot (when the Navigator was pre-occupied with more critical phases of his mission) was required to monitor the HF (high frequency, long range) radio and periodically record the receipt of any coded message from the Command Post, and then using the crypto key for the day, carried on-board for every mission, to authentic and decode the message for the Aircraft Commander... noting the call receipt in the Navigator's logs. The broadcast message received went something like this, [This is] "Skyking, Skyking; Do not answer. Bravo, Kilo, Sierra, Juliet, Tango. Authentication – Seven, Kilo, Zulu, Alpha", "Repeat: Skyking, Skyking, Do not answer. Bravo, Kilo, Sierra, Juliet, Tango. Authentication – Seven, Kilo, Zulu, Alpha; Over and Out".

[This long range communication capability was often used in SR-71 operations to encode and pass classified messages from mission aircraft to higher headquarters, reporting critical information (like aborted missions, successful critical refueling, aircraft crashes or attacks, etc.)]

Once authenticated and decoded, this message typically would routinely indicate that "all was normal", but the capability existed of announcing that an enemy attack was underway and alerted crews already aloft to their Strategic Integrated Operations Plan (SIOP) to initiate the counter-strike wartime attack mission, or to return to base, etc.

I was flying in 1970 in the KC-135Q tanker operations one fine day out of Okinawa, Japan, in support of the SR-71 "Blackbird" mission. In the KC-135Q, the sideways-facing Navigator position was directly behind the Co-Pilot seat on the right side of the cockpit, and the Aircraft Commander (Pilot's) seat was about two feet left of the Co-Pilot. The KC-135Q aircraft were equipped with 2-VHF (line-of-sight) radios , 2-UHF (medium range) radios, a secure-voice encrypted UHF radio for talking to the SR-71, and an HF (global, very-long range) radio, plus two intercoms (one exclusively for though-the-boom communications, when the SR-71 was taking fuel, and one for communications with the other tanker crew positions). Each crew position had a small bank of toggle switches provided in an "audio mixer box" which allowed each crewmember to select which of the numerous radios and intercoms that he wanted or needed to monitor at any given time, and which ones would be blocked from his reception. The ambient inflight noise level in the cockpit of the KC-135 was sufficiently loud that all crew members typically would have both ears covered by their headsets and would use the boom-microphones on their headsets as the only effective means of inter-crew communications.

As anywhere else in life, in any group there are always one or two extreme-personality "characters". It happened that in my squadron there was a very senior Major who was an aircraft commander and who had a reputation of being "short of a few books in his library", if you know what I mean. For discretion, I will identify him as Maj. T.

We were flying as Maj. T's #2 wingman with a third tanker in formation with Maj. T's aircraft leading the three-ship tanker cell toward the coast of South Vietnam when this incident occurred, as reported later by his crew navigator. We of course only heard the final transmission, because the rest of the story occurred inside Maj. T's aircraft, on intercom.

On long over-water flights, the aircraft were typically flown on auto-pilot with the Navigator providing periodic headings for the pilot at the controls to take (even though the pilot could pass the heading control directly to the Navigator by the flip of a switch). As Maj. T was leading the formation, his Navigator was responsible for the navigation of all three aircraft in the formation and was particularly mindful to maintain good navigation position.

Maj. T's navigator had directed a heading of (let's say) 270 degrees (West) and after 20 or 30 minutes had detected that a changing wind current was pushing the formation north of the intended flight path causing a right drift from desired course. He keyed his intercom switch and said, "Pilot, this is Nav. Come left to 260 degrees", and then went back to his navigation duties. After several minutes, he looked up at his gyrocompass repeater and noticed that they were still flying on a heading of 270 degrees. He punched his intercom and said, "Pilot, this is Nav. Come left to 260 degrees. Acknowledge". He received no response, either verbal, by wave of hand or by change of heading. He tried again, and once again received no reply. So he reached over and tapped Maj. T on the shoulder and shouted the revised heading "cross-cockpit" without using the intercom. Maj. T immediately changed the auto-pilot to the new heading, so the Nav. went back to his routine.

A half hour, or so, later the Nav. triggered his intercom and said, "Pilot this is Nav. Come right 272 degrees". This time he watched his gyrocompass to see if the pilot responded. Again there was no response. About this point he was getting exasperated. He tapped Maj. T again and shouted the heading change "cross-cockpit". He then queried Maj. T if he had not heard the heading change. Maj. T replied, very nonchalantly, that he had turned his intercom switch off so he could monitor the SAC Command Post frequency for the periodic transmission. The Nav. reminded the pilot that this HQ SAC message traffic was the Navigator's responsibility to record, authenticate any messages and note the transmission in his nav-logs, for the record.

Apparently, Maj. T decided to ignore this reminder and shortly thereafter again failed to respond to his Nav's latest heading change request. This time, his Nav., being totally exasperated in noting the lack of proper crew discipline, loosened his seatbelt, raised up so he could see the Aircraft Commander's mixer box switches, and confirmed that the Intercom switch was again OFF, and only the HF switch was ON.

So he reached up, switched his transmitter selector switch to the HF and transmitted, "*Maj. T, if you don't come right to 280°, we're going to get **way the hell off course!***" Needless to say, Maj. T heard the HF transmission, as did the other aircraft in his formation, and everyone else around the globe, who were in fact monitoring that frequency – including the SAC Command Post in Omaha, Nebraska, who responded, "Calling Sky King, say again"! The look on Maj. T's speechless expression was priceless (according to the telling by his Nav later), but the point of the lesson was noted, and the lesson learned!

Case of the Super-Sonic Tanker — The KC-135A (and KC-135Q) were both original configurations using the J-57 turbojet power plants with water injection for take-off. Both had a maximum operating Mach (speed operability limit, "Vmo") of 0.86 Mach. This is a design limit established by Boeing and certified through analysis, wind tunnel testing and inflight testing, which establishes a safety margin that will avoid control and/or structural damage.

During the Vietnam War, we were occasionally tasked to support other combat missions than the SR-71. On one of these missions, I was piloting a KC-135A aircraft belonging to another squadron, while operating out of Kadena AFB in support of B-52 "Arc Light" bombing missions over south Vietnam, when I discovered that the aircraft I was flying had encountered and survived a Mach-1 over speed in a combat evasion dive. The KC-135s by this time (in 1970) were 12 to 15 years old. The cockpit control wheels originally were equipped with a plastic hub medallion, which had a Boeing logo in the center (like the horn disc on an old car steering wheel). Over the years these had often been broken, or "removed as souvenirs" and local air force base machinists had fabricated replacement caps out of turned aluminum circular blanks that snapped over the wheel bolt and was removable, without tools, by a gentle tug. Often times, when in an unfamiliar airplane, while cruising at altitude over long boring segments over water the pilot or copilot would snap his yoke cap off to look underneath to find the occasional Crew Chief's favorite nude female photo. *(Boys will be boys)*. When I popped the Pilot's cover off, there was a neatly printed placard inside identifying the aircraft tail number and stating it "had exceeded Mach 1; VN" on a specific date. I showed this to the crew, and asked the Boom Operator to check the "Form-781" Maintenance Log Book carried on board and see if it identified any details.

The "Boomer" came back to the cockpit with the logbook open

in has hands and recounted the log entry found for that date. It stated that the aircraft was operating above 20,000 feet over the Gulf of Tonkin (between Hanoi in North Vietnam and Hainan island off the coast) on a "fighter refueling anchor" awaiting any fighter arrivals that might need refueling, when he received a radio notification from a USAF Ground Control Intercept (GCI) radar site south of his position that there were "Bandits (enemy aircraft; MIGs) outbound from Hainan Island, on an intercept with his orbit position".

Taking Evasive Action

The tanker pilot, with the assistance of the GCI radar, began evasive maneuvers. When the MIGs continued to close, the tanker pilot directed the boomer to stow the boom and headed down to lower altitude in an accelerating dive heading for cloud cover and ground clutter to mask his position from the MIGs. In the ensuing dive the aircraft instruments indicated that they had reached Mach 1.03 and the corresponding buffet and abrupt sound change had substantiated the indicators (although the observed instrument readings may not have been absolute and accurate in this trans-sonic zone).

According to the maintenance record, the aircraft was thoroughly inspected after the incident even though the airplane seemed to fly normally after the incident, according to the crew. The maintenance inspection reported that both wingtips were damaged by permanent twisting at their leading edges. The wing tips were changed (as were all four engines, for precautionary reasons), according to the log book.

I personally saw these records at the time, but did not think to record the tail number, or the specific date.

SR-71– Related Flight Incidents —

SR-71 Tangles with a Thunderstorm — After refueling the SR-71 in a 3-ship tanker formation (a split offload from two tankers plus an airborne spare) we headed to U-Tapao Royal Thai Navy AB, Thailand (near Bangkok) to ground refuel the tanker formation before returning to Kadena AFB, Okinawa. On the ensuing return flight to Okinawa, we heard the encrypted "Sky King" radio transmission from our sister refueling cell, that the SR-71 had crashed shortly after his high and fast final refueling on his return flight home to Kadena.

Upon our arrival home (Okinawa) several hours later, we were ushered into a briefing room and told of the accident and sworn to ultimate secrecy on threat of 10-years in prison and a $10,000 fine -- Typical disciplinary action for leaking information involved with the Top Secret program and its missions over the combat zones of Southeast Asia. (Part of the "Official Secrets Act").

Important things to know about the SR-71, in understanding this story:

Before the SR-71 became operational (at Mach 3.2+ and altitudes above the stratosphere, up to 85,000 feet), "*common wisdom*" was that thunderstorms all topped out at a maximum of 65,000 - 70,000 feet. The SR-71 flyers discovered and verified that thunderstorms were frequently seen to top-out well above the SR-71's maximum altitude (85,000+ feet, particularly in the tropics of

Southeast Asia.

Unlike any other multi-million dollar aircraft in the Air Force, the SR-71 had no forward-looking weather, or targeting radar. His radar was side looking and down looking only.

The SR-71, despite its high speed and streamlined configuration was designed without any speed brakes or in-flight drag devices (that might be used to pitch the nose down).

The SR-71 had a very precarious stall characteristic because of the broad flat chines running down the sides of the fuselage and the very far aft center of pressure (lift) on the aft located delta wings. If the nose got too high and the airspeed dropped below stall speed, the aircraft would fall tail first, the engines would flame out due to loss of inlet air flow through the engines, and there was literally no recovery (no way to get the nose down to allow the wings to regain lift in a dive, so a potential relight of the free windmilling engines could be accomplished).

Note Broad Chines and Aft Wings

Back to the story of the thunderstorm encounter . . .

The SR-71 came off the refueling track heavy (with a full fuel load, as you might expect). As it started its climb back to "high and fast" from the tanker track at 26,000 feet and subsonic it encountered a rapidly building large thunderstorm a few miles distant and right in the middle of its flight path. In order to do its recce mission, the SR had to navigate on a precise preplanned computer-defined route, for the onboard sensors to know exactly where the aircraft was relative to the target data that it was tasked to photograph or "recon". Therefore, a large deviation around the thunderstorm cell would likely exceed the computer defined path. And the pilot felt sure that at his acceleration, he could outclimb the thundercloud.

This was the "grand-daddy" of thunderstorms and it was climbing faster then the heavy SR-71 was, and it had no plans of topping-out at around 70,000 feet. The pilot ran out of airspeed; the SR-71 stalled and started fluttering like a falling leaf, tail-first, as the engines flamed out. At this point the Pilot and his RSO (Reconnaissance Systems Officer) had no option but to take the "nylon elevator" to safety, and so they ejected after declaring their emergency to the tanker leader, from which they had just departed.

The good-news part of the story is that both crewmembers, using their rocket ejection seats, landed safely in a rice paddy by a road that led to Bangkok and U-Tapao AFB (a Thai-owned and SAC operated air base). The two crewmembers walked out of the field, in their Mercury astronaut-type full pressure suits, with their moon helmets under an arm, flagged down a "baht bus" (a three-wheel Thai motor scooter that served as a cheap taxi cab charging only one Thai baht per short ride in Thailand). The baht bus took them to the guard gate at U-Tapao, from where they were escorted to the SAC Command Post on the base.

Once there, they reportedly picked up a secure phone line and called their SR-71 Command Post at Kadena to report their accident and safe recovery, but loss of the aircraft. Then they placed another call to our joint-home base Command Post at Beale AFB, just north of Sacramento and got patched through to their wives to let them know they were OK. These phone calls all took place before we (the tanker crews) even got back to Kadena after the four-hour flight from our refueling stop at U-Tapao, and before we were threatened against any disclosures of the classified incident. So much for the "Official Secrets Act"!

SR-71 Emergency Landing and Recovery — During a routine SR-71 training flight over the northwest United States, the pilot, Col. Charlie D, experienced fluctuating oil pressure on one engine while "high and fast". He checked a pre-planned alternate landing base for a precautionary landing, and shut down the engine, but discovered that the winter weather at his preferred choice, had brought the approach weather minimums down to an unacceptable level. So he checked on a secondary alternate, which was Hill AFB, Ogden, UT. Upon contacting the Tower he was informed that their runway (13,500 ft long) was partially snow covered; the snow-cleared portion shorter than he preferred due to its 4,800 foot runway elevation, and had an undesirable cross wind. But it was all that was available.

He noted that the far end of the runway ended abruptly at ridge line and fell off several dozen feet into a gulley and highway that crossed the end of the runway, which had no arresting barrier ... this was enough to add even more pressure to the landing.

I was called at home by the Beale Command Post to gather my crew and report for an overnight mission to Hill AFB, with an accompanying tanker, to recover the SR-71 that had made a successful emergency landing at Hill AFB. Between the two tankers we would be carrying spare landing gear wheels with tires, replacement brakes, replacement landing drag chute, sufficient JP-7 for the return flight after several preliminary engine ground runs, a "Buick start cart" for ground starting the SR engines, two 50 foot lengths of 6-inch ground refueling hose, tool kits, and a dozen or so SR-71 maintenance specialists.

Our trip was uneventful to Hill AFB, but we were surprised to discover that this was not to be a simple one-night stay. The cause of the fluctuating oil pressure was undetermined and would require potentially extensive trouble-shooting and repair capability was uncertain.

Meeting with Col. Charlie D provided substantially more details about the incident. He informed me that he was a relatively "new guy" with the SR-71 operation, and that he had entered the program — unlike most SR pilots — with no supersonic time (B-58, or F-104, etc.), no test pilot time, no astronaut training, no fighter experience, nor high altitude (U-2) time. He had been a long-term B-52 pilot.

After encountering the fluctuating oil pressure, shutting down the questionable engine and diverting to Hill AFB, with all its deficiencies, he decided to make a single-engine low approach to preview the runway environment before making his final approach and landing. His first reaction was the experience of initiating the low approach go-around on one-engine. He described his surprise at how difficult the aircraft was to handle with all that weight, and all his available thrust on one side of the aircraft. He said he really struggled to keep the aircraft under control under the rarified pressure altitude of over 5.000 ft runway elevation, and cold air density, as he flew around the runway pattern. He planned his approach to land close to the cleared portion of the runway end for maximum runway length availability. His flatter approach angle would bring him in for a higher speed approach, which also helped with more rudder control. His added speed caused him to land long, and an equipment malfunction caused his drag chute to jettison after only a very brief jerk of drag on touch-down. As he approached the cliff drop-off at the end of the runway, he was still going too fast and the blowing snow on the runway was defeating his braking action. As a last ditch attempt to avoid going over the cliff, he slammed hard on the brakes on the side of the failed engine and goosed the running engine's throttle, to initiate a ground loop. The brakes locked and the airplane swapped ends avoiding a crash. But the three tires on one main landing gear blew, and the aircraft ground the wheel rims on that gear flat, almost to the axle. This detail had apparently been known prior to our departure from Beale, because we had a complete set of replacement wheels and brakes onboard.

When we arrived, the SR-71 was already inside the hanger and ready for maintenance and the two tanker crews with the SR-71 crew retired to the barracks and then to the NCO and Officer's Clubs for dinner, while the dozen maintenance crew got to work with inspections and repairs.

The replacement of wheels, brakes, tires, and drag chute were intensive but routine. But checks on the oil pressure proved baffling – was it a leak, a failed gauge, a bearing or seal failure, a pump failure, low oil content, or any one of several other possibilities? Maintenance systematically tried all of the obvious factors working through the night, with nothing conclusive being found. The next day they ran a series of system static pressurization checks; none indicating the problem source. So next was the necessary test of running the engine up to high power. This required towing the aircraft outside and for the tanker to ground-transfer the necessary JP-7 fuel to the SR-71. This involved positioning the tanker nose-to-nose with the SR-71, but aligned at a 90° direction to the SR-71, and connecting the 100 feet of refueling hose between the two aircraft. We had to start two of the tanker engines with a ground pneumatic (high pressure air) cart, and then run up the two tanker engines to relatively high power to get enough hydraulic pressure to run the tanker's aerial refueling pumps, to transfer fuel to the SR.

Then using the 1,000-pound Buick Start Cart we brought with us, with its two tandem linked Buick 430 cu. in. engines, they started the offending SR-71 engine, with the cowling open and a direct reading pressure gauge attached. In order to open the SR cowling, there is a hinge line on the inboard top of the cowling and an opposite row of special heat-treated fasteners, on the bottom of the cowling. When these fasteners are removed. The entire top half of the cowling, including the outboard portion of the wing, rotates over the top hinge as a complete assembly (resembling the folding of the wings on a Navy aircraft carrier plane). Once returned to normal, new fasteners are required and they must be torqued and then re-heat-treated in place with a special electric–induction heating tool, before supersonic flight can safely be flown. This special tool is not sufficiently portable with its power source to be carried on a recovery tanker, so it must be done after returning to a home base. This meant that the SR would have to fly home at altitudes limited to around 30,000 feet and at subsonic airspeeds, similar to the tanker.

A characteristic of all SR-71 aircraft is that while on the ground, the SR leaks fuel due to the nature of airframe heat expansion at supersonic speeds, and an inability of the designers to find a suitable "caulk-type" sealant that can handle the extremes of temperature and remain pliable through-out the extreme skin temperature regime of the flight. The aircraft grows as much as 9-inches in length at supersonic speeds, due to structural thermal expansion, and can lose as much as several hundred gallons of fuel when parked overnight. The fuel is captured in huge flat "cookie-sheets", when hangared. Base Fire Chiefs, unfamiliar with the properties of the unique JP-7 fuel, can become quite nervous when they see this much fuel under the aircraft. But are difficult to persuade that the fuel spill did not constitute a severe fire hazard.

About 50 gallons of JP-7 was spilled during ground transfer and was captured in a concrete basin adjacent to the ramp. Even after explaining the fuel properties, the Fire Chief was concerned and unbelieving that the fuel could not be ignited without the addition of liquid rocket oxidizer fuel. He became a believer when he threw a lighted rail-road flare into the puddle of spilled JP-7 in the concrete catch basin, and the flare was extinguished by the fuel!

The maintenance team, after three full days of trouble shooting and repairs, finally determined that the oil pressure issue was a false alarm caused by a faulty sensor and not actually low pressure. We finally were able to top-off the SR-71, and launch him for the "Low and Slow" return, and followed him home after a successful launch. After three days of TDY, we all returned home and were ready for a good night's sleep.

As a foot note, during my time flying tanker support for the SR-71 from 1968 to 1972, fully one third of the SR-71 fleet of 33 aircraft were lost – never with any related deaths, and never from combat. All losses were caused by the extreme nature of the airplanes speed and performance parameters combined with weather or maintenance related failures.

Wing Chief of Safety Assignment — Nearing the end of my 5-year duty at Beale, I was selected by our new Wing Commander, Col. Y, to become his new wing Chief of Safety, after the previous two Safety Chiefs had received consecutive unsatisfactory ratings in Safety Management during HHQ no-notice inspections. After selection for this responsibility, I was immediately sent to Carswell AFB, Ft. Worth, TX for a two week SAC Safety Management Course. The Wing CO, with my agreement, planned that I would return for three months of local assimilation under the current Wing Safety Officer who was retiring at the end of that period. However, upon returning from the training class at the end of the two week course I discovered that just before my return, the Wing had received a third no-notice SAC Safety Office Inspection and again been rated unsatisfactory! Col. Y immediately informed me that he and I, after lunch, were headed to brief the 14th Air Division (SAC) Commander, B/Gen H, (the same General, who had flown with me on my "Mission from Hell', above), and define to him "what I was going to do to rectify this deficiency" (for which I had not even seen a copy of the report, much less, the inside of the Safety Office!). I soon discovered that when you are challenged to recoup from three-in-a-row "UNSAT" ratings, you are in a virtually "can't lose" situation, because there is no way to go but UP; I had three prior individuals, before me, who were unable to succeed, and I would have everybody's support to make it happen – no excuses accepted. But I feared that my less-than-satisfactory personal experience with Gen H from my "Mission from Hell" trip to Kadena less than 6-months previously, would leave me severely handicapped in his confidence in me for this important assignment.

Fortunately, I had learned much about SAC Safety Management at the Carswell course. And I was fortunate that the Wing did NOT have a poor safety record! The problem was that the involved paper work responsibility was so complex, involving Safety Management for three flying squadrons (two tanker and one B52 squadrons) plus all of the base maintenance units from munitions, nuclear weapons, missiles, armament, ground safety, infrastructure facilities safety and all or their various Safety Categories, etc. (a dozen in all). The course taught me the SAC Safety Regulations, which supplemented USAF Safety Regulations and then a system of how to organize by each squadron and unit, with files using 3-ring binders and safety category tabs unique to each, to resolve the documentation problems.

The failure on each of the prior inspections had been created during an inspection by the following similar scenario: The HHQ Inspector would say something like this, "In accordance with Sac Safety Reg. "SAC- XXX", page and chapter, the Safety Office is required to accomplish very specific actions at certain intervals, for each unit and Wing or Base safety activity. Have you met this Requirement?" When the response had been, typically "Yes"; the next question was, "Show me the documentation for such and so squadron or subject", and then another, and another. In most cases the Safety Chief believed he had accomplished the required items, but due to the massive different categories in each of two dozen and more squadrons and categories, combined with a less-than-adequate administrative staff, the documentation was often inadequately completed, and that which had been completed could not be located quickly for review, or was less detailed than fully required. Based upon the systems I had been taught in the SAC Safety Course, and with the help of a newly added senior administrative NCO specialist, I was able to pull all these things together during the next 90-days. The next follow-up inspection at the end of that period resulted in an "Outstanding - Best in 15th AF" rating, and a virtual "gold star" on the Wing Commander's score card, and I was the "Hero of the Year" as far as the Wing Commander, and the Division Commander, were concerned.

A couple of examples of how the Commander's priority focus changed the environment:

On the very first daily morning meeting of the Commander's Battle Staff, he introduced me to his staff and informed all of his staff where he placed Safety in his priorities. These staffers were mostly full Colonels, and I a mere Major. He stated that when I spoke to any of the Staff regarding matters of Safety, that they should understand that I was speaking for *Him*, and that they should either comply with my directions, or come to him, for resolution. I was thus verbally given seniority over any of these staffers and sub commanders.

In another example of this new level of authority. Col Y. requested that I be a participant and advisor at all of his daily and special battle staff meetings. In one meeting, as the various staff officers were making their presentations and reports, I followed a young Captain's report on Wing Cost Savings, who spent several minutes reporting his initiatives to reduce electrical power usage in the Wing's office facilities by removing one of every two fluorescent tubes in all of the Wing's buildings corridors and other non-critical working spaces with a tally of several hundreds of dollars saved per year throughout the base.

I had a much more costly and serious safety matter to brief, as followed the previous report. The day prior, a B-52 routine training mission had been compromised by an oil pressure loss on one of its eight engines shortly after take-off. As was typical, the Flight Manual called for the engine to be shut down and the aircraft landed "as soon as practical" after reducing fuel weight to within the maximum safe landing weight. The aircrew involved a flight Instructor flying with a fully qualified crew, but offered a second level of advice to assist the crew, if needed. According to normal crew protocols, the crew contacted the Command Post, and advised their intent to abort their mission (delete the scheduled aerial refueling, shorten the intended navigation leg to just enough to burn down to maximum landing weight, eliminate the planned low altitude missile simulated bomb runs, and land after about 4 hours of flight. The Assistant DCO (Deputy Commander of Operations; a senior Lt. Col.) was on duty at the time and was contacted by the Command Post Controller for notification of the "emergency". This individual was a "gung-ho SAC officer more interested in filling all the training squares than using common sense and safety considerations. Despite the onboard Instructor Pilot's pushback, the ADCO ordered him and the crew to continue to fly the preplanned 10-hour mission including the low-altitude cruise missile bomb practice, and the aerial refueling, and disregarding the flight manual recommendation to land as soon as practical. Even though reminded by the Instructor Pilot that flying high speed low altitude bomb runs would over-temp the shutdown and oil depleted engine from the high RPM windmilling and could cause further engine damage, potential destruction of the engine and potential related airframe damage. The ADCO "pulled rank" on the Instructor and ordered him to fly a mission over five hours longer than the original safer plan. Which the Instructor complied with and then filed an Operations Hazard Report with my office that would find its way to the Wing Commander and on up the chain of Command to SAC HQ. This ADCO had a habit of making and enforcing this type of situations on tanker operations as well as bomber and other operations, so I chose to take issue with this at the Battle Staff Meeting, as an extreme example of very poor decision making and order of priorities.

I opened my comments by offering praise for the Cost Savings effort of the previous officer, but contrasting his efforts with the poor judgment and priorities that ultimately cost the Wing over $100,000 in engine replacement/overhaul cost and unnecessarily opened the potential for a much more significant accident or loss of life. As I made my comments, the ADCO became flushed and was flexing his jaw muscles and fists, and I am sure that he would have struck at me, if we weren't in the meeting. Col Y, looked at him sternly, and stated that if he ever did such a foolish directive again, he would be fired and removed from the Wing immediately (and any potential for future advancement in the Air Force.) [Please recall the similarity of this incident with "***An Opportune Training Lesson***", page 181, above.]

When It Rains, It Pours — My Guardian Angel is still working full time on my behalf!

Simultaneously, (but purely by coincidence) with my elevation into the Wing Safety Office, I received almost immediate notification that I had been selected by Military Personnel Center, MPC, for a prized assignment, in 6-months, to AFIT (Air Force Institute of Technology) for a 2-year Masters Degree in their Industrial Engineering program. And then a day or two later another notification was received that I had been nominated by HQ USAF for a SPECAT (Special Category) NATO Pilot Exchange Program to the Canadian Armed Forces. This assignment was to fly their newly acquired Boeing 707-300 series aircraft (some of which had been converted with dual wingtip-mounted Beech hose-and-drogue aerial refueling stores – developed and in use by the US Navy, as a centerline mounted "Buddy Store" –) and the assignment required a KC-135 experienced and high-time Instructor Pilot to train and develop the Canadian Forces aerial refueling tanker and receiver aircraft capability.

The Canadian assignment was considered an "overseas assignment", which was a family-accompanied two-year assignment with additional extension potential. Furthermore, I was deemed the highest qualified of the four candidates selected for consideration. If I accepted, all I would need was a personal letter of recommendation from a General officer in my chain of command. (That would be B/Gen H, 14th Air Division (SAC), whom I had successfully impressed by the Safety Office Inspection results, and who was also the officer that I had displeased, as described in my "**Mission from Hell**" anecdote.

Result... I declined the AFIT assignment without prejudice, (which I really did not want, since it had a following assignment to a non-aircraft related position as Deputy Base Commander, i.e. Chief of a Base physical plant's facilities, and would not lead to follow-on assignment (in this cycle) to either aircraft flight test, or aircraft maintenance pathways, which would better utilize my aeronautical engineering degree, and my prior military experiences. (Taking this option would allowed me to reapply for the AFIT assignment, if desired, after completing the Canadian assignment, but with no guarantee of acceptance). I drafted my letter of recommendation of appointment for B/Gen H, who signed it with only minor personalized editorial comment. Leaving the Safety Office in outstanding condition, I was off to Canada with my family six months later, in the summer of 1976 to a pilot's dream assignment, and one for which I had been recognized as uniquely qualified to fill.

CHAPTER 6
NATO Exchange Pilot — Canada

Canadian Military B-707 Tanker (1973 - '76) — My assignment as a NATO Exchange Pilot attached to the 437 "Husky" Transport Squadron, of the Canadian Armed Forces (CAF), began upon my arrival in July 1973, to (Canadian Forces Base) CFB Trenton, Ontario. The Base was the headquarters of the Air Transport Command *[later, in 1975 to be redesignated to Air Transport Group]* containing two CC-130 Hercules squadrons and one CC-137 (Boeing 707) squadron, and several medium-sized, 3-engined executive FalconJet command transport aircraft, in residence.

Ontario Province Geography — The city of Trenton, is located on the southern edge of the Trans-Canadian Highway 401, approximately 75 air-miles directly north across Lake Ontario from Rochester, NY; it is 100 air-miles east-north-east of Toronto (largest city in Canada and capitol of Ontario Province); and is 140 air-miles south west of Ottawa (the National Capitol and home of the Canadian National Defence HQ). The geographical crescent these three cities formed was nicknamed by the "locals" as the "Canadian Banana Belt", due to its shape and the relatively mild winters "as compared to the rest of Canada, and the US immediately south of Lake Ontario".

Though Canada has approximately the same total land area as all of the total 50 states + DC, at that time it had only 11% of the population of the U.S.; 90% of its population lived within 200 miles of the U.S. northern border. Proportionately, the entire Armed Forces of Canada (Army, Navy, & Airforce, combined) was only about 20% of the size of the USAF alone (in 1975)!

On one early mission in my assignment there, we landed at Goose Bay AFB, Labrador, and the Canadian crew on board with me were astonished, proclaiming, "Goodness, (at Goose Bay AFB alone) they have 10 times as many Boeings – i.e. tankers -- (about 20 USAF KC-135s) sitting idle in the parking area, as our entire Canadian Boeing fleet" (five 707s, only two of which were tanker modified)!

Exchange Officer Housing in Canada — Because we were not Canadian citizens, we were not allowed to purchase residential property in Canada. By pre-made arrangements, upon arrival we obtained the rental residence vacated by my USAF predecessor. It was a very nice, but dated, custom-built three-bedroom ranch with a full finished basement located in the Trenton development of Carrying Place, consisting of about two-dozen homes, or so, on a finger-bay (Bay of Quinte -- pronounced "Kwin-tee") at the western end of the finger. The eastern end of the bay, 28 miles to the east, formed the delta onto Lake Ontario. The town of Trenton, and CFB Trenton were side by side and about 5-miles from the western tip on the north side of the bay where we would be living. The navigable Trent-Severin Waterway (A.K.A. the Trent River) passed from the bay through Trenton and meandered northwest about 240 land-miles through 44 locks, to Lake Huron's Port Severin (which is only about 90 air-miles, direct "as the crow flies"). The Trent-Severin then continued on north to the St. Laurence Seaway. Lake Ontario lay parallel to the Bay of Quinte. Our new residence had a 200-foot long by 35-foot wide boat slip dredged into the back yard with an 8' by 12' floating dock, similar to those of the residence-lots on either side of us. Having previously scouted the environment before leaving California, we came prepared by bringing a new 200 HP Mercruiser V-8 powered Cobalt, fiberglass tri-hulled ski-boat, which we had purchased new on an end-of-summer sale in Chicago, enroute from California to Ontario.

Our new 1973 18-foot Cobalt Inboard Ski-boat in backyard slip.

Arriving in late summer with 2-kids (and 2-cars) plus our new boat, Pat and I were planning for a wonderful 2 to 3 year tour in Canada on the bay.

Joys of Life on the Bay Waters of Lake Ontario — My first "significant Canadian experience", as a resident on the Bay of Quinte, occurred while getting settled into our new residence. I was anxious to get my new boat into the water and docked in our slip. However, our predecessor had no boat, so the slip had become over-grown with seaweed during his two-year assignment. The Canadian retired major and pilot living next door informed me that it was a very simple job to clear the slip, using a small 15 HP outboard row boat and a steel bedrail tied from its ends to form a Y-yoke with 25 feet of ski-rope. The technique used was to drop the bedrail over the stern of the small boat at the mouth of the slip, and then slowly drag it in toward the beach-end, then detach the boat and drag the cross-wise bed rail to shore by hand. The load of seaweed in one pass could weigh several hundred pounds, but as it was slowly pulled up the ramp slope at the beach- end, the load would quickly lighten as the water drained out of the seaweed. He kindly offered me the use of his boat and rig, described above, and said I could quickly do the job, single-handedly.

I was struggling with the first pass, and as I was manually hauling about 2-cubic yards of seaweed up the slope, I heard some female giggling behind my back. As I turned around to see who was laughing, I came face-to-face about 20-feet away from three approaching, bikini-clad young ladies (sisters, aged 18 to 22) who turned out to be daughters of my new Canadian expatriate neighbors, who had just returned from 5-years living in southern California, and were now residing two doors south of our rental home in Carrying Place.

The girls had observed my new 18-foot ski-boat on the front driveway and wanted to make our family's acquaintance as "boating-buddies", and offered to help me quickly clear the slip. With the extra hands, the four of us had the slip dragged clean of about 15 cubic yards of seaweed in little more than 2-hours time. Then I quickly hooked up my car to the boat trailer and we drove my rig over to the Trenton municipal boat ramp about 5-miles away, and launched the boat into the water. I had never driven this boat before, so I was learning as I went. (The Cobalt was only slightly larger, but at over 3,000 pounds, over 3-times heavier than the outboard ski-boat I had owned in Chicago and California for eight years earlier).

We all hopped into the bow cockpit, after the launching and I cruised out for a ride around the western end of the bay. As I opened the boat up to full throttle, it accelerated to slightly over 30 mph with the bow in the air and the hull planning on the aft 3 feet at the stern. I saw a large 30-foot cruiser motoring across the bay in the dredged deep channel ahead and decided to head toward it and then turned to cross about 25 feet behind the cruiser, in order to hop the cruiser's wake. I had often done this on water skis behind the wake of smaller boats with my previous 17-foot ski-boat. As we approached the cruiser's wake, I failed to consider the 5-foot height of its wake with the 3-foot trough at its center, and as we crossed the wake at full speed. My near- 4,000 pound Cobalt became completely airborne, with engine screaming as the prop came clear of the water. I had instantaneous visions of crashing and losing control upon impact – potentially destroying my new boat and possibly injuring myself and three Canadian guests, or even killing someone! But I was pleasantly surprised and relieved when the very stable tri-hull design came down very softly with a well-cushioned impact on the opposite leg of the cruiser's V-wake, and no variation of heading! With my heart in my mouth I glanced to see the three girls in the bow cockpit ahead of me with their mouths agape, eyes as big as saucers, laughing crazily and yelling at me over the engine roar, "Do it again"! With apologies, I said, "Never again", and regretted my foolhardy stunt! But later, they and my family did spend many pleasant boating opportunities with water skiing and cruising over the summers of my tour.

On a later occasion, we did validate the rock-solid construction of the Cobalt's hull. With the three neighbor ladies in the bow cockpit, and Pat and our two youngsters in the main cockpit with me, we were cruising near full speed northbound from the Bay up the Trent River, riding the narrow buoy-marked channel. I was scanning the river bank looking for a marina to pull into and buy some gas and refreshments. With the bow high in the air, and the neighbor girls in front of my windshield, I failed to see one of the 800-pound (estimated) steel channel buoys until just before impact. Each buoy had a flotation chamber that was about the size of a 55-gallon drum in size with a larger diameter steel flotation collar, which floated almost fully submerged. Above the flotation chamber was an orange painted, cone-topped steel pipe about 6-inches in diameter that protruded about 3 or 4-feet above the water. I quickly swerved to avoid the collision and went just left of centerline over the top of the buoy as I chopped the throttle. The buoy was forced to submerge upon impact a mere couple inches left of the center-keel of my Cobalt and about three feet aft of the bow. The submerged buoy made a couple thumps along the keel and emerged from the right side of the transom completely missing the out-drive and propeller, thank goodness! The only damage done – other than to my ego – was a golf ball-size chip in the gel coat on the left side of the bow-keel at the point of first contact, and a small blemish on the right side of the hull at the transom. Had it been a lesser boat (like my prior 17 ft, Fiberglas ski-boat, for example) the buoy would have likely penetrated the hull like a torpedo! (***This speed boating thing could become more dangerous than flying!*** *Mainly because it was a lot less disciplined, on the operator's part).*

437 ("Husky") Transport Squadron Aircraft —

The 437 Transport Squadron, to which I was assigned consisted of five newly acquired stretched Boeing 707-300 series (ultimately designated "707-347C") built to airline specifications. The five 707-347C aircraft were "convertible" passenger/cargo capable aircraft with a large forward left-side cargo door, reinforced flooring with imbedded pallet-roller tracks and folding overhead bins, as-well-as track mounted seat rails for quick conversion. These aircraft were ordered and deposits paid to Boeing by Western Airlines in 1970 for an expected added route sector, which became unneeded after an economic downturn. Western Air Lines forfeited their deposits and Boeing then offered the five new 1972 production aircraft to the Canadian Government applying the forfeited order deposits as a discount, for a quick sale.

(The Canadians referred to these aircraft as the "*Boeings*", in their small Air Force). These B-707 aircraft had replaced an aging fleet of 12-Canadair CL-44 swing-tail 4-engine turboprop transports.

Canadair CL-44, RCAF Predecessor to the Boeing-707

These new 707 aircraft could readily be converted from full 177-passenger, to full cargo configuration in less than three hours, or to 50-50 special mixed configuration missions, or with 76 all –1st class passenger 2-by-2 seating and an added third galley or bar in the middle for major VIP Embassy missions— or any special configuration in between.

The last two delivered of five were modified with even additional convertibility of added fuel system plumbing, valving, pumps, wing-tip plumbing, and mounting points for quick-install & removal of Beech Refueling Pods with hose and drogue refueling capability (originally designed for the US Navy as a fuselage-centerline "buddy refueling" store for carrier aircraft operations). Other tanker modifications included, special internal intercoms, added fuel transfer counters and electric control for the refueling pods at the Flight Engineer's cockpit station, and added radio communications with air-to-air TACAN (bearing and range indicating avionics).

Retracted Beech Refueling Store with Ram Air Turbine Pump seen on the Nose (looking much-like 25' torpedoes)

Boeing 707 Transition Training (30 days) – My new CAF Squadron Commander, Lt. Col. Max H, proposed that, since I had arrived with so much "Boeing" pilot and Instructor time (nearly 2,000 KC-135Q logged Pilot time, including over 500 Instructor Pilot hours), that there would be no requirement for me to go through their B-707-347C Transition program. I countered that the two aircraft types – though appearing very similar -- were substantially different in weight, engine performance, and systems configuration, as were the crew manning and aircrew operating procedures, and I suggested that my efficiency and skills would be far greater, and more quickly standardized with theirs, if I took the CAF formal transition course. He favorably agreed to that suggestion, and I entered the 30-day Boeing 707 transition-training program, taught locally at CFB Trenton, in August '73. After the transition, and "flying the line" for a couple of months of scheduled commercial airline-style passenger and cargo operations, I found myself getting very bored with the routine and grew anxious to get involved with the fledgling aerial refueling operations (which upon my arrival were only accomplished briefly once every six months.

Boeing 707-347C (also known as CC-137, in USAF Parlance)

Unlike the "integrated crew" concept of SAC, where each crew generally always flew together with the same crew-members, the Canadian concept closely paralleled that of the USAF's Military Air- lift Command (MAC) and commercial airlines, where crew composition was randomly composed on each flight from a pool of qualified members from each specialty (pilots, copilots, navigators, flight engineers, etc.). Each concept has its advantages and its disadvantages.

I had to get accustomed to this difference in procedures. For example. in KC-135 operations, the entire 4-man crew preflighted the exterior and interior of the aircraft before each flight. Also military aerial refueling missions are highly complex and unique with advanced Air Traffic Control coordination for the multiple aircraft formations, and time- constrained mission requirements, yet highly variable parameters of weather, varying fuel transfer considerations, failed fueling contingencies, etc. This meant that we did detailed flight planning for a couple, to several hours the day before each mission, and then went through Base Operations the day of the flight for a mission briefing, weather briefing, and filing of flight clearances. In SAC operations the crew were transported to the aircraft to arrive 2-hours prior to take-off to conduct all of the inspections and checklists outside the aircraft and inside the cockpit, assisted by ground maintenance crews.

With the Canadian equipment and operations being more repetitive and routine (excluding aerial refueling missions), and their use of a Flight Engineer on the crew, the routine missions were pretty well "canned", using standardized recurring flight plans which nominally fully used Air traffic Control electronic airways. Interval times and routes were typically very consistent, day-to-day. The Flight Engineer (with the help of a ground crew chief) performed most of the exterior and interior cockpit preflight inspections and checklists, leaving the cockpit switches and configurations set to the Start Engine Checklist. This meant that the rest of the flight crew (pilots, and navigator crewmembers), typically didn't arrive at the aircraft, until after the cabin crew and passengers were loaded, and about 15-minutes prior to the scheduled or designated take-off time.

Upon arrival to the aircraft, the pilot and navigator crewmembers, would stash their jackets or uniform blouses and caps on the coat rack in the cockpit, sit and buckle-up their seat belts & shoulder harnesses, and pick up a one-page checklist card and verbally cross-check and respond that each item had been completed, equipment turned-on, switches properly preset, everything functioning, and fuel tanks serviced. The Flight Engineer, by this time had completed the Take-Off Data Card computations from the flight performance charts using the fuel tank readings, and routine mission profiles items noted, for the pilot's use. As a result of this segregation of duties, I found the CAF pilots often did not did have as in-depth systems knowledge with the many aircraft systems and calibration procedures, as were crews in SAC operations and training (having had only initial ground transition training in their operations). And they often did not have the depth of knowledge of the underlying details that create confidence and can become extremely useful in analyzing the impacts of unexpected changes, failures of equipment and changing weather or mission requirements.

The typical scheduled passenger mission (excluding aerial refueling), consisted of the aircraft being configured for 177 passengers, in an all 2nd class seating arrangement with 3-airline seats on either side of a narrow center aisle. The passenger seating had typical oversize overhead bins for ample storage of carry-on luggage. Opposite the front airline entry door, on the left-side and aft of the cockpit bulkhead; and on the right side (looking forward) there were two forward lavatories facing the aisle, aft of which was a large galley on the right capable of preparing hot meals and storage for cold beverages. On the forward left side, behind the boarding doorway there was a typical small airline closet next to the lavatory, immediately aft of which was a "crew rest" area consisting of a triplet of seats facing aft, then a five foot wide crew table, then a triplet of seats facing forward – this area obviously accommodated 6-crew seats; plus there were four-fold-down single seats on the passageway walls two each adjacent to the front and aft passenger entry doors on the left side of the fuselage, typical of most commercial airliners. Counting the jump seat in the cockpit just aft and between the two pilot's seats, this accounted for 11-total crew seats in addition to the four used by the primary cockpit crew (2-pilots, navigator, and flight engineer). We almost never carried more crew than a total of 12 of the 15 "crew-seats" available. There also were two more lavatories in the tail plus a second large galley opposite the left aft passenger entry door.

Impressions of Flying the B-707—

A Larger, More Powerful Aircraft than the KC-135 —

The commercial B-707-347C aircraft (of the Canadian fleet) were manufactured in 1972, and had 17 years of technological improvements from the earliest versions of the B-720, which was the equivalent of the KC-135 airframe in geometry, systems and engines.

The 707-347C airplane had 11% more Max. Take-off Weight (333,600 pounds, vs. 301,600 pounds for the KC-135A/Q); had 39% more take-off thrust (19,000 lbs per engine times four vs. 13,700 lbs per eng. with water injection, times four); had faster acceleration due to the low-bypass <u>fan engines</u> vs. no fans; had 30% less runway length required for comparable take-off gross weight (due to more power and greater acceleration and wing area); had 15% greater wing area due to 11% greater wing span (146 feet vs. 131), and added size of inner wing chord area; and had significantly higher engine reliability due to newer engine technologies. *[The enhanced 707-300 wing was lengthened by adding 2- new wing-root plugs that added 7.5' spanwise length on each side to make the 15' longer wingspan, and also had an elongated fuselage chord, which added an increased total area.]*

This wing also incorporated hydraulic full span leading edge flaps and larger trailing edge flaps for greater lift at slow speeds (i.e. take-offs and landings). This enlarged and enhanced design carried a max. fuel tank capacity of approximately 155,000 lbs of fuel (but all the fuel was carried in the wings, none in the cargo hold areas, or above the floor line, as in the KC-135) *[total KC-135 maximum fuel weight capacity was 50,000 pounds more (but over the years as its empty operating weight grew from the original 98,500 pounds to over 105,000 pounds, this reduced the available max. fuel available overall for full take-off weight by the 7,500 pounds empty weight growth). The B-707 fuel efficiency and improved take-off performance more than offset the amount of fuel available for A/R transfer].* This increased power and lift (and improved quietness) made the 707's flying seem more like a sports car than a pick-up truck.

The CAF 707 configurations were built with enhanced structure in the floor and had quick convertibility using built-in flush seat-tracks and large cargo side door allowing either full passenger configuration or full cargo configuration, and any configuration mixes between the two, which could be customized for mission specifics.

The two aircraft versions (newer 707-347C and lesser-powered, older KC-135) had familiar handling characteristics, but the KC-135A and Q versions had much lesser overall performance in take-off, range and climb. The 707 systems were more automated and the take-off and operational ***reliabilities*** were far greater in the 707, and the degree of soundproofing, the more highly advanced heating and air-conditioning provided a second or third generation of improvement.

Astonishing 707 High Performance Take-off — Shortly after completing my Canadian 707 transition training at CFB Trenton, Ontario, a truly astonishing experience happened to me, which exemplified the performance difference. Being used to flying the KC-135 tanker with its original non-fan, straight turbojet engines, with water-injection for take-off (rated at 13,700 pounds max thrust, each at sea level), I was really enjoying the Canadian 707 with its up-rated low-bypass fan-jet engines that provided 19,700 pounds thrust each (a 66% increase, overall), for an aircraft that was only 15% heavier at maximum weight.

It was my first take-off in winter conditions, on the short 30-minute flight, returning to CFB Trenton from Ottawa after-dusk, after an all day flight with multiple passenger stops enroute from Vancouver. The outside air temperature was – a frigid -10°F and we had only about 30 passengers (less than 20% of a full capacity) on board with a light fuel load, so the airplane take-off weight was probably only about 200,000 pounds (compared to its maximum take-off weight of 333,600 pounds).

Before take-off, I preset my altitude-warning indicator for a 10,000 foot level-off for the short flight, and upon Tower clearance advanced the throttles to take-off power. The airplane took off in the cold dense air almost as if was being launched from an aircraft carrier's catapult. Due to the standard Air Traffic Control rules, maximum airspeed was constrained to a maximum of 250 knots (approx. 290 mph) until reaching 10,000 feet. Once airborne I pulled the nose up to keep my airspeed at 250 knots, compared to what I was used to from the underpowered KC-135; things were really happening fast. Concentrating on the visual activity beyond the windshield during my after-dusk initial take-off and climb, I suddenly caught a glimpse of my altimeter during my instrument cross-check and realized I was already almost at 9,000' planning to level at 10,000', and my vertical climb speed indicator was pegged at its instrument limit of 6,000 feet per minute!

I hauled all the throttles to idle as the altitude alert sounded. I reported on crew intercom, "Passing 9,000 feet for 10,000," as I pushed the nose over to stop the climb rate. In after-sight, I calculated a few minutes later that I had had only six seconds to level off without shooting right through my altitude. The weight in the seat of my pants went to almost zero, as we all caught our breath. The Navigator asked me if I knew how fast we were climbing. (Obviously not; I never expected this kind of performance!) Based upon his stopwatch time from brake-release to 10,000 feet, with allowance for time to accelerate from start of roll to lift-off, he informed me that we were climbing an average of slightly over 10,000 feet per minute. (That's faster than many fighter aircraft with after-burners can climb from take-off to 10,000 feet!)

This push-over created an almost zero-G lightness (maybe only 0.25Gs). There were a lot of light-seated passengers and cabin crew in the back of the airplane. Thank goodness they all were still buckled in by their seat belts, and yet we still went to about 10,600 feet before leveling off and easing back down to 10,000'. This definitely is not the way to keep passengers comfortable, especially military wives and children, *or VIPs*!

That was my first true appreciation of the power of these modern fan-jets on this princess of an aircraft – especially compared to its seventeen year-older KC-135 "cousins".

The Canarsie, NY "High Performance Approach" — We may not have had the thrills of aerobatics and afterburners, but in my KC-135Q operations with the SR-71, and many hours flying the Canadian 707, we did do some pretty amazing heavy-jet flying … near wing-tips-overlapped formation maneuvering, and fascinating skills during irregular take-offs and landings. We, the "transport weenies" and "trash haulers" did some very amazing things in our "heavy metal" machines.

Though it didn't involve "combat" or an "emergency", I had

one occasion while flying VIP passengers with the Canadians in the 707-347C that reflected my advanced experience and training in the KC-135. We had a planeload of about 100–Canadian Air War College trainee officers (mostly Lt. Colonels and full Colonels) and their ladies, and were flying from Ottawa, Canada to New York's Kennedy International Airport for a class tour enroute to Washington DC. I was the mission Aircraft Commander and was in the left seat. We were cleared upon arrival for a "Canarsie (NY) approach" to JFK Airport, which used a "non-precision" ADF (airborne direction finding) approach beacon (meaning, with-out positive control radar, or electronic direction and distance info). It was unique, and similar to the "Checkerboard" approach in Hong Kong where the aircraft had to home in on the approach beacon at an inbound heading that was close to 90 degrees off from the runway's heading.

[The approach beacon is usually located on the extended runway centerline about two miles before the touchdown point. The Canarsie Approach beacon was about 3.5 miles out and 4.5 miles south west of the extended runway 13 Right. The Canarsie approach chart called for the aircraft to approach the beacon on a track of 043° (flying north east at roughly 90° to the runway intercept and crossing Canarsie at 1300 feet, continuing on the same heading for another 2.6 miles then turning right to intercept the extended runway centerline while in the turn – touchdown was about one mile from the rollout at 13 feet above sea-level. See Approach Chart graphic on next page, below.]

When passing this approach beacon, the approach required a fairly brisk 90° right turn at a distance of less than two miles to the runway. The published approach altitude established a crossing of the beacon at 1,500 feet and then using a standard 3-degree glide slope inbound to touch down. Unfortunately, on this particular arrival, Approach Control had restricted us to holding at 5000 feet at an above-normal approach speed until crossing the beacon (for some undefined reason unknown to me).

I did something (from my SAC experience) that no Canadian military pilots (nor most commercial-trained pilots) had ever before witnessed in a 707-class heavy-jet transport aircraft. We were in visual daylight conditions and as I approached the beacon passage, I called for gear-down and half flaps (higher drag) and reduced power, and began to slow the aircraft, as I proceeded the 2.6 miles to the turn point beyond Canarsie beacon. The turn came about a minute and a half past Canarsie and I racked the airplane to 30° right bank around to align with the runway, and I was cleared out of 5000 feet (and cleared to land) once crossing the beacon. I reduced to almost flight idle, called for full-flaps down, and started a 3,000 fpm (foot-per-minute) descent rate (a very high rate for so close to the ground for a heavy aircraft). At about 1,500 feet I started easing in the throttles, as I reduced my sink rate to approximately 500 fpm (knowing that it often takes nearly 30 seconds to spool up engines from flight-idle to normal thrust). I descended onto the glide slope from above, to compensate for the high crossing of the approach beacon, and crossed the end of the runway at about 140 knots (20 knots faster than normal), but rolled it on with a real "squeaker". Immediate use of full thrust reverse after touchdown on the main gear, while the nose was still in the air, brought the aircraft smoothly down to a taxi speed with only about half the 12,000 foot runway used.

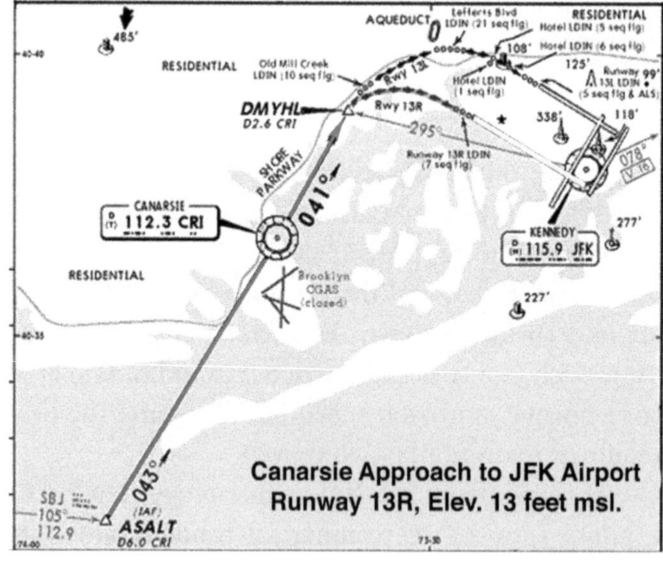

Canarsie Approach to JFK Airport
Runway 13R, Elev. 13 feet msl.

It was certainly a rapid elevator ride for the passengers, but my experience from the KC-135, never failed to impress my Canadian counterparts with what a fully experienced pilot can do in the heavy commercial 707. I am sure that Boeing Commercial instructors would not approve, either. For them, it was all about "passenger comfort", not maximum performance, no matter how well executed.

Being only "airline trained", my Canadian crew had been taught that you dare not get into a high descent rate close to the ground (a good rule) and that the engines wouldn't spool up quickly from flight idle to produce good thrust and sink control (also a good safety consideration), and feared that the approach I was given with the altitude restriction over the beacon could not be safely made. Also, although both the KC-135 and B-707 were similarly designed and had similar true performance, Boeing had never flight-test certified the B-707 to the extended performance limits that the military had in the -135s. and like in my early KC-135 operations and experience, I had only been taught a limited version of the aircraft performance envelope and was fearful of exceeding "normal limits" (and passenger comfort was seldom a consideration in SAC operations, because we seldom flew any passengers). But my enhanced SAC Instructor training had provided the extra experience to know the true limits and stay within them.

The 100-plus passengers in the back of the aircraft gave me a round of applause after we touched down and were duly impressed — as were the rest of the crew. Even the tower commented on the approach and thought we might have to make a go-around due to Approach Control's high initiation restriction above the normal published altitudes. My SAC experience in flying support with the SR-71, my in-theater combat tactics experience in the EC-47, and my SAC IP Course training at Castle AFB (where we learned to fly the limits of the envelope) had all contributed well beyond what typical routine crew capabilities would be and I received many positive "gee whiz" comments from that flight. It also gave me memories of my earliest Tower Control challenges in the TC-47 where the Tower almost had me overrun by a Boeing 707 on an O'Hare Approach!

I overheard some of the Canadian Colonels "bragging me up" for giving them and their wives a "special approach" (supposedly, in there estimation) to get a birds-eye view of the Statue of Liberty, off to the side of the arrival approach! Though not the case, I appreciated that they enjoyed their perceived "special treatment".

Standard Mission Route Structures (excluding A/R) –

Following is a description of the more routine flying operations of the B-707 Strategic Airlift functions of the Canadian Armed Forces:

Each week the Squadron flew two complete trans-Canada "scheduled airline-type" passenger operations, which originated and terminated at the CFB Trenton facility, with a subsequent crew-change for each following segment.

All Canadian military personnel and Canadian Government civil employees (at Headquarters-Level positions) were able to avail themselves of these routine flight schedules on a no-cost reserved seating basis for themselves when on "official travel", and for their dependents, on a space available basis when on "personal travel". Each operation began in mid-morning and flew from Trenton to Ottawa (National Defense Headquarters, and Canada's Capitol) about 30 minutes flying distance, with generally only a partial load of its 177-passenger capability. After a short turn-around it continued eastbound to CFB Goose Bay, Labrador, Newfoundland. Then a short hop to CFB Halifax, Nova Scotia, then back to CFB Trenton. The 5-member cabin crew provided full passenger catered hot meal-service on any leg which lasted more than about two-hours. (in those days, it was far more than "kibbles & bits" snacks, or box lunches). Arriving back at Trenton in mid–afternoon, the full crew would be replaced by a fresh crew for the next segment, which headed westbound to the western Canada seaboard. (This first segment involved two meal services and returned to CFB Trenton in about 6-hours from departure, including the ground stops). *[I was able to periodically take my wife, or one of my young daughters on this short work day for familiarization and motivation to see what I was doing on my job as a transport pilot.]*

The second segment began with the first stop again at Ottawa, Ontario, and then proceeding westbound dropping off passengers and picking up additional ones at CFB Winnepeg, Manitoba, then on to stops at CFB Edmonton, Alberta, then to Vancouver International Airport, BC, and then remaining overnight for crew rest at CFB Comox (on Vancouver Island), a 30-minute flight off-shore from Vancouver. The next morning having chased the sun across three time zones westbound to Comox, we started early at about 8 AM (local), after a 5 AM get-up, for the flight eastbound with stops back through Vancouver, CFB Edmonton, CFB Winnipeg, Ottawa, and finally CFB Trenton arriving home in the late evening some 12-hours travel plus stop-over times. This was an exhaustive two-day trip completing the second segment.

The aircraft would then continue from Trenton, with a crew change, "down east" as with segment one, described above for another circuit.

Another regularly scheduled trip, once per week, was the trans-Atlantic flight to Europe. This flight departed Trenton about 9 PM on Thursdays (as I recall) and flew first to Ottawa, then across the Atlantic into the approaching sunrise for landing at Gatwick Airport, London, UK, arriving about 9:30 AM (London/Greenwich Mean time), passing through customs and refueling, then proceeding on with some passenger changes, onto CFB Lahr, Germany (on the southwest corner of Black Forest region, about 12 miles south of Strasborg, France, on the Rhine river border.) The itinerary was established such that our plane full of passengers would arrive about noon, so they would have time to arrange transportation to other areas at mid-day and not saturate overnight temporary quarters on CFB Lahr before proceeding to their final destinations.

At Lahr, a crew change would be made and the aircraft would

proceed on to Nicosia, Cyprus (Turkey). Meanwhile the initial crew would go into crew rest for the next 48-hours until the aircraft returned from an overnight in Cyprus, and then would fly a reverse course back to CFB Trenton through London. *[I would typically be scheduled to fly one of the Trans-Canada segments each week, and one of the trans-Atlantic round-trip missions every other week (when not otherwise involved in an A/R missions).]*

Additional occasional missions would occur over the calendar year, including an average of three or four annual global Embassy resupply missions of 10-days duration, which were combined with VIP training and familiarization for the cabin crew members. Occasional Global VIP Canadian Government missions occurred each year, carrying Members of Parliament, which were accompanied by a large contingent of staff and Press to other various global regions. I performed as Aircraft Commander involved with one for the Minister of Trade and Commerce with an entourage of about 30 government staffers plus about 20 members of the Press. These used especially configured 707 "VIP aircraft" converted to all 1st-class seating for 80 passenger occupants and special alcoholic beverage arrangements and added galleys for the VIP catering and stop-over at 1st-class hotel accommodations for all (passengers, aircrew and maintenance support personnel), and also carrying dual flight crews and onboard spares of sufficient size to provide self sufficiency for the semi-global trips. My VVIP mission was to South East Asia and included stops in Mexico City, Honolulu, Singapore, Kuala Lumpur, Sri Lanka (formerly, Ceylon), Hong Kong, Bangkok and Manila. *[I also was scheduled as back-up Aircraft Commander for the Queen to Canada on her 1975 10-day visit.]*

Several global VIP training missions were flown each year, which served to familiarize both the flight crews and the cabin crews with all the logistics and protocols for carrying VIPs and VVIPs anywhere in the world, combined with Embassy supply runs. During my 3-year tour, I made two of these special training flights crossing the Equator 4-times and crossing both the North and the South Poles at least once each. These missions were special motivation and incentives given to the top performing and most senior crew-members in the Squadron, with an opportunity to live like dignitaries and experience tourism and shopping like the VIPs we typically supported, staying in international 5-star hotels and having the best catered VIP in-flight menus and service available. Since these had only 437 Squadron personnel on board, they served as training opportunities for the flight crew and the cabin crew to operate with full VIP amenities and coordination. Cabin crew "trainees" operated as 1st class food preparation and wait-staff to the others using fine crystal, silverware and linens with fruit juices served as "mock wine" to ensure all VIP protocols were learned and used with VIPs and Royalty. They also provided incentive crew composition to award outstanding performers in the squadron, and break-in new crew-members with special ceremonies in flight for celebrating equator crossings and other special polar crossing ceremonies.

Other Special Missions occurred each year like ferrying Canadian Forces personnel to Australia through Honolulu, Hawaii (more details to follow on Page 239), and transporting a plane-full of Canadian Sr. Officers and their spouses, from Ottawa to the USAF Air War College in Birmingham, AL (as previously mentioned in the Canarsi Approach anecdote).

The addition of the A/R mission, for which I was responsible, introduced other unique travel opportunities during trans-continental missions into the US and trans-Atlantic missions to northern Europe, the UK, Germany, Norway, and other NATO allied countries. (more on this later).

Flying these multiple roles, exposed me to far greater international and global travel than in SAC. I had the opportunity to visit over 40 nation/states internationally and globally, though many visits were only a three or four hour refueling stop. But many involved two or more days with ample time for tourism, shopping, and exploring different cultures. *[The Canadian crews had the saying, "The whole world is nothing but a series of 12,000 foot concrete runways, with a bed at one end and a bar at the other".]* You can well understand with a flying schedule task as described above, how one could get that impression!

For health reasons, when traveling outside of Canada, each crew member or support crew member was authorized (and encouraged) to purchase, duty-free, case lots of alcohol in advance at the rate of one 2-liter bottle, or six-pack of beer, per day of travel outside Canada (average cost of $3 per bottle for name brand liquor). This liquor allotment plus other snack and food supplies carried by the crew and managed in bulk by the Load Master, always made for some fun-filled crew parties in the hotels (which typically provided a complimentary party room when we arrived with a traveling crew of up to 40 or 50 persons lodged two per room (including our carry along maintenance teams). This was officially encouraged by Higher Headquarters in our secondary role as "friendly ambassadors of the Canadian government".

Due to the nature of our international travels, we also carried a safe onboard with at least $20,000 (up to $50,000, depending upon duration) in US cash, plus a Canadian Govt credit card, and a Canadian Govt. Impress Book (Canadian "petty cash" Check Book), with authorization to purchase fuel, replacement parts and services for aircraft support, up to the cost of a replacement engine. ($100,000 US, or more). These funds were the responsibility of the Mission Commander (aircraft commander) and administratively delegated to the crew First Officer (co-pilot) for handling and monitoring. *[This cash operation often gave rise to active competition from fuel and servicing vendors, who would race to the aircraft ramp upon our arrival with special offers of "metropolitan-phone-book sized" books of S&H Green Stamps or other incentives for the 120,000 pounds (~19,000 gallons, worth as much as $40,000 US, of JP-4 jet fuel and food catering services), which were of course turned in to the Canadian Govt, upon our return home. And there were always interesting transactions in money changing in various foreign countries with US Dollar* *advantage being far greater value than native foreign currencies, when crew members were shopping in various countries.]*

Unique Special Assignment Benefits—

Because of the relatively small numbers of the Canadian Armed Forces (compared to the US military), there were substantially less <u>internal</u> rules and regulations; *[And arguably a lesser number of disciplinary infractions and no "social engineering" within their services].* As a result, the CAF had no prohibition of crew members carrying their wive's and families on board any transport suitably equipped for seating, meals and toilet amenities, on most missions (non-combat, etc.) if seating availability permitted and passenger protocols (excluding Aerial Refueling and VIP, etc.) were not circumvented. I therefore had ample opportunity to take my spouse and/or my maturing children on many flight opportunities, so they could become familiar with "my office" and my military pilot duties. On overnight travels (even globally) I had only to pay for their catered meals (a max of $10 per day per person during aircraft operations), and any incremental bed-charges in the luxury accommodations that were always arranged in top 4 and 5 star hotels (which were also provided for on a minimal cost basis on "training-familiarity" and global missions).

[For example, on my mission to transport Canadian troops to Australia, my responsibilities began at Trenton, and ended in Honolulu when a second aircrew (which flew "dead-head" to Honolulu) to make the second segment from there to Australia and return with a plane full of Australian exchange troops bound for exercises in Canada. My responsibilities resumed after three days in Honolulu for the continuation back to Trenton at the mission conclusion. I was authorized and approved (along with three other Canadian crew officers) to bring our wives along since we knew we would have no flight duties during this three-day lay-over in Hawaii. (All expenses paid, except as mentioned in the above paragraph)].

[In another example, I was able to take one of my two girls (at a

time), or my spouse, with me on several occasions to ride in the cockpit jump-seat during the six-hour round trip mission from Trenton to Nova Scotia and back].

[And I took my wife to Europe on two occasions, where we deplaned at London, stayed and toured for a week while the augmented crew proceeded to Lahr, Germany. We then proceeded to Lahr when the next aircraft came through the following week and spent a week holiday in the Black Forest and Switzerland (by rented car belonging to a Canadian NCO based at Lahr) for the second week; and finally reconnecting with the scheduled flight returning to Trenton after the time spent in Lahr (and Switzerland). My days off were charged to "personal leave", and of course our meals, lodgings, and rental cars were personally paid by me for my added family expenses. By the time my tour was ending, my girls were now 8 and 11 years old, and they and my wife accompanied me on a similar trip as previously described above. Now that was certainly a unique opportunity that none of us will ever forget!]

Humorous Story; Flying in French Airspace (1973) — I had an experience in flying with the Canadians in their Boeing 707 aircraft that offered a challenging and somewhat comical bit of Canadian pilot ingenuity. This occurred on one of my first routine trans-Atlantic missions, which were sometimes flying under the auspices of NATO (with a NATO call sign) and other times using a "Canadian Military" call-sign, depending on our specific destination and what agency or authority had ordered the mission. On this specific mission I was serving as a relatively inexperienced "CAF" copilot on an aircraft using a Canadian call-sign.

We were flying over France from England's airspace carrying military passengers and dependents. Our route arrived in Europe after an overnight flight from Canadian National Defence Headquarters in Ottawa, Ontario, Canada landing at London's Gatwick Airport, where we took on fuel, deplaned some of our passengers, and boarded some new ones. From London, we flew across France into Germany.

[The standard International language for all Air Traffic Control Agencies is English, for all nations operating under ICAO Standards (International Civil Aviation Organization, which was established in 1944, by the United Nations). However, the French air traffic controllers were often cantankerous dealing with non-French aircraft -- particularly military.]

As we were handed off from the British air traffic controllers to the French frequency, I changed the radio to the proper frequency and heard the French controllers talking to other aircraft very clearly, sounding close at hand. Of course, most of the time, they were communicating in French – air traffic controller, and aircraft, alike – and we had no idea what type of aircraft, or what altitude, or proximity to us they might be. This is one of the primary reasons for the International standardized traffic control language. As I was new to all this, and becoming familiar with proper format, I called, "France Control, this is Canadian Military 513 at Flight Level 320, requesting IFR passage through your airspace for Lahr, Germany". We already had an international ICAO clearance all the way from London to Lahr over this flight path at the specified altitude of 32,000 feet above sea level. This initial check-in was only a required formality while in their airspace, and I knew that they should have received the hand-off location and altitude of our flight clearance from British Air Traffic Control.

Often in typical fashion, they would talk to everyone else, but not respond to English speaking aircrews (the Canadians were having some recurring diplomatic issues with France at the time). I tried again, with no response. Before I attempted contact for the third time, my Canadian pilot explained a trick that the Canadians had often used, that worked every time over the many months that I flew through French airspace. The third time I called, I reported in at 10,000 feet lower -- Flight Level 220. At this point, they figured they had me in a violation, and quickly responded, "Canadian 513, Say again flight level". Now, at least I had two-way communications and I quickly confirmed that we were at FL 320, the correct altitude, and they could no longer feign that they weren't hearing our transmissions!

[Operating in France or French-Canadian territories the spoken French language sounded totally different than the way it was printed on maps and signs, because the French language is spoken very rapidly and they run words together where there are often syllables omitted, certain letters are silent, and phrases sound nothing like what we might expect to hear. (e.g. As pronounced, "Mamselle" is actually spelled Mademoiselle; "Ver-sai", the city is actually spelled "Versailles"; and "Rahm-boolay", the airport, is actually spelled "Rambouillet". Quite confusing, for the English spoken translation! French language is not phonetically spoken, as is English (for the most part).

CANADIAN AIR REFUELING OVERVIEW—

My Introduction to Canadian Military A/R — The CAF Squadron had already accomplished two joint Aerial Refueling (A/R) two week training exercises, about 6-months prior to my arrival, one with each of the two CF-5 Fighter Squadrons (one English speaking, in Cold Lake, Alberta, the other French speaking in Bagotville, Quebec). Also, about a month before my arrival, under the guidance of my USAF predecessor, they had accomplished their first and only trans-Atlantic mission involving 2-tankers accompanied by four CF-5s per tanker, from each of the two CF-5 Squadrons. The NATO support exercise flew the formations from Canada to Norway and return. Amazingly, luck was with them and they had no incidents in the crossings, but I learned they recognized that there were many things still unknown that needed better definition.

My first semi-annual two-week refueling course for combined tanker and receiver initial qualification and proficiency training, was conducted after my six-months familiarity with normal transport operations. The previously trained A/R crews conducted the training for me along with other new members required to increase the A/R mission capability and crew resources. Upon completion of this course in Jan '74, I was presented with a Certificate of Training, and a two-foot tall stack of CAF A/R documentation, and training aids and told it was now "my program" to more fully develop and implement. I was designated as CAF "Air Refueling Operations Officer" with responsibility for all aspects of its accomplishment, including publishing the CAF nation-wide tasking "frag-orders", defining and allocating resources from any and all *participating* Canadian Armed Forces units globally, and negotiating airspace clearance allocations (both Canadian domestic and international, including US). These responsibilities carried the authority and responsibilities of a B/Gen within the CAF. This operation was not only new to the Canadian Air Force, but also largely to Canadian and European Air Traffic Control systems, and other ICAO agencies, *(as I was to later discover)* so my training and operational responsibilities went much further than just aircrews, as I had first envisioned.

Although I arrived in Canada with nearly 500 flight hours of instructing in USAF KC-135 tanker operations and unique SR-71 tactics and procedures, the Canadian aerial refueling concept, and virtually all of the equipment, crew procedures, and tactics were totally different than the "refueling boom" procedures and aircraft parameters with which I was intimately familiar and fully proficient; though my operations with the SR-71 had certainly taught me to be flexible and capable of adapting to "thinking outside of the box". Virtually, the only thing that was consistent between the Canadian and the USAF modes of A/R was comprehending and tailoring the development of the importance of crew-coordination and A/R discipline.

My first overall management experience that I had gained from my Canadian A/R Training and Certification Course, for which I was now responsible, was the need to substantially upgrade the depth and standardization of tactics used in the training program. I found the first week ground school portion of the course was thorough, detailed, and content-rich. However, this involved both tanker crew members and CF-5 receiver pilots, most of whom had "zero" perception about the "what, where, and how" of either what aerial refueling was all about, or of the new procedures, tactics and safety issues they were about to confront.

When you place one very large, less-agile aircraft into formation with four relatively small, highly-agile aircraft, in very close proximity at altitudes up to 30,000 feet and speeds around 500 MPH (equivalent ground speed) in a three-dimensional and highly dynamic environment, every participant must be keenly aware at all times what to expect, and of whom is in charge, in order to accomplish the job successfully and safely.

This group of trainees had been lectured on many highly visual aspects of A/R using hand-drawn, very crude chalkboard images that could not be readily reproduced for later review, nor adequately and efficiently integrated into their A/R experience and memory. Much of this instructional material provided for use in the second-week's "flying performance" segment of their A/R training, would be their first opportunity to see A/R "alive" for the first time, and convert this ground lecture into performing the highly precise and disciplined skills of a choreographed aerial ballet. This was demonstrated by my observation that each new receiver pilot took anywhere from three to six attempts before accomplishing their first successful "contact".

This provided me an emphasis to develop and implement a training movie that captures all of these various details in a deeply realistic visual way, combining explanatory animated graphic images integrated with actual movie footage from various viewpoints that provided a real-life view of what the graphic was trying to portray. This product would need to visually show with various views as seen by each participant, what the A/R looked like. It had movie cameras in a chase airplane, a receiver cockpit rigged with pilot's-view camera, cameras inside the tanker from the tanker Observer/ Controller perspective, and integrated computer-graphic images of the critical actions. This was the impetus of what culminated into a 35-minute color audio-visual, dual-use (Public Relations and

Training) 16 mm motion picture: (More details on this later.)

With considerable help from my Squadron Commander, I coordinated and obtained through higher command channels for the services of the Canadian National Defence Film Board to produce and accomplish this monumental undertaking.

"Operation High Test" Video Title

CAF Aerial Refueling Concept — The CAF concept of A/R initially was that of solely accompanied "mother hen" flight formation, with a CF-5 receiver formation of 2 or 4 "chicks", accompanying the tanker "hen". That meant that the tanker (which became formation leader) not only provided fuel management for the formation of receivers, but also navigation, route planning, all communications with Air Traffic Control, and guidance of the whole formation from initial accompanied take-off down to the formation final landing.

Boeing 707 with Two CF-5 Fighter Receivers

The level of A/R proficiency was minimal at the beginning, and no one in the A/R operation solidly knew what to expect, even on routine procedures, since the "routine" was not yet fully developed, defined and codified through training, discipline, or documentation. Since the Tanker was the formation lead, the tanker AC and all tanker crewmembers needed to have a substantial understanding of both the tanker's and the receiver-aircraft's operations and limitations, so that all refueling crewmembers had a standardized expectation of what was to happen both in normal and abnormal emergency procedures.

Tanker Mission Crew Manning — The tanker crew consisted of the normal B-707 commercial airline type crew — Aircraft Commander, Copilot or First Officer (both of whom were usually AC experienced and qualified), Navigator and Flight Engineer, plus the Cabin Crew – a Load Master and 2 or 3 Flight Attendants (as the norm). For A/R operations, the cockpit crew was supplemented with an additional and specially trained Tactical Navigator, and a 2nd Flight Engineer, both of whom were dual qualified in normal and A/R procedures and responsibilities for their crew positions. These two additional A/R crewmembers performed duties as A/R Observers/Controllers –analogous to a Boom Operator – each with some additional responsibilities. During A/R operations, the tanker interior had two (one on either side of the tanker) Observer/Controller's positions, each of which had a rear-facing table and crew seat, on either side of the 707 fuselage about halfway aft of the wing trailing edge and the interior rear galley near the tail. These positions were equipped, each with table lighting, an intercom control panel with use of radio communications through the primary radio (as controlled by the pilot's selected inter-plane communications frequency) and interior crew inter-communications on the tanker. These rear-facing positions also provided relatively unobstructed vision of the refueling store (pod) on their respective wing tip, throughout the extended range of the hose and drogue, and the receiver when he was in the pre-contact position (about two aircraft-lengths aft of the extended hose and drogue). In addition the Observer/Controllers had to also be visually aware of the receiver(s) on the opposite side of the tanker, by eye contact and visual cues with their opposite counterpart using visual and hand signal cues and communications inter-phone, communications with the cockpit and inter-plane communications to ensure that all active A/R crew had complete positional awareness of where every aircraft was located in the formation, particularly during A/R operations. *(The tanker A/C could – at best – see only the receivers on the left side of the tanker, and as far aft as the limit of the trailing hose/drogue on the left side, yet needed at all times to be cognizant of the position of every aircraft in the formation. So the two Observers were his eyes, and situational Controllers.)*

Though the CAF had only two tanker aircraft, we kept a pool of trained, certified and current crewmembers to man eight mission-crews (since many of our operational missions carried two separate crews on each aircraft — a primary crew, and a secondary "dead-head crew" for the next mission segment). Each crewmember trained a minimum of once every 6-months for two weeks to maintain currency and familiarity of updated or new procedures. Flight crews were scheduled on a rotationary basis, similar to normal transport missions and were not kept integrated together (unlike

SAC). So intense standardization was critical to the integrity of the operations, and repetition was the key to training proficiency.

Aerial Refueling (A/R) Tactics —

[The tactics and procedures described here are as they were implemented during the early evolution (mid-1970s) of Canadian A/R based upon the relatively low experience and proficiency and minimum annual A/R flight hours flown, and certainly may NOT reflect those used in later years (1980s and beyond) of Canadian operations and the evolution to newer tankers (Airbus A320s), advanced hose drogue A/R systems, and advanced receiver aircraft types (F/A-18), as used in the later years].

The Controller on the right side of the tanker; facing aft (Tactical Flight Engineer) had a copy of the CF-5 receiver's technical systems flight manual -- and had full knowledge of the receiver's aircraft systems and operations to the degree that he could advise any receiver pilot of circuit breakers to check, switches to activate, and aircraft emergency procedures, if/when needed. The controller on the left side of the tanker; facing aft (Tactical Navigator) had full knowledge and document access regarding receiver flight and fuel performance, and was responsible to continuously log each receiver's fuel state, fuel burn performance and coordinated with the primary Navigator in the tanker cockpit with reference to how long the recommended time interval was between aerial refueling brackets. "Brackets" were defined and updated along the formation's manual map plot and logs by the primary tanker Navigator, so that each of the "chicks" could be assured that refueling would commence at a point and all receivers could be topped-off by the end of the "bracket" at a fuel state, which would provide sufficient fuel to proceed to an emergency landing location – with predetermined landing-reserves on <u>a single-engine</u> ***[known as "Bingo" fuel state].*** Further, the brackets (with defined MDP, *Minimum Diversion Point*) could be achieved, using only a single hose on the tanker (for the total number of receivers). And every receiver was trained so he knew what to expect and where each receiver would position himself and sequence his position relative to the tanker and his sister "chicks" in any of a number of different abnormal and/or emergency situations – but never without prior permission/direction from tanker (AC, or designated Controller). This rigid discipline was necessary for flight safety and situational awareness. Practical knowledge of these safety procedures were rigorously trained and practiced, especially initially while A/R experience and proficiency were relatively low.

Accompanied Take-off Procedure — The original A/R tactics for formation take-off that were in place at that time (by command of the tanker AC, as cleared by the Tower for formation taxi and departure) were such that the flight of two – or more typically, four – receivers would taxi-out together followed immediately by their tanker. Upon Tower take-off clearance, the fighters would make a formation take-off (2 by 2, at 15-second intervals between pairs) and enter an immediate downwind leg in fingertip "Vic" echelon formation (like the fingers of the right hand with fingers straight and tightly together). After the fighters launched, the tanker would pull onto the runway and hold.

Once becoming airborne the fighters would climb to 1,000 feet above the runway (visual pattern altitude) while reversing direction onto a close downwind leg, paralleling the runway. As they joined into 'Vic' positions and upon coming abeam of the tanker (which was now ready to roll) holding on the runway, as viewed from their downwind position, the fighter formation Lead would call, "Abeam" and the tanker pilot would then advance to T.O. power and begin take-off roll – acknowledging "Husky rolling" on the radio. As the tanker became airborne, retracted flaps and gear (climbing straight ahead on the runway heading), the receiver formation would reverse course again and request clearance from the tanker to join on the tanker in echelon formation (typically with 1 and 2 on the tanker's left wing tip, and 3 and 4 on the tanker's right), while the tanker maintained a maximum of 250 Knots in the climb until all fighters were joined up.

At that point the tanker, upon climbing through 10,000 feet, would call for formation to advance to climb power and accelerate together up to 300 Knots while continuing the climb to the ATC "Block altitude" for the formation of FL280 to FL300 (a moving block of airspace between 28,000 and 30,000 feet above sea-level. After established in the climb, the Tanker would command the formation to switch to the briefed secondary "inter-plane frequency", while keeping the tanker's primary radio tuned to Tower or other ATC (Air Traffic Control) frequency to reduce radio communications clutter between A/R formation and ATC, and other aircraft on the ATC frequency. Once leveled-off, the formation Leader, (now the tanker) would advise the receivers of the time for the first bracket and permit loosening of formation spacing (typically for about 15 minutes after top-of-climb). Approaching the first bracket, the formation Leader (tanker AC), would request the receivers to tighten the formation for refueling.

Mother Hen, and Four Chicks (each with Dual-Underwing Tanks, plus white Centerline Travel Pod)

Operation of the A/R System —

The tanker fuel system is controlled by the tanker Flight

Engineer, through electrical controls for the appropriate fuel valves and pumps to pressurize the lines up to the fuel pod(s). Sensors in the Beech store(s) keep the fuel hose depressurized until the receiver makes contact and the receiver pilot pushes the drogue forward into the refueling zone marked on the hose(s). The receiver must move forward to push the drogue forward about 5-feet to the first orange band, then further forward to center the white band at the bellmouth. (The two orange bands are about ten feet apart; the white band is in the middle and fuel transfer can be conducted anywhere between the inner and outer orange bands, with the white band as the target optimum mid-point.)

[The following several graphics are frames from ***"Operation High Test"*** *movie.]*

Hose Markings:

<u>Top Orange,</u> (when pushed into bellmouth) = Fuel Transfer Valve Opens and Ram Air Turbine (RAT) Pump is Armed (on nose of store).

<u>White</u> (when at bellmouth) = Optimum mid-range for Aerial Refueling.

<u>Lower Orange</u> mark (when at bellmouth) = Max. Forward Travel, beyond which will cause slack hose, and fuel transfer valve closure.

When the hose is anywhere between the top and bottom orange markers (at the bellmouth), the fuel Transfer Valve will be open, and if there is fuel pressure to the A/R pod from the tanker's pumps, fuel will flow to the receiver aircraft. The fuel pressure also pressurizes three roller-cam locks that engage the Drogue onto the grooves on the end of the receiver's probe. The greater the fuel pressure, the stronger it holds on. During intentional, or accidental disconnects, the fuel flow will automatically be terminated and drogue locks released as the receiver pulls the hose aft of the upper orange band (approximately 5-feet from full hose travel).

Sensors in the system also detect the fuel backpressure in the hose. If the hose pressure rises above limit pressure (i.e. receiver tank is full or the receiver contact had reached either Orange marker), the system closes the fuel Transfer Valve and releases pressure on the Drogue/Probe lock mechanism. If the hose sensor pressure detector senses low pressure (i.e. receiver tanks are low and hose is within the A/R zone limit) then the RAT (Ram Air Turbine) will activate and further boost the flow rate through the pod and into the receiver tank(s).

So the tanker's system fully automates the transfer process as long as the receiver pilot keeps the hose pushed into the mid-zone between the orange marks. And it unlocks the drogue and the hose depressurizes anytime the receiver pilot falls outside of the refueling zone. This leads to minimal fuel spray on contact or disconnect, and minimal force on the hose, drogue and probe automatically if anything physically pulls the drogue from the probe. Red, green, and amber lights inside the bellmouth, also inform the receiver pilot of the switch operations, whether automatically, or manually controlled by the Controllers. A shaded floodlight in the bellmouth also illuminates the hose markings during night A/R.

Preparing for A/R in Flight— Once closed into tight formation (as shown on Pg. 250, above), the tanker would extend each hose and drogue wingtip Beech 1080 A/R store separately while insuring that no receiver was directly behind the extending (or retracting) store. Typical planned onload for each receiver's refueling was about 1,800 to 3,000 pounds (~ 6.5 pounds per gallon) per CF-5 receiver, depending on whether they were configured with a single centerline drop-tank or two under wing drop-tanks. Several additional variables (wind, route in-relation to proximity of emergency landing sites, receivers' external-tank configuration, winds aloft and weather, flight turbulence/visibility), would determine when subsequent refueling brackets were required – typically about one-hour between brackets and each planned bracket based upon single hose tactics (assuming suitable relatively smooth refueling altitude) would require only 20 to 30 minutes total, to refuel 4-chicks to full tanks during a single-hose procedure.

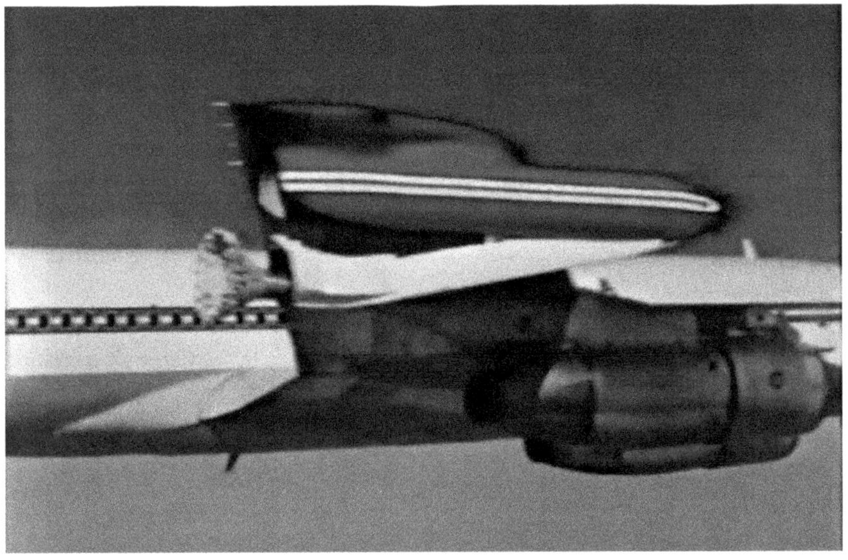

"Right Boom Extending", Radioed by Rt. Observer

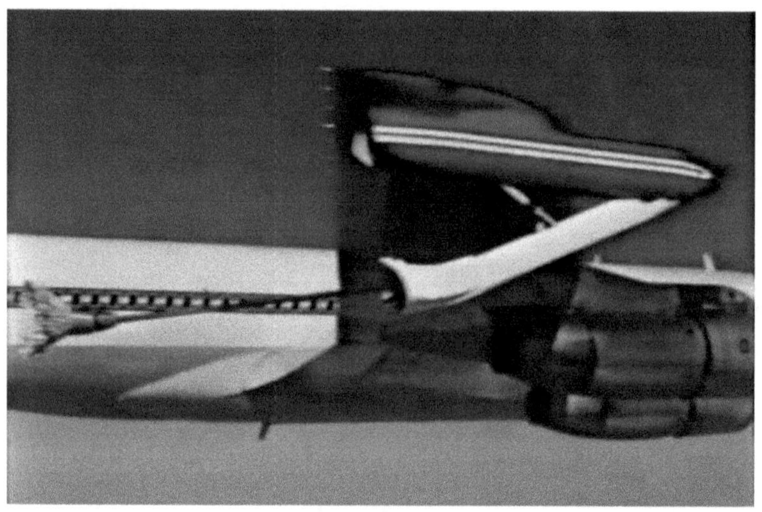

Mid-Extension

Boom & Hose (near) Fully Extended (Note Hose Markings)

Once both Beech refueling stores were extended, the tanker A/C would transfer command on inter-plane frequency to their related Controller, for each pair of receivers on their respective wing-tips. The tanker can safely refuel two receivers simultaneously. However the approach to contact was done separately, making sure that only one receiver at a time was cleared to advance to contact and until that receiver was in stable contact and receiving fuel. Typically the refueling sequence was left wing – #1, then right wing #3. Once the receiver closest to his respective wingtip was cleared behind his drogue, his wingman would "tighten" into the vacated close-to-tip position ready for his subsequent turn for a "drink". When each receiver completed his onload, he was cleared by his Controller to the "outboard echelon" on his respective side of the tanker aircraft. As refueling proceeded, and the second aircraft would be moved over behind the drogue ('basket") the vacated position would be filled by movement "sliding" into the wingtip position and he would then be back in original position in the cycle. When the wingmen finished refueling on each side, and were cleared back to his respective <u>outboard</u> echelon position all receivers would be back in their original positions after top-off. The tanker crew would then retract the A/R stores individually and the receivers were allowed to loosen formation (weather permitting) by sliding out to twice or three times the normal separation distance, for some relaxation until the next bracket.

Sounds complex, but is really a very choreographed and practiced rhythm, and is consistent through all receiver movements around the tanker.

Receiver's #3 and #4 awaiting clearance to move separately, in sequence behind the right hose. (Note Hose Markings).

After all four receivers had been topped off, and both hoses retracted, the Right Controller (Tac. Nav.) compared fuel consumption for each receiver against planned figures and then the Primary Navigator would calculate time and distance to the next refueling bracket. All fuel transfer data and next planned bracket timing was then passed to the receivers. Typically, each refueling bracket would be about 30-minutes long (based upon systems functioning normally and two receivers simultaneously refueled on each store) and would occur with about one hour after the previous, so that the receiver pilots would have about an hour "rest" between refuelings. Turbulence or in-the-clouds weather could often make refueling more difficult and fatiguing to complete and would cause the bracket intervals to shorten. The final refueling was planned to be within about 30 minutes prior to start of descent, to have the receivers all near full fuel for any possible landing contingencies.

Upon approaching destination, the tanker AC would initiate formation pre-descent checklists about 40-minutes out, obtain destination weather and expected runway approach type, and initiate formation descent. He would call the formation when reducing power and provide intended descent airspeed. He would also call appropriate configuration changes prior to making them so the receivers would know what to expect and maintain close wing distance from the tanker and each other, as configurations were changed. (e.g. "Huskies, approach flaps—approach flaps – Go", or "Huskies, landing gear, landing gear — Down"), and at appropriate locations on approach would direct the receivers to switch over to Approach radio frequency, so they could anticipate approach heading and altitude maneuvers. Upon breaking out below any weather ceilings into positive visual conditions and at, or inside, the final approach fix with all aircraft on approach or tower frequency, the tanker would call the fighter formations advising them of runway in sight and repeat the controller landing permission while initiating a tanker pull up and go-around. *[The tanker always landed after his receivers, when on an accompanied approach, to allow for receiver fuel contingencies.]*

Other Unique A/R Receiver Considerations —

Reference the Boom Bellmouth, not the Drogue —

When approaching the drogue for contact, there was frequently some degree of airflow turbulence. So the drogue might be bobbing around due to the tanker wingtip bounce or air turbulence, and therefore the drogue would not be in synchronization with the ambient airflow, and could be at a higher rate of oscillation than the wing tip. For the receiver pilot to try and focus on the trailing hose-drogue would therefore be aiming at a less stable reference, than using the bell mouth of the boom for reference, and this would invariably lead to a miss or an off center contact with the drogue resulting, in a tip-off.

This effect can quite visibly be seen in the subsequently produced A/R movie, ***"Operation High Test".***

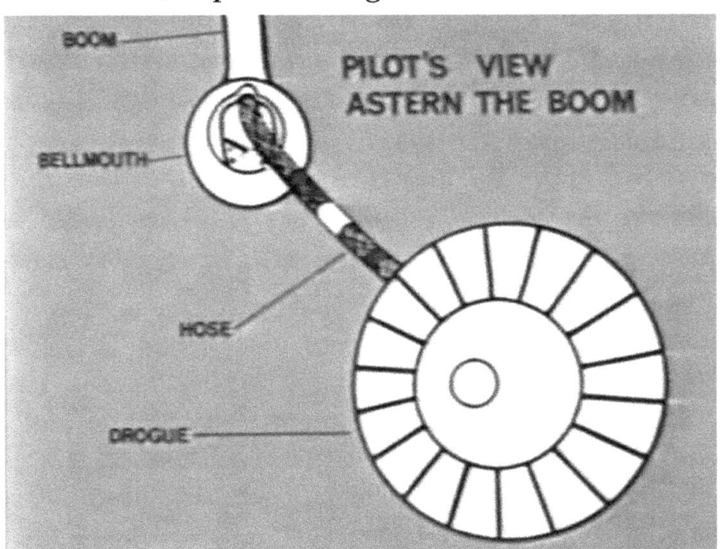

CF-5 Pilot's View when Probe Aligned with Drogue Approaching Contact, on Tanker's Right Wing

Immediately ahead of the drogue, there was a length of about four feet of steel pipe attached between the metal-sheathed hose and the drogue swivel. The drogue swivel was also weighted with 40 lbs of ballast. These two pieces of structure were provided to prevent undue bending (and inflight failure) at the end of the hose, and to assist the hose to free-fly further below the wingtip vortex. Without the added ballast, a large undampened drogue-oscillation of nearly ± 3-feet (6-feet total top-to-bottom oscillation) could occur. A tip-off could easily be of such severity that the 45-pound drogue could smash a windscreen, puncture nose skin, or even cause airflow blockage of the right engine inlet on the CF-5 receiver that could cause an engine flame out. Tip-off could not always be prevented, but they were something to be avoided as much as possible.

[In training, we occasionally encountered tip-offs that would bend one or two the collapsible drogue "feathers" outward. These conditions would usually require discontinuing the use of that drogue until ground repairs or replacements could be made, due to the significant drogue oscillations. Sometimes we would also encounter heavy turbulence and wing-tip oscillations, which could also cause up to 6-foot diameter drogue oscillation. Amazingly, a very few of the CF-5 Instructor Pilots became sufficiently proficient that they could match their aircraft flight with the oscillations using the bow wave effect and make completed contact and lock-on. I wouldn't have believed it, if I hadn't personally observed it!]

Stabilizing the Drogue with Receiver Bow Wave –

During early testing and training with the CF-5 A/R it was observed that at refueling airspeed there was a sufficient airflow around the CF-5 nose that would cushion the airstream as the drogue approached close to the skin. Using this bow wave–effect and a deliberate pause in closure speed as the drogue came abeam the twin-50 cal. machine gun barrels on the top of the nose, would momentarily capture the drogue and stabilize the oscillations so a brief thrust would send the probe right into the center of the drogue for a successful lock-on!

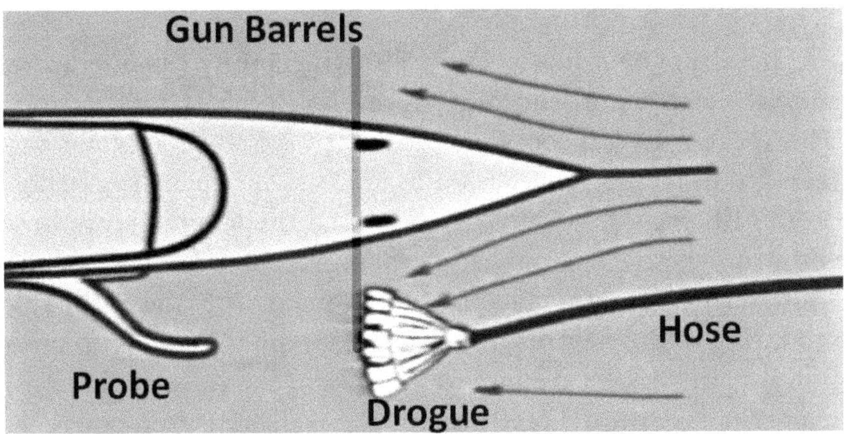

Drogue captured by Bow Wave of CF-5 when abeam of Gun Barrels

Drogue at the Pause at the Gun Barrels
(Camera Nose Installed on this photo)

This brief pause also prevents the receiver from approaching too fast, which almost always causes a tip-off and unsafe over-run of the tanker.

Effect of Tanker Wing Airflow —

The nature of airflow over the 707 wing, created an interaction anomaly with the extended hoses on the Beech 1080 A/R store. This created several considerations that were apparently not corrected during the tanker modifications. The spanwise airflow on the Boeing's 35° swept wings caused the wingtip store hose and drogues to splay outward, when extended. Because of this "outboard hose splaying effect, combined with the right-side mounting of the A/R probe in the CF-5, the right wingtip position was the easiest contact to make, and the pilot could easily maintain a position directly astern the right refueling pod.

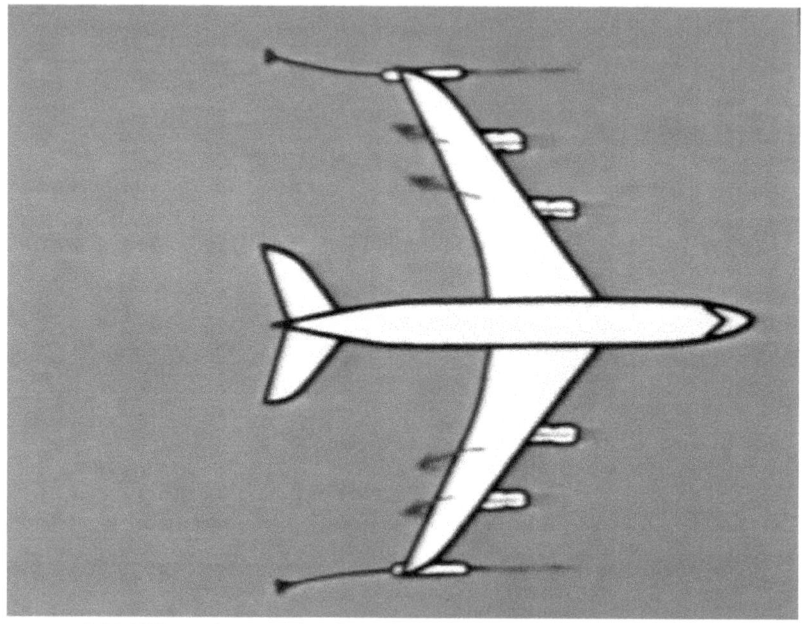

35° Wing Sweep Airflow Splays the Drogues Outboard

On the other hand, approaching the left wingtip drogue position found the CF-5 displaced about 2-feet left of the refueling pod alignment. This caused the reference view of the boom-bellmouth to be in a different location. Once capturing the drogue during "contact" the natural tendency was to fly right to align with the pod. However this caused the airflow to set-up a condition called "skip-roping" of the hose, once the contact was made. Correction was required to move left, outboard from the more familiar position directly astern of the pod, as compare to the naturally neutral position on the opposite (right) wing.

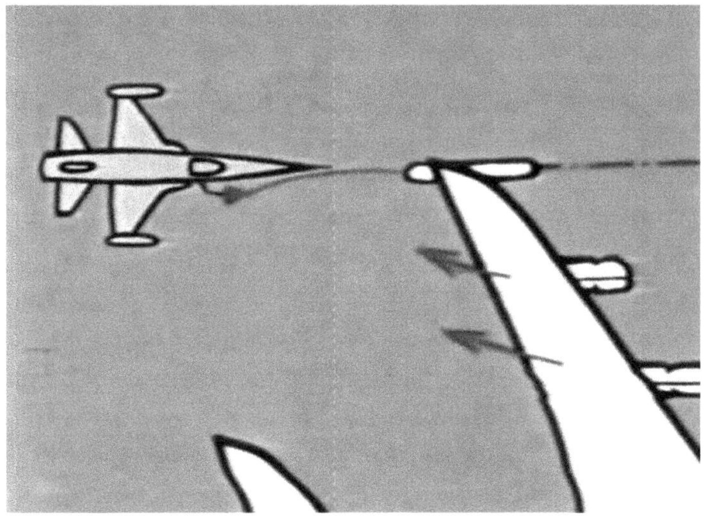

CF-5 position adds to the outboard float of the left drogue, making contact more difficult, and causing hose "skip-rope".

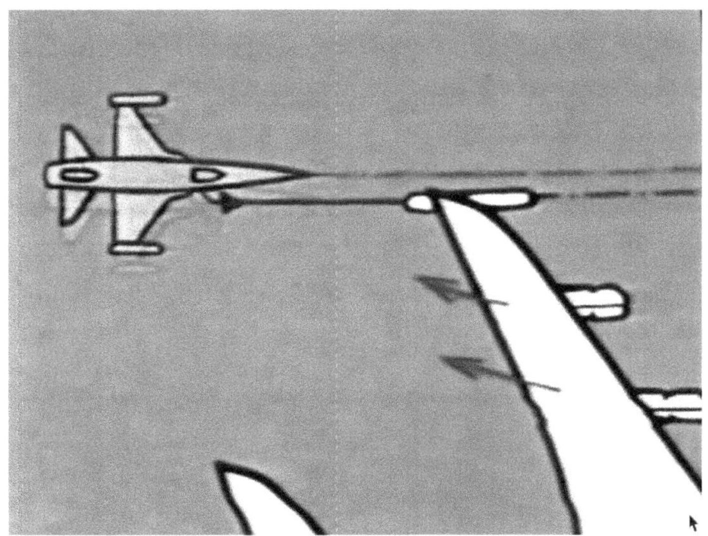

Once Contact is made, Pilot must move left a couple feet tostop the hose "skip-rope".

[The Canadian B-707 A/R Modification was the first of several Beech 1080 A/R wingtip mounted pod installations. They were also applied to a dozen Iranian tankers, and numerous other "third-world" small 707 tanker fleets had both the Beech stores and the KC-135 type centerline boom. (Specifically, the Iranian Tankers also had the addition of wider aft viewing A/R Observer windows on each side of the tanker combing the span of two standard 707 windows, for enhanced safety of control and operations throughout the refueling envelope, based upon the Canadian "lessons-learned" and my recommendations to the USAF and Boeing, on the Iranian contract). I participated with the USAF and Boeing in recommending certain modifications to both systems and airframes for the Iranian Tankers, which may, or may not have been implemented in other subsequent international B-707 tanker sales. One example in addition to the enlarged viewing window, was the paint scheme on the Beech store. In the original delivery, the Beech stores were painted white with a narrow red striping. In weather, we found the store became invisible in the clouds and the receivers had difficulty maintaining visual position. Reversing the colors, making the Beech store bright red with white stripping, greatly improved in-the-cloud visibility of the stores. Another improvement applied to other sales was to add electroluminescent lighting down the side of the Beech store for better night-time reference lighting. Most of those other than Iran, were not processed through the USAF, and most had different configuration variations from the Canadian version. These apparent overlooked considerations required fixes, where possible, and caused minor performance degradations that were "lived-with" due to the cost of redesign and test. I will mention them in passing to suggest the complexity of the issue and the ingenuity with which engineers and operators coped with these issues.]

The Dihedral Effect — The wing dihedral is a factor that provides inherent lateral (rolling) stability in flight by inclining the wingtips above the horizontal attachment point at the fuselage. In the B-707 this is an angle of about +10° to +12°. (The wings flex upward by plus-or-minus 2-feet at changing airspeed/lift, or turbulence.)

The Beech A/R store was designed as a centerline installation under the belly of Navy fighters for carrier "buddy-tanker" operations. So it was hung vertically from the belly mount. When attached to the B-707 wingtip, they were hung perpendicular to the lower skin of the wingtip, (to make them interchangeable on either side), which meant that the booms were not vertical with the horizon (i.e. gravity vector in aircraft level flight), but were angled outward like two legs of a tripod. This placed an additional side load on the pod's booms when retracted, which prevented the booms from extending by gravity when the boom hoist released the up-tension on the boom retraction cable. This was a relatively simple fix – the addition of a spring-loaded "sling-shot" cable across the tunnel that the boom retracted into on the pod – which forced the boom out of the tunnel when the boom hoist was released.

Another issue was for the pilots flying in contact with the refueling hose, regarding their peripheral visual references used to maintain coordinated formation flight on the tanker during refueling contact.

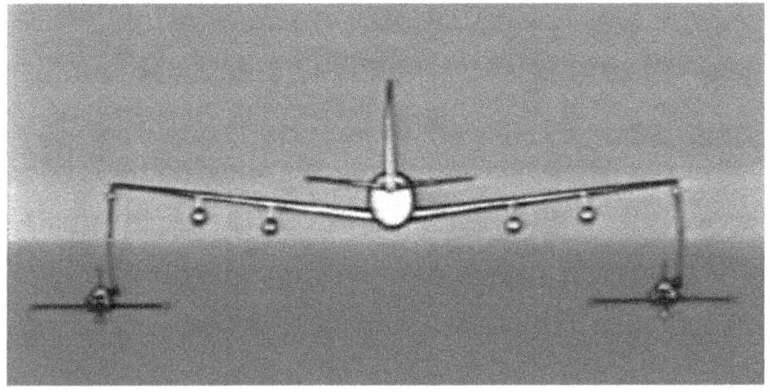

Refueling Stores are mounted perpendicular to bottom of the wingtips; With visual horizon, orientation is clear.

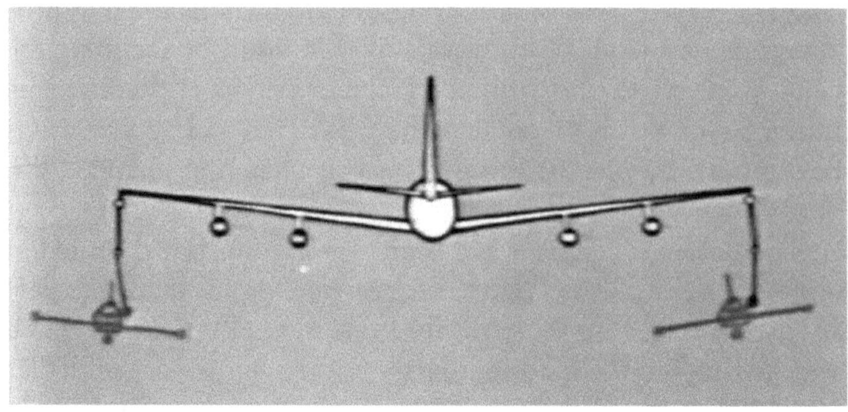

With obscured visual environment (clouds or darkness), CF-5 "horizon" becomes the dihedral angles of tanker's wings, causing disorientation, and fighter cross-control.

When flying in obscured visibility, the receiver pilots automatically tend to perceive the tanker wing as a horizontal reference. This requires banking in one direction to align with the wing dihedral, while applying opposite rudder cross control (to keep from turning). Once disconnecting from the hose the receiver aircraft tends to slide inboard toward the opposite receiver and can set up a potential for pilot vertigo and a mid-air collision.

Hazard of Wing Tip Vortex —

When typical fighter pilots in combat are given a radio call to "Break, Break, Break", combat maneuver training has taught them to go to max power (afterburner), climb and bank sharply away to escape potential attackers or missiles. This is done almost instinctively as a reaction. Conversely, in A/R an emergency such as too fast an approach to contact, or potential of a mid-air collision, the emergency separation call is "Breakaway, Breakaway, Breakaway!" The required reaction to this situation for the receiver is to quickly <u>decelerate</u> (power to idle) speed-breaks as necessary and <u>rapidly descend</u>. If the receiver pilot does a "Break", rather than a "Breakaway", he will climb right up into the powerful wingtip vortex, which will throw him in toward the tanker and potentially into the vertical tail. So this is totally new reaction that he must react to correctly.

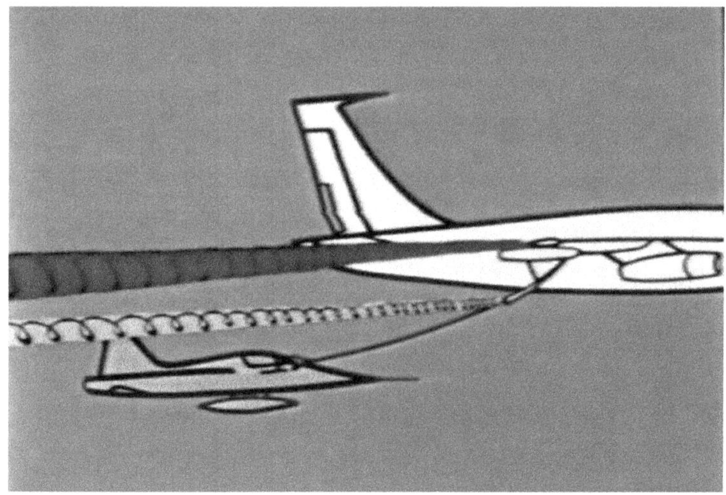

Weak Vortex from Boom Bellmouth can affect attempting Drogue Contact; Strong Wingtip Vortex Can Flip Receiver Up and In Toward the Tanker Vertical Tail

Solving Some of the A/R Unknowns —

One of the first impressions I realized after my initial check out, was revealed when I learned of the assumptions used during the initial trans-Atlantic A/R mission. First, the F-5 airframe was new to the A/R capability (at least in the Canadian CF-5 version knowledge base). The only available data showed how high it could climb on one engine after take-off at full fuel weight -- and that was only about 10,000 feet (or less with dual external tanks). ***[There was no performance data available for the aircraft that defined the maximum altitude that the aircraft could maintain at heavy weight on one engine (including use of after-burner) if the engine failure/shut-down occurred at cruising altitude, nor for what distance it could fly, or how long it could fly from that point.]***

Therefore on the first trans-Atlantic mission, (before my arrival) the emergency contingency procedure that was planned and briefed was that the tanker and all of its "chicks" would retain formation integrity (over-water) and descend and slow as necessary (even if entering cloud conditions, icing, and/or turbulence) and remain in formation to an emergency landing base. This could potentially cause the loss of the entire formation. And with refueling, there was an added potential that the refueling operation could precipitate inadvertent engine failures due to ingestion of debris or blocking of intake air by a drogue tip-off during attempting to make contact in rough air or in icing conditions.

So early-on in my A/R responsibilities, I developed a plan where we could do performance testing from 30,000 feet, by actually having the CF-5 pilot shut-down one of his engines, after topping it to full tanks, and then documenting how low we would actually have to descend on this worst-case critical engine failure, and under what conditions we could refuel during single-engine descent, and to what altitude he could then maintain at full-up fuel state, after refueling during descent. We were amazed and pleasingly surprised to determine that we could start an immediate descent out of 30,000 ft. by reducing formation speed by a mere 25 knots during descent, while bringing the disabled CF-5 into contact and topping him up in the descent for a level-off at 20,000 ft or above, and arriving at full tanks with a Bingo-fuel range of 500 miles to an emergency landing location. We implemented this emergency tactic and practiced it in every refueling training session so every CF-5 pilot and tanker crew was familiar and proficient with this tactic.

Growth in A/R Crew Proficiency — In the beginning of my tour, annual aerial refueling operations consisted of less than 5% of the 437 Transport Squadron's total annual flight hour allocation; a token, part-time operation. As the hours of experience accumulated over the first year of regular training, we were ultimately able to develop our tactics from our original "accompanied cross-country" mode to operate a prepositioned tanker orbit in a geographical area ("gas station orbit") and make rendezvous with one or more formations of CF-5s in the more conventional manner. This had the practical application, for example, of scheduling a tanker to proceed to an orbit point over Hudson Bay and rendezvous with up to four CF-5 receivers, from Bagotville AB, Quebec, configured with the camera nose. Once topped–off with fuel, the four-ship formation could accomplish mid to low altitude photo recce passes of Baffin Island and other upper Canadian Arctic islands looking for unpublicized incursions or Soviet exploitation, then return to the tanker for a top–off and second run; or return to Bagotville at termination. By the end of my Canadian tour, A/R allocated tanker hours had increased to more than 15% of the total annual flight-hour allocation (as compared to 5% at the beginning of my tour.) Considering that was accomplished by just two tankers – of the total five B-707s in the CAF fleet, that was a considerable increase of operational capability – and mission expansion.

B-707 Beech Store Failure Incident — An unusual incident was encountered with the Canadian B-707 tanker operation when an inflight structural failure of the internal mechanism in one of the Beech wingtip refueling stores occurred during boom and hose extension.

Normal hose & drogue deployment;
One engaged, the other approaching Contact.

Fortunately, during my tenure while developing the refueling training procedures, we had considered contingencies for this type of situation and had "table-flown" them during my training classes, though they had never actually been previously encountered in flight, nor simulated in practice training. In anticipation of this potential type of failure, we had fortunately implemented a normal procedure of never retracting or extending the booms and hoses with any aircraft directly behind the booms, in the event that something could fail, or fall off, during deployment or retraction. And we developed and practiced procedures for refueling from a single hose, should one fail or be damaged during a mission.

This incident occurred nearing the end of my three-year tour, in the summer of 1976. We were flying a daytime 4-receiver (CF-5) tactical reconnaissance mission over Hudson Bay in the arctic. During the second rendezvous and refueling while extending the two Beech refueling stores, as the four-ship fighter formation rejoined the tanker from a low altitude photo-recon operation, the store on the right wingtip experienced a catastrophic internal failure, disabling it from further use. We were able to turn toward home base at Trenton, Ontario, while conducting "single-hose" emergency refueling of all four receivers using only the operable left refueling store. Once the CF-5s were at full tanks and were within range to proceed to their base in Quebec Province without further refueling, they were cleared to depart the tanker for home.

The tanker continued enroute back to CFB Trenton, Ontario, knowing there was little means to either remove the detachable stores at CFB Bagotville, nor parts support there, and the inflight handling of the tanker was without difficulty. We proceeded to troubleshoot the failed Beech store and were able at least to retract the boom into the up-and-stowed position using the built-in boom-winch, however the hose/drogue failed to retract into the store due to the nature of the failure, leaving the fully deployed hose and drogue (about 32 feet in length) trailing behind the retracted boom on the wingtip.

While still more than an hour away from landing, the Trenton Tower was contacted through coordination with Air Traffic Control, and Emergency fire fighting teams and rescue crews were alerted for our upcoming precautionary emergency arrival. We were informed that the airfield had no runway foam capability for our arrival, so we had to make alternate plans to avoid the potential for sparks from the extended fuel-filled flex-steel hose and its attached drogue, which might start a fire upon touchdown with it dragging on the paved runway. I also requested that the Tower alert the Safety office to arrange for a videographer to film our approach and landing for Safety and training purposes (as well as any potential accident or incident investigation, that might ensue). This was not a failure mode that we could simulate for inflight training!

During our return to CFB Trenton, I decided that it would be judicious to make a low 20-foot pass over the runway to determine a safe aircraft offset-alignment, in order to put the failed right refueling store and drogue over the grass, and not potentially get the dragging spiral steel-encased hose and drogue in contact with the runway side marker lights (a potential to cause further structural damage to the mechanism or resulting flailing of the hose, or possibly causing the aircraft to be dragged off the runway). These sturdy runway lights were spaced every thousand feet and aligned approximately 15 to 20 feet off the edge of the runway. Since I could not see the right drogue's position from the cockpit, this would need some close coordination from the onboard right A/R Controller to help me determine safe references by which to fly. The aircraft landing weight was approximately 240,000 pounds (76% of maximum Take-Off weight), which would require a touchdown speed in excess of 120 knots. A second and more significant concern was a short runway crossing at a point approximately 3500 feet from the touchdown point of Runway 06, the active runway for the existing wind direction. If I was unable to land and stop the aircraft before reaching the Runway 31 crossing, there was a concern in my mind, that the extended hose and drogue would be dragged across the pavement, again raising the possibility of sparks and abrasion which could possibly wear through the steel casing of the fuel-filled hose, and initiate a fire hazard.

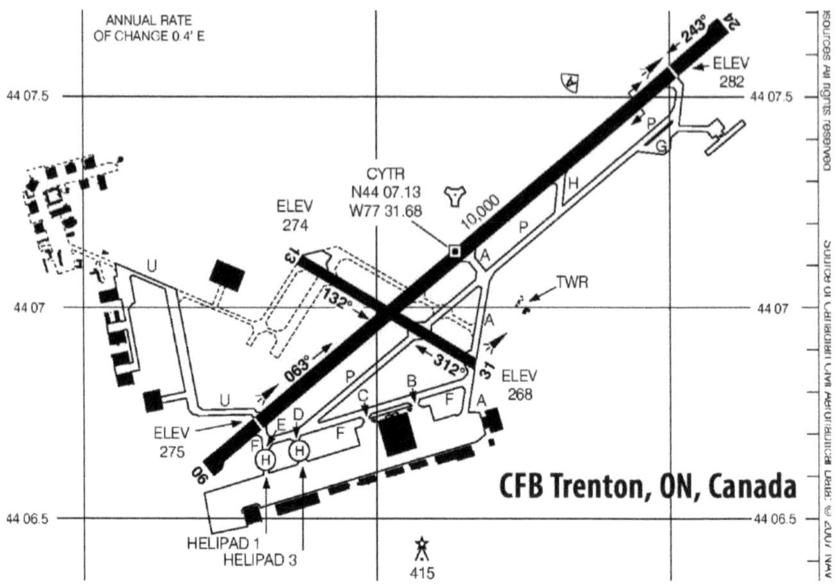

CFB Trenton Runway Layout

I felt that under these circumstances it would be prudent to push the aircraft systems to their limit and use maximum anti-skid braking on the main gear as soon as they were on the ground. Combining this with maximum power on the thrust reversers, gradually easing off the power as we slowed below 40 knots (the usual minimum speed for reversers on landing), which was limited to minimize damaging ingestion of grass and debris into the engines. Neither of these procedures was a normal, nor regularly practiced tactic, so it was an added risk. I was successful in stopping the aircraft completely just before the drogue reached the edge of the intersecting runway surface on my second approach for full stop landing – quite a short landing for the aircraft weight and landing speed. Despite the weight and higher touchdown speed, with the benefit of the low pass to get everything aligned safely, I touched down at the target lip of the runway, applied the thrust-reversers to full power on touching down with the mains, immediately thereafter retracted the full flaps to gain more weight on the wheels and gradually eased in maximum anti-skid braking. The aircraft was safely stopped at the intersection of runways which left the deployed hose just short of climbing onto the pavement.

Much to my disappointment, even with nearly two hours notice before landing, the Base was unable to get a video film photographer on scene before our landing, to document the "incident" for safety and training purposes.

Upon examination after landing, maintenance personnel determined that the refueling store failure was caused by a major structural break in the hydraulic "strut-support forging" that slides internally on a track to retract the hose, as the boom is raised by its internal hoist. The Beech refueling store required a major overhaul. But the dragged hose and drogue were restored to flight operations without any maintenance except for removing grass divots from the "birdie's" bottom fingers.

Good Show Safety Award — This emergency incident was documented in the "CAF Flight Comment" Safety Magazine, and ultimately was the basis of my award by the Commander of Air Transport Group.

Maj. Charles Miller (USAF), receiving "GOOD SHOW" Safety Award Certificate from B/Gen Henry, CO, Air Transport Grp (RCAF) (1976)

Maj C.L. Miller

FOR AN OUTSTANDING CONTRIBUTION TO FLIGHT SAFETY, AN ACCOUNT OF WHICH APPEARED IN FLIGHT COMMENT AND IS TRANSCRIBED HEREUNDER

BOEING CC137

Maj Miller was Aircraft Commander of a CC137 tanker conducting an Air to Air Refuelling mission with four CF5 fighters. The mission proceeded uneventfully from home base of the fighters at CFB Bagotville until arrival over Rankin Inlet on the northwestern shore of Hudson's Bay, where the CF5s were to do a photo recce. While deploying the refuelling hoses for a final top-up prior to descent, the starboard boom and hose assembly extended to its maximum with a severe thump. Subsequent attempts to retract the hose were unsuccessful and the assembly remained jammed at approximately 32 feet extension.

The fighters were topped-up from the port refuelling pod, carried out their mission and were escorted back to home base using the port pod for enroute refuelling. After exhausting all possibilities to retract the boom and hose assembly and verifying the safe handling characteristics of the aircraft at approach speeds, Maj Miller and crew flew the tanker to home base and carried out a low approach and overshoot to allow visual examination of the jammed pod by technical personnel.

Maintenance personnel verified that nothing additional could be done to retract the assembly and emergency vehicles were alerted for the subsequent landing in the event that residual fuel in the hose caught fire. Maj Miller landed the aircraft to the right of the runway centerline, allowing the starboard wingtip and refuelling hose to extend over the grass, touching down and stopping so that the hose and refuelling basket did not make contact with any part of the runway. The skillful landing resulted in no damage to the aircraft, refuelling hose assembly or aerodrome lighting facilities.

Investigation revealed that the hose response strut had failed, causing the drogue assembly to travel, damaging and jamming the internal mechanism of the refuelling pod.

The resourcefulness and professional skill shown by Maj Miller and his crew in troubleshooting a serious in-flight emergency and in effecting a safe emergency landing deserves Service-wide recognition for a job well done.

Editor, Flight Comment

DFS.

"Good Show" Certificate presented by B/Gen Henry, Commander Air Transport Group (1976)

Canadian Air Traffic Control Induced A/R Crisis —

Here is just one example related to military aviation, how an obscure difference between US and Canadian ATC procedures led to an in-flight emergency involving a five aircraft, aerial refueling formation, and a potential International catastrophe. But first a little necessary background, would be appropriate to the story:

As a part of the Canadian Aerial Refueling development program, during my first two years, we would conduct a joint training session for tanker and fighter-receiver flight operations every six months, consisting of both ground school and in-flight exercises for two tanker crews (6– refueling qualified crew members for each tanker) and 8– fighter crews (1–pilot for each fighter). These training sessions would provide currency refresher training for those already qualified members, and opportunities to do initial qualification on new additional or replacement members. In between these typically 10– to 12–day duration, six-month trainings, we would periodically participate in international exercises into the US and trans-Atlantic round-trip missions into Europe staging through Goose Bay AFB (SAC), in Labrador, Newfoundland.

Initially, as previously described the first year or two of the Canadian aerial refueling program, we flew all our A/R missions as totally accompanied flight from take-off to landing. On this type of tanker-accompanied cross country flight, since the fighters had only a single voice communication radio, the tanker would maintain radio communications with Air Traffic Control (ATC) (on the tanker's number 1 radio), while the fighters and tanker would stay tuned in to a pre-determined *inter-plane* frequency (on the tanker's number 2 radio) for coordination of navigation info, fuel state, refueling brackets, refueling tactics, formation or gear and flap configuration changes, etc. In this manner, the tanker was the formation Leader and the tanker crew provided all navigation, ATC contacts, position reports, and was the "mother hen" for the fighters.

The fighter pilot's primary responsibility was to maintain proper formation position on the tanker and his wingmen. In this manner we could maintain required formation communications without congesting the traffic control airways with unnecessary chatter and distraction. Since there were six tanker crewmembers actively involved in the formation refueling and progress, and four fighters on the wing, the communications within the formation and among the crew could be intense and was very disciplined, particularly during critical stages of refueling.

Now for the details of this incident …

On one session in my second year during the winter months, we were holding our two-week training class at CFB Cold Lake, Alberta. At the end of the 2-week session, after all participants had flown about half a dozen training flights each, in the local training area. We planned to end the session with one tanker and four fighters on a day/night cross country flight from CFB Cold Lake to CFB Trenton, with the CF-5s to return (using auxiliary 'dead head" pilots carried outbound on the tanker. The CF-5s return to Cold Lake would be done in a couple shorter legs, without tanking the following day. Due to the short winter days, the last half of this approximately 5-hour, 1,800-mile flight, would terminate after nightfall, so it would be good example of many different mission environments and conditions.

The formation took-off during daylight, the fighters joined-up in "Vick" close formation, on the tanker wings during climb, before entering the clouds (which had been forecast). We found it necessary to level off below the intermediate overcast after take-off at about 6,000 feet, and remained at 250 knots until the "chicks" were all in formation on the tanker's wing, under the cloud bases. We then called our beginning climb and advanced throttles to climb power. To the stated amazement of the CF-5 pilots, they commented that our immediate acceleration was greater than their ability to stay on the wing, as they went into afterburners to try and keep up! We pulled away about a half mile in the climb before they were able to regain position. ***This was a very clear indication of how effectively the fan-engines moved a large mass of air***

very quickly, and substantially improved the performance of our "heavy jet", as compared to that of the non-fan turbojets that I had flown on the KC-135, as well as those used on most fighter engines, of the day (even though they had after burners to assist in their acceleration and total thrust).

The formation of 5-aircraft broke-out on top of the overcast cloud ceiling at about 12,000 feet in the climb (with tops increasing to about 25,000 feet, enroute), and we would cruise at 30,000 feet on top of a winter undercast. Once above the cloud tops, we conducted 3–refueling brackets across the route. During the initial portion of the flight, we had been in and out of the clouds at our 30,000 foot cruising altitude. After the third refueling was completed (about 3.5-hours into the flight, and darkness had arrived), we crossed from Winnipeg Center into the Toronto Center for Air Traffic Control and were cruising in Instrument Flight conditions (IFR) with formation clearance and an airspace "block' altitude reservation for the formation of FL270 to FL310 (27,000' to 31,000') as typical of all A/R formation flights, for inter-formation safety. This would ensure vertical separation in the event of need to quickly separate, especially during refueling and/or during join-up maneuvers.

Our approach conditions, at CFB Trenton, were forecast to have clear night conditions for the last 50 miles before landing. Inbound to Trenton we planned to start descent at 100 miles west of Trenton (just after passing Toronto) and would lead the Vick formation for an "accompanied approach" down to 1,000' elevation on final runway approach heading, at which time the tanker would level off and the fighters would have visual contact with the runway and take interval spacing as previously described for an "accompanied approach".

As we crossed into Toronto ATC and checked in on the new frequency, the new controller in Toronto Center (apparently an inexperienced controller to formation refueling operations) prepared to hand us off to Trenton Approach. We requested clearance to start an enroute descent for our approach to CFB Trenton. When he realized, shortly after the formation began descending into the clouds, that we were a formation of a tanker plus 4-receivers the Controller directed us to separate the formation *immediately* stating that Canadian Air Traffic Control regulations prohibited formations with more than 4-aircraft flying within controlled airspace. We informed him that we were in the clouds, and had already filed and been cleared as a tanker plus four "Chicks" with a 4,000 foot moving block of altitude. We had already obtained the necessary authorizations. Further, that we could not break up the formation for safety and control reasons. But he kept insisting!

As mission Commander, I then informed him that if he insisted, we would attempt to accommodate him, but not immediately, because if we broke up the formation we would have to first reposition all fighters on the same side of the tanker while descending through clouds (for their departure from the tanker-lead formation), and then would have to obtain new and separate flight plan clearances for each of the fighter aircraft, and obtain a new radar transponder code for each to be tracked by ATC and Approach radars (we had the only transponder turned on at that time). I explained that we would then switch them over individually from inter-plane frequency to the desired ATC frequency with their new flight clearance and current position in hand. Additionally, we would have to give each fighter his current position information (relative to Trenton, heading and distance) and current navigation radio frequencies, because they were flying using the tanker's navigation, not ground or radio aid reference info. As I was negotiating these points with the uncompromising and uninformed ATC controller, I heard a loud roar off our right wing followed by an immediate Mayday call from #3 fighter (closest on our right wing), stating that he had experienced a sudden loss of airspeed, a stall warning alarm, an abrupt pitch down and a cockpit full of warning lights and alarms. As he declared his emergency to us, he had instinctively gone into after burner on both engines, and was pulling ahead of the formation rapidly "trying to regain safe airspeed and separation"! By standard protocol, #4 stayed on his wing. Talk about a busy couple of minutes in our cockpit, not to mention theirs.

A few moments later, the #1 fighter (closest on our left wing) experienced the same symptoms and circumstances, and broke away from the tanker formation, with his wingman (#2) in after-burners!

It took only a few moments for our (the tanker's) refueling Controller (tactical Flight Engineer), to figure what was going on. He correctly diagnosed that the two aircraft (Fighter lead #1, and Section Lead #3) were both "photo recce" configured birds, with camera-noses, which had different Pitot-static system configurations than the other two wingmen (which had only machine guns rather than cameras in the nose). Our Flight Engineer assessed that the likely issue was that moisture had accumulated in the Pitot system (airspeed measurement system) on the two camera equipped CF-5s on our descent through the clouds, and that when we descended into warmer atmosphere, accumulated ice had been ingested into their "pitot" tubes causing a blockage, which in turn falsely indicated loss of airspeed and impending stall. This in-turn had caused the low-airspeed stall warning alarm and had shutdown the two camera-nosed CF-5's stability augmentation system (SAS). This cascading sequence shifted to "slow-speed flight" mode – causing much greater elevator and aileron control surface movements resulting in over control of pitch inputs from their pilot's – not to mention the added distraction of all the additional alarms and warning lights.

Had these fighter pilots been aware of this potential and more proficient with refueling formation (especially at night and in-and-out of clouds) with the tanker, they would have fought their natural instinct to go into after-burner and try to gain airspeed. Because they were flying formation on the "big bird", they should have realized that if the tanker was not stalling, then they certainly were not! It was an instinctive trained response! And adding another degree of confusion, since they were flying at night and with "mother hen" doing all their navigation, and ground radio contact for them, they had been in isolation without awareness of the ATC situation being created, and without "situational awareness about their own location on the map".

As the two sections of the fighter formation, sequentially went into after-burner and pulled away from the tanker leaving us behind while we were descending, we were frantically passing Toronto Center frequency and radar transponder codes to the fighters. Fighter #3 and #4, which had been "formated" in echelon on our right wing when the incident started, ended up over a big illuminated "unknown city" (Rochester, NY) and had entered US air space with no clearance, and were "lost", not knowing what city they were over, nor its immediate location relative to Trenton. Only their "emergency" transponder squawk averted an airspace violation and possible collision with other known civil air traffic.

As Toronto Center established radio and radar contact with the four fighters – paired together, but each two flying in a different direction and altitude, they handed off #3 and #4 to New York Center in a minimum fuel state, and vectored the other two into CFB Trenton airspace where the base Approach radar made contact and vectored them into safe emergency landings. Unfortunately, the second CF-5 to land (#2 wingman) blew a tire on landing, which closed the runway until the ground team could tow it off the runway. Subsequently the other two, were also vectored back into Canadian airspace and were vectored to CFB Trenton, as well. Although we had already been cleared to approach and had proceeded to descend to 5,000 feet, (with plenty of fuel on board) we coordinated a delay for our approach until all CF-5s were recovered, in case we were needed to upload them with some additional fuel. It turned out that behind us about 10 miles, also holding in a pattern at 5000' above ground on an extended final approach east of Trenton's runway, while awaiting landing clearance, behind the four emergency recoveries and the Boeing 707 tanker ahead, was the CFB Trenton Commanding General piloting the military "corporate" FalconJet. Needless to say he was alarmed and requested a meeting with me while airborne for an update after he landed.

The next day, after my debriefing, he filed a formal complaint through Canadian National Defence HQ against Toronto ATC for setting off this fiasco. And I ended up on a two-week "air tour" briefing each of the major ATC Centers across Canada on the newly acquired aerial refueling mission, its tactics, procedures, and safety implications, and providing improvement in the awareness of air traffic control knowledge of aerial refueling priorities and safety considerations.

This precipitated Canadian ATC rule changes that accepted more than 5-aircraft when in refueling formations, and precipitated regulations more aligned with US ATC procedures for better integrating and upgrading communications with the centers and the local approach controls so that each had advance notification of what was coming their way, rather than an unexpected hand-off only at the time of control area transitions.

We all learned the importance of making sure that all formation aircraft were keeping up with their position and enroute electronic nav-aids and Center frequencies along their flight path. And fortunately, due to the cool heads of the inflight refueling tanker crews and the four-fighter wingmen, major accidents were averted and no International airspace violations were processed. Canadian air traffic control had finally arrived into the 20th Century!

CAF Training/Public Relations Film — In order to improve the efficiency of Aerial Refueling Flight Training, it was apparent that conducting initial training with hand-drawn graphics on a white-board during ground school was "less than adequate". So with my Squadron CO, Col Max H's assistance, I collaborated with the National Military Film Board of Canada to produce a training film that would give the pilots a more visual look at the operation from many different viewpoints. The result was a 35-minute sound and color training movie, which had the dual purpose of including both PR (community public relations) and training. The film was titled ***"Operation High Test"***, with the opening scene of a "tasking order" to deploy 4 CF-5s to a NATO Base in Norway via a trans-Atlantic A/R mission following the preparations and the detailed flight activities including accompanied-formation take-off to final landing in Europe. Imbedded inside this script was a flight training segment, which displayed the classroom situation followed by a pilot's-eye view of A/R, the tanker-receiver interactions and coordination, and the technical aspects of hose-drogue refueling from wing-tip mounted equipment, (using the graphics and film footage described in the previous several pages).

To my amazement, the movie required tremendous resources for the inflight filming segments including the use of several dual-cockpit chase aircraft for the exterior photography, interior camera positions from the CF-5 pilot's perspective, and views from inside the tanker. It filmed scenes using footage of both CF-5 squadrons as well as both tanker aircraft. Several distractions were discovered at the time of editing because one receiver squadron's pilots wore white helmets; the other wore orange. One squadron's aircraft were equipped with dual drop tanks; the other used single center-line drop tanks. And over the extended 18 months of filming, the background changed from summer to winter and back. These all contributed to a lot of technical inconsistencies that had to be edited out of the "enroute mission-portion" of the film, due to the single-day timeline for the flight from Canada to Norway and created a lot of wasted film on the cutting-room floor.

During and after the 18 months of filming, it required another 3-months of music, scripting, audio editing, and production time with a total of more than 60-hours of filming to produce an integrated and technically continuous film of only 35-minutes duration.

Observed proven results of this video training tool were remarkable. In the earlier training, as mentioned, a receiver pilot initially would require as many as five or more attempts to make their first successful A/R contact and fuel transfer. In classes, using the training film, an average of about 65% of new CF-5 pilot trainees were successful on the first or second contact attempt. This substantially increased their confidence that it could be easily done with the several new perspectives they had gained from seeing the film. It reduced the amount of flying time to achieve training goals. And they could also preview the film prior to the commencement of the training course, for additional preview insight.

CAF Air Refueling Procedures and Tactics Manual — Another major accomplishment was my responsibility to compose a formal Canadian Armed Forces Aerial Refueling Manual, as an illustrated reference and training guide. It took me over six months to complete this detailed task, describing every unique aspect of tanker and receiver refueling operations, including those detailed in this book; (Some of which were still being developed or refined). All the while, I was performing my other conventional transport scheduled flying, as well as A/R duties and operations. These details included explanatory drawings of each of the various formation positions, describing standardized and emergency maneuvers and the precise protocols to be used between receiver aircraft and tankers. This approximate 150-page document (published under Canadian military formats and regulations) was then translated into a duplicate, illustrated French version, which was co-printed back-to-back, into the same binding as the English version (by our administrative personnel), and formed the basis of all aerial refueling operations in the CAF for the decade to follow.

[This Canadian Exchange assignment had proven to be my "most fun" and probably the most rewarding flying assignment due to the very much expanded opportunity for global travel and the substantially increased authority responsibility and higher level of experience.]

Chief of Defence Commendation Award —

At the culmination of my extended three-year tour with the Canadian Armed Forces, I was honored for my service by General Dextraze the top ranking 4-star Canadian general. This award (shown below). was presented to me by CAF Maj. General G.A. McKenzie, Chief of Air Doctrine and Operations. The presentation was accomplished in the office of USAF Brigadier General Pete Piotrowski, Commander of the 552nd AWACS Wing Headquarters, at Tinker AFB, OK. The Canadian team making the presentation arrived with a one-day notice at Tinker AFB several months after my reassignment from Canada. The arrival of a Joint Canadian/USAF AWACS contingent arrived on an AWACS aircraft from Cheyenne Mountain, Colorado, the North American Aerospace Defense (NORAD) Command Headquarters,

Up to that time, only once previously had this award ever been made to a non–Canadian Military Member! I was permitted to retain this foreign recognition by HQ USAF and to wear it on my USAF uniform for all occasions.

A somewhat unique, and proud moment —

The 552nd AWACS Wing was the largest active duty "tenant" on the Oklahoma City Air Logistic Center, where I was then assigned. Tinker AFB and the Logistics Center (where I was assigned was commanded by a Lt. General. But the NORAD AWACS with numerous Canadian senior Generals wanted to present the award in the Commander's office, of the highest operational flying unit, the AWACS Wing, and I was requested to appear in dress blues for the presentation, along with an entourage of OCALC senior officers (also in dress blues).

However, the Canadian generals were in their Class B short–sleeve uniforms on the arriving AWACS aircraft. Due my prior direct personal contact with these Canadian officers, through my A/R responsibilities, and the smaller and less formal environment of the Canadian Armed Forces, they greeted me with an informal "Hi Chuck!" upon entering the USAF Wing Commander's "blue suited" formal setting, much to the amazement of Tinker's senior contingent. This provided me quite an auspicious recognition!

USAF Lt. Col. selectee, Chuck Miller receiving Commendation, presented by CAF Maj. Gen. McKenzie in Ceremony at Tinker AFB.

The Chief of the Defence Staff
The Canadian Armed Forces

commends

Major C.L. Miller USAF
437 Transport Squadron

In recognition of his outstanding contribution to the Canadian Forces Air Refuelling Program whilst on exchange duties with the Canadian Forces. Major Miller's leadership, resourcefulness and professional skill have greatly aided the Canadian Forces' accident free air refuelling operations in both staff and operational functions. Major Miller is a credit to his country and to the United States Air Force.

Ottawa Canada
August, 1976

Chief of the Defence Staff

Canadian Chief of Defence Staff Commendation

CDS Commendation 3-Oak Leaf Device

CHAPTER 7

"Flying A Desk" — AF Logistics Command

Reassignment to OCALC, Tinker AFB, OK (1976 – '81)

In the final days of my Canadian assignment, my name was published on the USAF list of selectees to Lt. Colonel. Military Personnel Center (MPC) contacted me to ask what type assignment I wanted upon leaving Canada. I knew that my window of opportunity to attempt to reclaim the formerly offered AFIT assignment for a degree in Industrial Engineering, had passed. So I first suggested a Tanker Squadron commander assignment in SAC. The SAC Personnel response was that I had been out of their system too long (three years) and expressed no interest in my returning in a Commander's capacity, and my promotion made me too senior to return to a basic cockpit assignment.

I had worked on several development programs in Canada, as an adviser to Boeing as they pursued more 707 tanker sales to foreign allies and I suggested to USAF's Personnel Office that my aeronautical engineering and technical experience might be of interest to Air Force Systems Command (the command responsible for most USAF Research and Development of aircraft and systems). Systems Command Personnel responded similarly to SAC, that I already had too much rank with no Systems Command experience to be brought in as an a entry-level candidate.

I then proposed that assignment to the Oklahoma City Air Logistic Center (OCALC), at Tinker AFB, in the C/KC-135 Weapon System Management Office (aircraft fleet maintenance, modifications and logistics), might be a good match for my extensive experience in KC-135 and Boeing 707 operations and management. That suggestion was accepted, and put into motion.

The OCALC was one of five huge air logistic industrial centers scattered around the ConUS, with OCALC being the largest under the AF Logistics Command's HQ. Each had a working and management population of around twenty to 22,000 employees in residence, of which typically 95% were Civil Service engineers, technicians, logistics experts, and administrators (also known as "bean-counters"), and five percent were USAF uniformed personnel that formed the interface between the industrial/corporate complex, and the military operational users of the aircraft and equipment. Each Center had a large industrial base, which included aircraft, engine, and equipment overhaul, refurbishment and systems modifications responsibilities, as well as worldwide logistic support for their assigned "weapons systems" (i.e. individual multi-command global aircraft fleets) and subcontract management of thousands of large and small vendors. The Logistic Center as the parent unit of Tinker AFB also had numerous other USAF units co-located there, the largest flying unit there was the USAF's only AWACS Wing (Airborne Warning and Control System). There are also numerous other USAF National Guard and other services tenants located there.

While in "transient leave" getting my housing and family relocated to the Tinker AFB area, I was working on getting my new home, in an adjacent subdivision to the base, organized. I was called in to the Center by the Colonel heading up the Engine Division. He made a strong plea for me to join his organization under urgent need. I told him that I knew a whole lot more about the KC-135 aircraft and its operations and issues, to which I had already been assigned, than I did about its related engines. In response to his request, however, I agreed to become the J-57 Engine Manager (used on the KC-135 tankers, B-52 bombers, F-100 and other "Century Series" fighters, in various configurations -- some with after-burners, etc.). Once on that job, I soon found myself as nothing more than a "Blue Suit go-between" while the Civil Servant bureaucrats made all the decisions and held tightly onto their historic knowledge of airframe and systems issues and logistic resources. After 90-days (by Jan '77) of being in a job without a substantial purpose, I negotiated with the Directorate's senior Colonel, to get myself transferred back to the C/KC-135 Organization where I believed I could make a more substantial contribution. In that assignment I would be third in the line of succession, while still wearing Major's oak-leaves on my collar (but Lt. Col. selection "already in my pocket"). The non-pilot Lt. Col in the #2 slot was within a few months of retirement, so upward mobility seemed soon to be available.

During my prior assignment (1968-'73) with the KC-135Q at Beale AFB, my primary focus had been on learning all about the tanker operational side of the mission and mastering my operational and tanker flying skills, then passing those skills and knowledge by instructing younger upcoming pilots and crewmembers. I had since accrued nearly 2000 logged pilot hours in the KC-135Q, which included over 25% as Instructor Pilot, and another 1550 pilot hours subsequently logged in 707-tankers, which included a similar percentage of Instructor Pilot hours in the Canadian 707 transport operations with "hose-and drogue" aerial refueling major responsibilities. Now I was about to gain an in-depth knowledge and responsibility for keeping the USAF tanker fleet operational and implementing new systems and modifications from my exposure to the operational tanker mission and capabilities of the newer and more capable Boeing 707-300 aircraft from my Canadian refueling operations. The KC-135 fleet, at that time, was in its 15th year in-service while I was flying it. It was now approaching its 25th anniversary as I entered the Weapon System Management of this fleet.

Structural Integrity Crisis – Wing Reskin Program — As I checked into the C/KC-135 Weapon System Management unit (in Jan '77), I found they were in the throes of a New Year's holiday crisis. One of the Washington DC based, VIP VC-135 passenger haulers was in Boeing for PDM (periodic depot maintenance) and an inspection had found two of three main wing spars with having major structural cracks – a major crash potential just waiting to happen, due to inflight wing failure! This particular airplane had one of the highest flight-times logged in the C/KC-135 fleet, but otherwise was in excellent cosmetic condition expected of VIP aircraft. However, the nature of carrying around Congressional and higher VIPs, and incurring a much greater frequency of take-offs and landings than most tanker aircraft, created a panic regarding the structural integrity of the entire 20-plus year old C/KC-135 fleet of nearly 760 aircraft. This made the tankers, which typically had only 65% of the flying time (8,000 hours) compared to the VCs, but were routinely operating at 35% heaver take-off gross weights, and many fewer landing cycles, caused especially more concern. This created a very strong threat that the entire C-135 fleet (which included C-135s, VC-135s, RC-135s, EC-135s, WC-135s, and NC-135s) and KC-135 tankers (by far the largest group, with 630 of the total fleet) could have major weight restrictions imposed, or even total grounding, until the problem could be inspected, analyzed, tested and a long-term, highly-costly structural fix implemented.

OCALC high-level management convened a high level ad-hoc engineering committee, consisting of members from the senior structural engineering leaders of Boeing, Lockheed, MacDonald-Douglas, ASD (Aircraft Systems Directorate, of Systems Command), and the Senior Civil Service Engineering Director and engineering team from Tinker. In recognition of my experience flying the KC-135 and my aeronautical engineering degree (with a major in aircraft structures) combined with my flight safety experience, I was selected as the (Administrative) Chairman for the committee, which also made me the "Face to the Blue-Suit community" for all briefings, "show and tells" and status reports of the problem with interim, as well as final resolution status-keeping. This meant I had become middle-man for keeping everybody at the top of the 10 Major Commands fully informed, which were operating the various -135 variants of the fleet. Their major concern: ***Grounding or major operating restrictions, telegraphed the***

potential crises to ALL users – "No gas passed = No weapons on target; loss of critical enemy surveillance and intelligence; and severe reductions in flight crew and maintenance proficiency and training AND the overall impact on military readiness!", not to mention the impending budget priorities and time resources to make the needed fixes.

I began to realize that the differences between the commercial 707 fleet and the KC-135 fleet were far more than differences in power plants, paint schemes, number of passenger windows and physical dimensions (and seating). I discovered that, at the time of the initial KC-135 development, the technology was still fairly simplistic. Boeing and USAF engineers had selected higher strength structural materials for the tanker wing structure by selection of 7178-T6 Aluminum for the lower wing skins – a material that was described as "stronger than stainless steel" – as compared to the materials used in the commercial 707 wings made of 2024, T-4 Aluminum, which had much longer "anti-fatigue" structural life. This decision was made upon recognition that fuel weight is significantly greater than traditional cargo and/or passengers. And translated to the comparison that the KC-135 had a maximum take-off weight of 301,600 pounds compared to the same –sized 707-720 of 275,000 pounds (which followed the KC-135 design by 2-years). This resulted into the higher wing-strength structure of the KC-135 being "less fatigue resistant" (i.e. was more brittle") and had an initially tested wing life of about 10,000 flight hours, as compared to the early 707 wing that looked identical, but had a tested fatigue life of 40,000 hours!

The problem manifested itself by nature that the fatigue properties of 7178 Aluminum lower wing skin used on the KC-135 (and other C-135 variations) from wingtip-to-wingtip was such that should a fatigue crack developed at a rivet hole, in the area of "wet-wing" fuel tanks, in many instances could "go critical" with less than a 1/8" crack development before the crack reached the edge of the rivet head (which could then cause a visible seepage at the rivet), but then over a potentially very brief time could continue to jump or "zip" to the next and then the next rivet, precipitating a catastrophic and near-instantaneous inflight failure. Ground inspection would often show a wet rivet, telling the inspectors that a crack had formed under the rivet head, and alert them to a potential impending major crack development, so repairs could be performed, immediately. However, in the center-wing area, it was not a wet wing fuel tank, but rather a bladder tank, plus the belly fairing concealed the visibility of any leaks unless removed (a major removal which occurred only during major depot maintenance, every three-to-five years).

Secondly, the reference to this being a "wing re-skinning program" creates a false impression of what the "wing-skin" in question really is. It is NOT just a contoured sheet of 1/16th inch aluminum wrapped around spars, stiffeners, frames, and ribs. It originally consisted of 29-panels of chemically milled and tapered panels that continuously varied in thickness from approximately ¾ inch to less-than ¼ inch with multiple splice joints and additional stiffeners at the butt joints. The replacement design took advantage of 15-year newer technology, which could now accommodate much longer skin fabrication lengths, with the end result being a reduction of the chem-milled panels to four on each side (from fuselage to outboard engine pylon), and five each across the belly to the wing attach points (13 total panels), all of which eliminated multiple butt-joint seams and stiffeners (structural weak points).

This was a very ingenious solution, which had already been under design and testing for several years by Boeing Military engineers. Since the interior of each wing consists of a number of "wet-wing" fuel tanks, the initial options to a "fix" were to either add additional skin thickness and interior stiffening to accommodate the lower strength of substituted 2024 Aluminum, thus reducing the wing-tanks' fuel capacity to that similar to the 707 design, **or** in the "worst case scenario", to enlarge the wing thickness on the outside to maintain original internal fuel capacity (a total upper wing skin and structural refabrication) and force the test and recertification of the aerodynamics and structural life of a drastically new wing design.

The picture in yellow, below, reflects the area of the "lower wing skin", and reduced number of panels that were replaced.

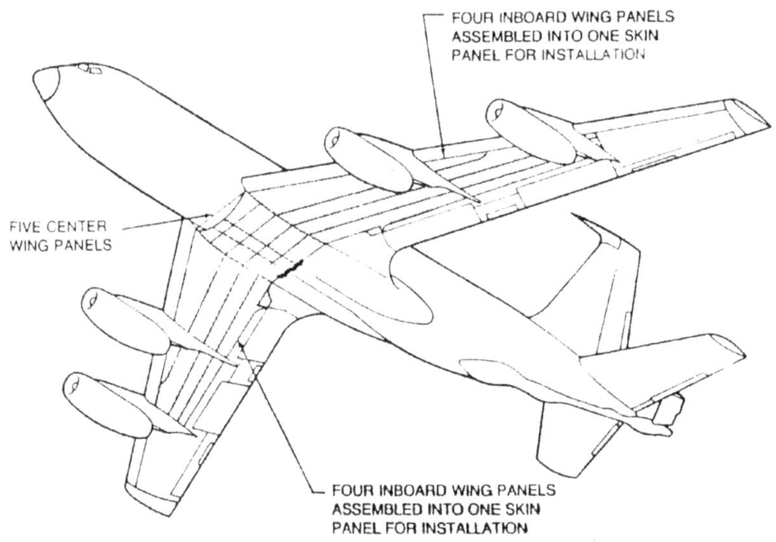

C/KC-135 Wing Reskin (ECP 405)

The committee's work took several months to develop an accelerated recommendation of action, while our technicians and engineers implemented a relatively inexpensive center wing acoustic crack detection system, and increased the detailed mission structural records for every tail number as interim help in knowing which aircraft needed fixes or specific inspections the soonest. In the end the committee recommended complete lower wing skin replacement (as shown in yellow above) on every KC-135 and every C-135 of every different special mission category using common structure – representing a fleet of over 750 aircraft -- (as described above, this accelerated a program which Boeing had already initiated and was under development, was only at first aircraft prototyping and test). After some analysis Boeing made a proposal for <u>their best efficiency</u> that would complete this modification (which initially required about 1-year per aircraft to complete) at a maximum rate of 30 aircraft per month. This would mean that at any point during production up to over 200 aircraft — 1/3rd of the fleet – at any given time), would be out of service for many months! This would mean not only a great financial cost per year, but that major wartime capabilities would be severely degraded (tankers and their receivers). My analysis – in coordination with the 10 user commands – concluded that four to six aircraft a month, would be an optimum compromise (accounting for build-up and overlap each month) and could be worked without totally destroying the aircraft mission capability — of all variations. Also a major Air Force budget constraint required spreading out the financial impact over many years. At the final rate recommend by the committee (6-aircraft input per month), this meant the wing re-skin program was projected to require over 12 years to complete (starting up in 1976 and completing in 1988), at a projected cost of over half a billion total "then- year" dollars!

As part of my job, I was tasked to prepare detailed white papers for Congressional staffers, and detailed briefings for all the 10-user commands, and Logistic Command and System Command, and the Pentagon up through the 4-star level, culminating after a multitude of dry-runs and refinements to a final compacted 1-hour personal "decision" briefing by me to the Secretary of the Air Force (SecAF), John Stetson for final approval. In preparation for this final briefing I drew upon a background resource of hundreds of multi-layer overhead-projection charts and graphics (before computers and PowerPoint), which I had adopted and used for the preceding working level and up-to 4-star briefings. My final briefing, hopefully, had to anticipate every possible question and be prepared to cover it – before it was asked in the presentation – and then have the answers, at my fingertips for instant response for anything that I had not included (or failed to consider in the decision process) in the presentation. I successfully completed my briefing in one hour and fifteen minutes, including Q&A, with the SecAF, achieving his concurrence with the detailed plan we had proposed and its operational and budget impact.

With the usual delays and changes in direction and priorities, this program was not completed until nearly a decade after my retirement. Of all the hundreds of briefings I had to prepare and deliver, there was only one — the one to the SecAF — that I ever had to have totally memorized (by repetition of many, many "dry-runs"), that compressed about 4-hours of detailed material, into less than an hour, and was achieved without one un-answered question by the SecAF.

Worthy of highlighting; all of these activities and responsibilities created multitudes of 60 to 80 hour work weeks, hundreds of written reports and white papers, preparation of dozens of detailed presentations and briefings with many trips all over the US informing the using commands of the status of the issue and fixes that were being contemplated so they could be informed and be making work-arounds for the contingencies that this issue created in their funding, scheduling, and numbers of aircraft remaining mission capable. These elevated work requirements and heavy involvement in resolution preoccupied nearly all my first 18-months in the new job. ***[My "higher guidance" had placed me exactly where I was most needed, at exactly the right time!]***

Introduction to Military Budgeting, and "Super Skirt"— As a byproduct of the above major USAF structural integrity crisis, I became involved in dialogue with the Pentagon in formulating an urgent un-budgeted funding requirement to immediately start-up the consequential structural repairs on the –135 fleet. Normal DoD military budgeting (in those years – and maybe still?) is a four-year long process. The military organizations first define what funds and resources are needed for them to accomplish their mission tasking (as tasked from the top down). In an ideal world this would involve the "operators" to define a "Statement of Needs" (a Requirement) followed by a "draft statement of work" in detail, defining what a provider/contractor would do and a specification of what their product "would perform and how it could be measured/evaluated". This in itself is a "humongous" and time-consuming task. *[Often times, the <u>Need</u> was very undefined, or a provider had discovered/invented some new and unknown technology with a capability that preceded the defined "need". This meant that in those cases, the provider/contractor would develop the Statement of Need <u>and</u> the Statement of work, as well as the definition of the Specifications.]* All these things would go into a "hopper" and be regurgitated by all the experts in the Pentagon down through the users, and ultimately to the Congress for the necessary funding.

Along the way, each element of the budget line item is relegated within the Pentagon to the specific military services (Army, Navy, Air Force, etc…) budget segments, and each service establishes a ranking or priority of where this line item (or program) fits into the overall portion of their "budget priority-pie". The Pentagon planners, by near the end of each Fiscal Year, will have developed a lengthy list of all the programs by relative priority of <u>mission</u> importance, which identifies the potential cost of each, projected out incrementally over the next four years, (and on into the future, as best speculated). This list also includes all of the items currently underway from prior year incompleted funding cycles, which are integrated into each annual total budget pie.

When the next year's budget "pot" is released by Congress to the Pentagon (and all other federal agencies with their portions and priorities specified), each agency then determines the size of their "portion of the pie" and runs down their established list until the total amount of funding runs out, and everything "below the line" on the list is either cancelled or postponed until the following year's cycle (in theory). *[In actuality, there is often a renegotiating of the line-up of priorities, and even formerly approved programs are adjusted, slowed, or cancelled to accommodate approval of new programs or higher priorities. In reality when you place an order for 100 aircraft (for example) delivered over a one year time period, the benefits of scale in cost, changes the cost of the project. (i.e. If the 100 per year rate cost $10 Million for each aircraft, reducing the number to 50 aircraft will cause each to cost substantially more, and would only represent maybe a 20% – rather than the simplistic 50% – savings due to cost of tooling,* *manpower and industrial facilities that is already sunk for the higher rate of production and materials.)]*

In the USAF (during my management responsibilities, 1976-1981), there was a specific office in the Pentagon for the USAF Weapons Systems Project Control. It was headed up by a very senior ranking Civil Servant who maintained knowledge and records for the budgetary details on virtually every USAF Weapons System (loosely defined as "fleets of like Aircraft"). She managed all of this with a huge three-ring-bound notebook(s) that was at least 6-inches thick detailing all the major upgrades, modifications, and periodic maintenance for each Weapon System, their over-all priorities in the bigger funding picture, and all of the break-downs of timing, cost, and mission. Her name is long-gone from my memory, but she was known in my "community" as **"Super Skirt"**, and she was either hated or loved depending on whether you were an intimidated and uninformed "faithful subject", or a strong and credible advocate for your own areas of responsibility. In my world with a 750 aircraft fleet that was very critical to USAF mission capability, second to only a very few, my Weapon System, without prior projection, had suddenly been elevated to the top of her misery index.

Budgeting with a Crystal Ball and Fuzzy Requirements; Winglets—

An example of how this budgeting process can be counter-productive was a Program Initiative, of which my organization was a participant. In the late '70s, there was a major push going on to focus on saving fuel. After Boeing and other technical agencies had done much research on different aeronautical methods to reduce fuel consumption, NASA, working with Boeing were looking for a good "proof of concept" vehicle to develop the "winglet program" upon, and the KC-135 aircraft was selected as a large base of aircraft which could be used at a "minimal cost per aircraft" to get the ball rolling. Conceptual analysis showed that the use of an 8 to 10 foot vertical winglet, added to each wingtip, would produce up to 10% fuel savings. Studies had shown that winglets created an "air-flow" fence that reduced wing-tip vortices on swept wing "heavy-lift" aircraft, thus reducing drag while adding lift. (Beyond this brief description, I will not try to further explain the why and how this really works. My focus here is explaining Budget practices, with this example.)

KC-135 NASA Winglet Test Bed with Instrumentation Probe

Since we were providing the test bed aircraft, OCALC decided to obtain aircraft modification cost data to consider this as a fleet-wide modification, should this prove successful and cost-effective as a future fleet modification cost.

Since the flight test data proved the scope of fuel savings, we solicited a cost determination for this modification based on our 700–plus potential aircraft fleet size. Boeing submitted planning cost (assuming they would be the kit producer and installer) and gave us preliminary cost quote in the range (as I recall) of about $60,000 per aircraft. (Certainly NOT peanuts, but with a viable big payback and reasonable cost recovery period). We used their quote as the basis for budgetary planning, and installation schedule timing (time per air craft to retrofit) into the future years to obtain funds. The program was funded by the Pentagon, beginning (as I recall) beginning in the late '70s; (Remembering the 4-year budget lead-time before funds would finally be available for start-up.

As the proof-of-concept flight tests drew to a successful close, Boeing had discovered that though the fuel savings expectations were achieved, that the retrofit cost was not as inexpensive as first believed. [If you look closely at the above photo, you will notice the extreme flexure upward on the wing(s) that addition of the winglets created. This in-turn reflects the substantial rebuild of the outer wing beyond the outer engine(s) as well as the connecting structure required to carry this added lifting load, without degrading structural wing life.

The resulting update to the budgetary planning cost was on the order of $2 million each (vs. $60,000) for the modification and installation, per aircraft. The point being, as you can see, that substantial budgetary machination takes place in the prioritization of funds and the rate of installation over long-term years, across many inter-competing aircraft weapons systems. This type of disruption and change in funding makes the budget-planners very upset when the "rob from Peter to pay Paul's" concept is in play, and causes great grief to those on both sides of the process.

[And in short, that is why you see winglets on most newer large commercial and military transport aircraft, but not on the KC-135 fleet – it is much easier and less expensive to build it with them on, than to retrofit them to an existing aircraft – not to mention the major disruption in the late budgetary scramble for priorities and funds!]

Back to the wing reskin application — After working very hard, in consult with all the 4-star Commanders and their staffs of the ten Operational Commands and Agencies to fine-tune an acceptable level of annual aircraft with wing reskinning over a 10-year or longer program, I was also doing a "management battle" with Boeing Military as the prime contractor for the wing re-skin program. I had been keeping Ms. Super Skirt in the loop on all the back and forth adjustments in the -135 priorities (including many other numerous funded life-extension improvements and efficiency mods on the -135 fleet, for equipment upgrades and their priorities) totaling in the billions of program-budget dollars. She in turn was doing a remarkable effort trying to wedge these newly critically identified -135 wing-reskin expenditures into her "Master Book", which involved "robbing from Peter to pay Paul" from critical B-52 bomber upgrades, and fighter fleet mods, and transport aircraft improvements, most reflecting the wear-and-tear of the recently ended Vietnam war. Through these ongoing machinations of available funds and priorities, my office received a grossly overstated budget proposal from Boeing Military for the newly implemented structural fleet "wing re-skin" program. After a very cursory level analysis on my part, I challenged Boeing's cost proposal based upon the fact that the outrageous cost was based upon their calculations of obtaining a large quantity of aluminum alloy billets used in the machining and manufacturing of the new lower wing skin structures. This required funding was for "long lead-time materials" needed for finished parts materials list items well in advance of each specific aircraft input to the modification schedule. My analysis showed that the number of billets that they identified as needed weighed more than 200% of the **total aircraft weight** of the number of aircraft that were to use the material, and challenged them to defend their numbers (and/or levels of scrap in manufacturing). They obviously realized they had been caught either over-padding the needed resources, or incredibly poor calculation of the resources needed. After several weeks they responded with a drastically reduced proposal cost and said it was an honest error in calculations.

When I informed "Super Skirt" of our revised (corrected) numbers, she was livid because she had already "robbed Peter to pay Paul" in several other Weapons Systems units, at the expense of this earlier "emergency" budget submittal. I politely reminded her that the error was not mine, but rather Boeing's, and that I was not willing to be "punished, or ostracized" because we had done our proper oversight and negotiations to minimize being over-charged. This singular event changed the total attitude of our relationship for the rest of my time in that assignment, and I had an enviable reputation with her that few other Weapons System Managers in all of Logistics Command could boast. This was seen in the very high marks my organization received from her office at each annual program budgetary review from the Pentagon.

[Senior managers cannot make good decisions if they don't have detailed long-term insight into the myriad of details of the problem. Do you remember "Lasting Leadership Example" from my first assignment at O'Hare in Chapter 3? It was the source of my actions, here.]

Additional Weapon System Manager Responsibilities—

In addition to my Wing Reskin "kick start" to my Logistics career. I was in charge of management and "marketing" (to Higher Headquarters) on most of the Major aircraft modifications suggested or requested for implementation on the SAC specific tankers, and in some cases the entire fleet. These included **Structural Integrity** mods *[Acoustic Crack Detection System; four fleet-wide, time-phased fatigue packages]*; **Electronic and Avionics** systems upgrades, *[Addition of Inertial Nav System, Doppler Nav System; Fuel Savings Advisory System (FSAS); Boom Interphone (tanker to receiver intercom when connected in flight); Fuel Control Panel Redesign & Upgrade; Radar & TACAN solid state upgrade programs; Upgraded VHF & AM/FM Radios, HF Radio Upgrade]*; **Tanker Capability Development & Enhancement** programs [*Initial R&D on KC-135 Winglet Program; Addition of Female Aircrew Latrine Facilities]*. For a fleet size of 750 aircraft, these major modification programs had individual multi-year budgets ranging from $1 million to $520 million and involving anywhere from 2-years to as many as 14-years to complete!

I also had oversight and liaison responsibility for structural tracking of fleet operational hours and take-off and landing cycles – by individual aircraft tail number, and scheduling of the 4-Year cyclic **Periodic Depot Maintenance (PDM)** overhaul programs; and tail number scheduling of structural mods on the basis of "worst case wear, comes first". I also performed quarterly duties as Primary Representative of Logistic Command and Co-sponsor of the ARSAG (Aerial Refueling Systems Advisory Group); an organization composed of all military inflight refueling operations – domestic multi-service and Allied countries – with an effort to standardize systems and specifications between all manufacturers and operators, and making every effort to maintain a sufficient mission capability (measured on "Equivalent Booms in the Air) to fulfill the US military requirement to fight an all-out war with use of aerial refueling, on two fronts simultaneously.

By the end of 1977, the second-in-command of the unit (previously described) had retired, and the Col heading the unit had been reassigned leaving me to single-handedly (blue-suit) perform the O-6 (full-colonel) duties of Weapon System Manager (WSM). During the remaining 3-years, I had several short periods of a different newly arrived SAC Colonel, that would "take over command" for a few months (to get a check mark on their experience card) and then move on while I maintained the continuity as "Col. USAF Tanker" expertise for Logistics Command, and the USAF.

Make no mistake. I do not suggest nor claim to have done all this single-handedly. But, as the C/KC135 Weapon System Manager, I headed up and had responsibility for leading and directing a Civil Service organization of more than 250 engineers, logistic specialists, technical documentation specialists, analysts, and administrative personnel, some dedicated to this fleet and some shared across commonalities with other aircraft and weapon systems. I had contractual and financial control responsibilities over a multitude of civilian contractors up to and including Boeing Military (airframe) and Pratt & Whitney (engines) and interface with 7 Major Using Commands, (plus NASA, US Navy, and The National Guard Bureau), involving aircraft support on 54 US and overseas Bases, and 27 unique and different Mission Designated Series (M/D/S) configurations. All involving an annual budget in my office in-excess of $1 Billion then-year dollars, and in conjunction with negotiations, dialog, and reporting to various branches of the Pentagon and other intermediate Higher Headquarters Commands (HHQ) and Congressional Staffers.

KC-135R Re-engining; CFM-56, (Beginning 1978) —

Most notable (after wing re-skin) of major aircraft modifications for the tanker fleet "under my watch" was the KC-135R re-engining program… a major power upgrade to the aging fleet. Prior completion of wing re-skin was a structural imperative on each aircraft for this program, and also a schedule-pacing factor for concurrent versus prior retrofit. [Wing reskin was prioritized by worst structural condition, by age and total flight hours first; while re-engining was prioritized by modifying each involved squadron together and sequentially to minimize intermixing two radically different aircraft in the unit].

This re-engining was a highly unusual competitive contract activity for two reasons. **The first** was that the Prime Contractor had been predetermined to be the original aircraft builder – Boeing Military Aircraft Co., which created a major conflict of interest due to varying engine characteristics and unknown performance (or uncompleted development) of two of the three candidates due to limited operational use.

Two engine candidates were produced by Pratt & Whitney – one with a long history of military operations and well established maintenance and support statistics, a version of which was already in use on the C-135B and RC-135s, and an up-rated version in use on the Lockheed C-141 transport – This was the JT3D family of engines providing anywhere from 18,000 to 21,000 pounds thrust, each with a 1.4:1 low-bypass ratio, small diameter fan (as compared to the original 13,700 pound thrust, non-fan engines requiring water injection to reach this level for one-take-off only, per flight). This was the "easy and inexpensive" upgrade, since most of the changes had already been engineered by Boeing on the above mentioned C-135 and RC-135 aircraft, and the engine's variants were already in-service elsewhere for more than two decades. [i.e. Least cost for Boeing and the USAF, but not incorporating the latest environmental, noise, and fuel efficiency technologies].

The second P&W candidate was the newer technology, JT8D-209 engine, under development for advanced twin-engine commercial jets, such as the aft fuselage mounted MD-80 airliner, and a potential upgrade for the tri-engined B-727 Advanced aircraft. The JT8D-209 had a slightly larger engine diameter with a moderate 1.74:1 low bypass ratio and provided 19,000 pounds thrust, each. At the time this was a new and more efficient engine, but its durability and maintenance had not yet been substantiated, nor did it have any military application experiences. This engine involved an increased amount of airframe modifications to meld it into the KC-135 airframe and systems, and thus would take longer to engineer and be more costly to develop and mature on the KC-135 application than the previously described JT3D candidate family. [In typical P&W fashion, this engine was never to see operational usage and required fixes and upgrades into the -217 version and higher, before going into wide-spread commercial applications].

The third engine was a product of CFM International, designated as CFM56-2 (military designation F108) and was a large diameter engine, with 5.5:1 bypass ratio fan, produced in partnership between GE (US) and SNECMA of France, and rated at 24,000 pounds thrust. GE provided the turbine (hot) section, which was a variant of the already developed USAF B-1 bomber engine, and SNECMA provided the fan and compressor sections. This was a much larger and heavier engine (compared to the two P&W candidates). The CFM engine had seen commercial service for about 2 years in the Douglas DC-8-92 (re-engined) aircraft (a contemporary aircraft with the B-707). It represented an order of magnitude of cost increase over the other two candidates, but had political and military advantages due to its B-1 engine components, and represented the highest revenue solution for Boeing in airframe and systems development and modifications for KC-135 usage. It was the most costly modification of the three candidates.

DC-8-92 with CFM-56 Engines *(NASA Photo)*

The second factor making this a very unusual competition was that Higher Headquarters AFSC unstated and unpublished primary priority was to develop and insert a high-technology engine candidate into a large fleet modification. Because of this unstated (and unjustified-cost specification) priority, it meant that the parameters of design, complexity, cost, and technical risk that the three primary operational and logistics panels had to deal with, and ground rules of the proposals, were different from what the competitors were required to submit in their proposals, and did not track with the foregone conclusions that the SPO and its higher headquarters had predetermined to be the winning answers.

This unique contract competition meant that Boeing would be answering all of the technical questions about how each candidate engine would be integrated onto the existing airframe, and providing performance and maintenance estimates and cost impacts for each configuration. It was also obvious that the prime contractor, Boeing, was supporting the "predetermined" solution, with the most complex and costly solution (for Boeing's ultimate financial benefit).

The Contract Source Selection process was conducted at Wright-Patterson AFB, Dayton, OH, during the Fall of 1979 through the Spring of 1980, under the direction of the Systems Program Office, **SPO,** of the Air Force Systems Command/Aeronautical Systems Division (AFSC/**ASD**), which provided oversight of Development Engineering, and over-all administration of the other four panels. The additional multi-member "panels" representing major technical expertise (five including the SPO) made up the activity — **Operations**, (SAC, chaired by Col Charlie D, a former SR-71 pilot at Beale AFB, CA, now from SAC HQ Operations, at Offutt AFB); **Flight Test** (Aircraft Systems Development test branch from Edwards AFB, CA), Flight Test Engineering; the **Systems Program Office**, **SPO** (System Program Office, **ASD/SPO**, from Wright-Patterson AFB), and **Contracts & Financials**, (ASD, also from WPAFB); and I served as the Committee Chairman for the 10 to 15-member **Logistics** Panel, from Oklahoma City ALC, which provided the most wide-spread and deep technical history of the KC-135 operational and structural conditions.

The Source Selection process took over 6-months (TDY to Wright-Patterson AFB, Dayton, OH, for my team, SAC's and Flight Test's) and was compromised by (proven, but hushed) improper doctoring of the LOG, SAC, and TEST committee's evaluations, by the ASD management team headed up by the ASD SPO ultimately under command of M/Gen Larry S, ASD/CC) over the Christmas break of 1979. With my inside observations on this corruption, and my reporting it to my Civilian Deputy Director (at OCALC/MM), Bill J, who was on the Source Selection Exec Committee chaired by Gen Larry S, the issue was elevated to AFLC 4-star Commander, Gen. Brice P. Although M/Gen Larry S was admonished by Gen Brice P, the meeting resulted in no change to the ASD preferred selection of the CFM-56 but was left with major restrictions to the rated thrust (reduced to 20,000 lbs), major development and design of an on-board APU capable of providing a war-time "quick-start" and live-aboard arctic and tropical environments *at a multi-million dollar item cost of manufacturing and installation arguably equal to the original total aircraft cost*; major systems mods (reduction of inflight minimum idle speed for approach and taxi speeds); major design changes to the rudder system to compensate for increased worst case control with critical high-thrust engine failure; change in MITO (extending Minimum Interval Take-Off intervals) procedure due to engine inlet-air intake disruption causing compressor stalls; reduction of aircraft max cruise speed and VMO (maximum operating Mach number), due to flutter generated by the bigger engine's weight and positioning higher on the wing for ground clearance; and other performance compromises, and cost over-runs. All these issues created a substantial time delay for prototype and flight test and major expensive mods to the end-design and installations. These added compromises in-turn, extended the time and tremendously increased the cost of the development, prototype and test ($180 Million for 1-aircraft), and settling out at a per-aircraft value of modification to exceed $35M, each (compared to an original aircraft value of approximately $3.5M, each).

KC-135R — High Bypass Fanjet (CFM56) Engines

In all fairness, as it turned out (program cost, and time to complete fleet modification, not-withstanding), this was a very successful program for the USAF. Largely because the engines, involving the latest state-of-commercial technology, were down-rated by 17%, and on-wing engine maintenance support was so refined that a majority of the modified aircraft performed for more than 15 years without ever requiring any engine removal. (Somewhat analogous to the improved reliability of using 240V rated light bulbs, powered by only a 120V source). Combined with commercial engine maintenance programs and annual upgrades in improved engine configuration (to commercial standards), plus commercial logistics of commonality with the DC-8 and B-737 engine families, as well as common hot-section components from the B-1B bomber engines, significant cost efficiency was realized.

Creator and Architect; KC-135E Re-engining, (Beginning 1980) — From the earliest stages of the KC-135R upgrade program, the operational (SAC) and Logistics community (along with Flight Test) predominantly preferred re-engining the aging KC-135 airframes with the most conservative approach, by using the well proven JT3D engine-family at the 18,000 pound thrust level. These three expert source "communities" were working the issue on the honest evaluation of what was absolutely the "best bang for the buck", with quickest modification to perform, and minimum cost and minimum risk, with minimal new supply and maintenance systems to develop, and minimum impact to the overall military budget. But Systems Command had hidden agenda to introduce the newest technology into the USAF in a large fleet of aircraft.

This obviously gave rise for a "proof of concept" parallel program to put the needs of the USAF and national security, on the front line — a comparison of the most costly modification Vs. the most conservative, taking into account the remaining longevity of the airframe and systems. But there was no obvious way to make this happen. However, suddenly I was confronted with an indirect way through a totally unexpected "unsolicited proposal". **Destiny** had suddenly provided the only possible way for this to happen, and **Destiny** chose me, with my unique background and experience, as the only "vehicle" to bring it to fruition. This became the most significant innovation that I personally *created and "SOLD"* to the Pentagon and tanker operations (SAC, AFRes, and ANG)!

In my role as KC-135 (Tanker) Weapon System Manager, my most primary responsibility was to fulfill a mission requirement that would provide sufficient tankers ("boom equivalents") so that the USAF could have sufficient capacity to support a world-wide conflict simultaneously on two fronts. Until this proposal arose, we had only sufficient assets to meet maybe 80% of this primary requirement, and the best existing means for improvement, with the optimum way to fill the requirement for more equivalent refueling capability ("equivalent booms in the sky"). The problem was being addressed by the development of the KC-10 (a DC-10 widebody derivative) tanker fleet of approximately 80 aircraft, and the KC-135R program (previously described). But both of these programs were very big budget efforts that took many years to bring the new capability to a viable readiness and logistic supportability status. The KC-135E concept, relatively speaking, had neither of these disadvantages. Here is the story of how this came about.

One afternoon in early 1980, I met with a visitor who sought me out in my offices at Tinker AFB with a very unusual proposal. His name was Mr. AB S. and he was a senior VP of American Airlines in Dallas, TX. He was on a mission to dispose of the American Air Lines fleet of highly maintained Boeing 707-100 and 707-300 (stretched) series commercial airplanes that were being forced into retirement because of pending FAA (EPA) noise and air pollution standards. He told me he had first been to the Pentagon and then referred to HQ SAC where he received essentially the same story. "The USAF does not buy used airplanes, no matter how good the condition, nor how reasonable the price". He described AAL's fleet of 75 707s, consisting of about 70% of the newer and bigger -300 series, with the remainder of the earlier and smaller 707-100 series (which airframes were approximately the same physical size as the KC-135, and which were largely built on the same initial USAF tooling). All were certifiably in "above average to excellent condition", since AAL had the highest reputation of maintenance and always used new and original structures and components in their repairs (not refurbished parts). All of these aircraft used the same common commercial engines (low bypass P&W JT3D-7s with pneumatic thrust reversers, and rated at either 18,000 or 19,000 pounds thrust each, depending on larger or smaller airframe) -- Basically the same engine as was used on the later C-135Bs, and highly similar to that used on the 21,000 lb thrust C-141 and E-3A military AWACS aircraft versions.

His initial marketing proposal envisioned that the USAF could use his offered airframes, at highly discounted prices, to become supplemental tanker conversions, and also have a VIP or cargo supplemental capability. With my personal insight of the KC-135 structural issues, and tanker systems design requirements, plus my experience flying the Canadian B-707-347C aircraft with knowledge of its advanced systems, I readily understood the complexity and cost aspects of modifying these airframes to tankers in the USAF mission roles. None-the-less, his proposal was very attractive at $3M each for the -300 series and $1M each for the smaller -100s. These proposed prices also included total refurbishment of the engines, brakes, and operating systems and updated airworthiness inspections on each airframe by AAL engineering and maintenance personnel to current FAA standards, plus the physical conversion of these aircraft to use in there new roles. *[Note: FAA Standards, are not equivalent to Military Standards, and each has unique requirements for the differing requirements of operations and maintenance.]*

I discussed the basic after-market expenses of adding all the specialized systems (additional fuel tanks in what were the existing baggage compartments in the belly bays, special plumbing for refueling systems, additional structural mods to add the boom pod and controls to the airframes, additional hydraulic pumps for fuel transfer, increased fuel management cockpit controls and panels, addition of cargo door and cargo rated flooring in the passenger compartment, and many other facets. An alternate plan came to my mind and offered a much simpler and substantially less costly alternate proposition of using the bulk of his offering as cannibalization candidates due to the major similarities of his airframes and many systems components for use in upgrading existing USAF aircraft basics with near-interchangeable more modern systems. He counter offered to retain the original proposal price, but including all the related transfer work to be performed by AAL Engineering and Maintenance facilities in Dallas and other AAL depot facilities in the U.S.

After also explaining the military budgeting system and the need to develop an internal requirements statement, to which the proposal could respond, and the typical 4-year lead-time in budgetary submittals, I told him that I would need some time to define these parameters in greater detail and submit them up through Higher HQ before a preliminary decision could be reached to more completely analyze the scope of the proposal. This was an unsolicited proposal, the likes of which had NEVER been entertained in the prior history of USAF acquisition, particularly involving so many potential aircraft assets. But the opportunity was too good to pass up without at least exploring it more fully.

With my unique experience and knowledge-base with both the KC-135 and the B-707, I accomplished a design "mini-study" of structural similarities and performance comparisons – a marketing approach – combined with a proposal-offer briefing and comparison of the increased fuel efficiency, improved off-load capability, and ability to operate the KC-135E from shorter runways (due to the added thrust, plus thrust reverse capability). In less than two weeks, I had developed the study and prepared the initial presentation, and began briefing it up the Logistics chain of command. With added refinements, as each level added their suggestions and questions needing answers, the briefing was favorably taken up to the Pentagon and HQ SAC. Less than 5-weeks after the initial dialogue with the AAL VP of Marketing I found myself briefing the Air Counsel in the Pentagon. This council consisted of about a dozen Maj. Generals and 2-star Senior Executive Service equivalents from each of the Major Commands that operated the tankers plus the Executive staffs from Logistics Command, AF Systems Command engineering and development organizations, including

Lt. Gen Larry S (mentioned previously with the KC-135R program), now president of the Air Council.

KC-135E — Low Bypass Fanjet (JT3D-7) Engines

The KC-135E Configuration – My evolving vision of what the (later designated) "KC-135E" configuration would consist of started with a KC-135A baseline (with wing re-skin completed).

[NOTE: All other baseline ongoing KC-135 Cockpit avionics and instrumentation upgrades were also performed on the "E model" re-engining program assets, where applicable for configuration commonality.]

The original J57 engines, struts (pylons) and nacelles would be removed and replaced with those from the commercial B-707 donor aircraft. This would also include the commercial thrust reverser systems. *[The engine strut-to-wing mounts were identical to those of the C-135B airframe. And the thrust reverser rigging would be simplified by exchanging the original throttle quadrant and power levers from the 707 donor aircraft with all of the related cables, pulleys and fittings; only minimal cable rerouting modification and cable-length resizing would be required due to the similar design but different dimensions, between the two aircraft.]* The horizontal tail planes would need enlarging to accommodate the added engine thrust.

[This could be accomplished by using the existing larger horizontal tail planes from the donor 707-100 aircraft, or by using the existing Boeing engineering used in modifying the KC-135A tail plane for the later produced C-135B USAF configuration. The larger, stronger elevator trim actuator for the tail plane would also be swapped from the donor aircraft.] The KC-135A fleet vertical tail had already been modified to the larger commercial design size, and structural attachment fittings, during earlier KC-135A upgrades.

The newer commercial donor aircraft had an improved auto-pilot with a full-time series yaw damper, and this system would also be transferred to the KC-135E. The KC-135A baseline had a main landing gear that had only a 4-rotor anti-skid braking system which operated only from the left pilot seat; the commercial donors had improved capability 5-rotor anti-skid systems operable from either left or right pilot's seat, and would also be used by cannibalization, as well as the heavier-duty main landing gear struts (which were fit-form-and-function essentially interchangeable with the original KC-A equipment).

The commercial aircraft donor engine struts incorporated a strut inlet housing incorporating a small engine-bleed powered turbine to assist aircraft pressurization, circulation and air-conditioning for the passenger aircraft on three of the four engines. These subsystems were deemed unnecessary for the tanker application and were deleted in the conversion. On the commercial donors, there existed two different nacelle fan inlet "sucker-door" configurations, the larger of which improved fan operation during take-off at the higher 19,000 pound thrust levels. Since the more numerous donor aircraft had the smaller "sucker doors", these were chosen as the "configuration-standard" for the KC-E fleet (and were common to the 18,000 pound thrust (per engine) rating of KC-135B, so Boeing already had the engineering and USAF tooling for this production), and the nacelle inlets were all demodified to this "revised standard". *[The primary advantage of these larger sucker-doors was more efficient take-off airflow on the higher 19,000 pound thrust engines, which were standardized and derated to the 18,000 pound rating to avoid further cost for flight testing certification on the KC-E configuration and maintaining flight manual operational performance commonality with the C-135B aircraft].*

Numerous other commercial systems on the donor aircraft were cannibalized and installed on the KC-135E, where there was an advantage in either performance, and/or available inventory of spare resources, and where minimal interchangeability issues were involved. All of the components taken from the donor aircraft were fully inspected and over-hauled or "zero-timed" as part of the proposal submitted by American Airlines, and incorporated by Boeing when they were ultimately awarded the contract for the installation work. The combined cost of this "cannibalization" re-engining, and the recovery value from recycling the unused portions of the airframes and passenger equipment, plus the acquisition of surplus available spare parts added up to an amount estimated at $15 billion in taxpayer savings, plus an inventory growth of some additional 20+ additional more-modern 707-300 series aircraft for special use (as summarized below).

My briefing was received with much resistance at the Air Council, due to its unprecedented approach, and their main focus on the acquisition budgetary concerns. With both the KC-10 and KC-135R programs potentially competing for the same funds, many of the panel members thought the funding competition to be too threatening to these two already ongoing programs. Too few on the Council were really focused on the urgent immediate need for more refueling capability to meet Wartime requirements. But the two generals representing the ANG and AFRes were very enthused, because if they applied this modification to their fleets of airplanes, there were great financial and operational advantages. Most of their KC-135 tanker pilots were also airline pilots familiar with the B-707 performance and procedures, and were operating out of noise and exhaust-smoke sensitive airports, and often with much shorter runways (than SAC's traditional tanker bases). These potential KC-135E aircraft were much more desirable than the "water-wagon" water injected J-57 engines of their KC-135A models. As my briefing approached its conclusion, the "Nays" were leading the "Ayes", until I made my final clincher. ***"In the time required and the costs involved for Boeing to do one KC-135R retrofit prototype aircraft (five years and $180M), the KC-135E program could generate up to 65 upgraded tankers, which could provide*** *(by Boeing's own analysis data)* ***more than 90% of the performance advantages and increased offload, at about 10% of the highly expensive KC-135R retrofit, per-aircraft)."***

At this point in my presentation the AFRes and ANG generals threw their influence into the discussion by reminding the Air Counsel that, "They both provided their own budget funding from State level resources – not from Federal funds — and that if no one else was interested", they were willing to proceed on their own dollars for this modification." They saw the immediate value in having common power plants in the KC-135E (familiar to the majority of Guard pilots and maintainers, and the advantage of quieter, and cleaner environmental engines out of their Civilian Airports, with shorter runway availabilities, plus their state's budgets savings for a substantial tanker upgrade.

This added consideration largely removed the concern by the Air Counsel that the KC-E program would negatively impact funding for either the KC-135R, or the KC-10 tanker programs (and fewer KC-A assets would require re-engining with the more expensive CFM56 configuration modification – which overall had a positive funding impact on that program).

Unpublished Kudos for the KC-135E Program — Recognition must be given to the high majority of the KC-135E tanker missions flown in the 1990s Desert Storm Gulf War that were flown by the AF Reserves and Air National Guard commands. These aircraft greatly altered the outcome of that conflict that would have not been possible with the existing KC-135As, and few KC-135Rs and KC-10s, then available. Further, this initiative was a further amplification of the practicality of using commercial engines and equipment on USAF line aircraft in contrast to retaining strict configuration management by the USAF, which in contrast "maintained the configuration" to commonality across the fleet to that of the earliest 1955 KC-135 version produced.

The budgetary savings of this 161 aircraft re-engining program using cannibalized 707 commercial assets resulted in an initial estimate in excess of 15 Billion then-year Dollars, in addition to entering the modified airframes into service over a period of less than 5 years.

[Of the original 161 KC-135E re-engine tanker aircraft, nineteen were later retrofitted to the KC-135R configuration (with the high bypass CFM-56 engines, at the end of the KC-135R schedule). Since the early 2000s, the remainder have been retired to AMARG (the USAF Boneyard) for storage, sale to Allied countries, relocation to USAF Museums, or recycling of parts, systems and components].

My assignment to Tinker AFB, was without a doubt my most challenging, most detail oriented, and most financially and politically intense of my entire career, with the highest responsibility for affecting and enhancing USAF capabilities.

My Career Ending Decision — I had become a pain in the backside of a very agitated Gen Larry S, a second time over. And due to my experiences of twice crossing swords over the two re-engining programs with Gen Larry S (who had subsequently gained a fourth star and Command of AFSC), I felt my promotion future was probably poisoned as long as he remained in-service.

However, what made it all worthwhile was that, ultimately AFRes converted 24 tankers to KC-135Es. The ANG converted a total of 114- KC-135As (1955 through 1958 KC-135A models), to KC-135E, plus two SAC -1957 & one AFSC -1959 KC-135As) were converted. All told, a total of 161 KC-135A aircraft plus an additional 24 J-57-powered EC/RC-135 and special mission C-135 aircraft (total of 187, in all) were converted with this unique program. This donor acquisition required purchasing not only the entire AAL fleet, but also the entire and less pristine 707 fleets of PanAm and TWA, as well as a number of smaller international airline company assets with much lesser maintained airframes.

However, in addition to these acquisitions, about 20 late-model B-707-300 series aircraft were applied from these acquisitions to special mission configurations as intact airframes (with subsequent further modifications), rather than as cannibalization donors. These additional pre-owned aircraft were to serve as the platforms for the original fleet of JointSTARS (12 to 14 aircraft), a replacement Airborne Laser test bed aircraft, several other special test-bed aircraft, and two additional Presidential VC-137 back-ups to the VIP 707 Presidential fleet at Andrews AFB, DC, (replacing existing VC-135s).

JointSTARS (707) E-8C Aircraft

(Photo Air Force Magazine, USAF Almanac, June 2018)

[Included in this package of acquired used 707s, ironically, unknown to me at the time, were the five CC-137 (B-707-347C) tanker/cargo convertible aircraft that I had formerly flown in Canada. These 707s had been replaced in Canada by Airbus A-320 tanker-modified aircraft.]

CHAPTER 8

Post-Retirement Civilian Employment

RETIREMENT CARICATURE —MAY 1981
PRESENTED BY OKLAHOMA CITY AIR LOGISTIC CENTER

My US Air Force Retirement —

I retired from the USAF in Jun 1981 after completing 20 years and two-months, and in promotion frustration. I had just completed the last 5-years of my 20-year active duty, as a Lt. Col. (O-5 level). I had spent the last 8-years filling O-6 (Full Col.) and O-7 (Canadian Brig. Gen.) job responsibilities with great accomplishments and distinction during that time, which I felt was not recognized by advancement appropriate to those accomplishments and responsibilities.

When I put in my retirement request, my OCALC Commander, M/Gen Jay E. asked why? I expressed my frustrations to him, and informed him that I had concluded I had advanced as far as I was going to, and that the sooner I entered a civilian career, the better my chances were of starting a new career at that younger age (42). He offered that if I stayed in, he would do everything he could to see that I was on the next O-6 promotion cycle. "*Too little, too late*," I thought! And Lt/Gen Larry S's influence on that promotion board was still above M/Gen Jay E. in the approval chain of command, so I felt unimpressed with the likelihood of further advancement. I also realized that if successful and O-6 promotion had been achieved, my most probable future assignments would be to the Air War College in residence for a year, followed by an assignment, as a new Colonel to either HQ AFLC, in Dayton, OH, or Logistics & Requirements in the Pentagon, in DC, neither of which would be attractive to me as a junior Colonel in a sea of Colonels that were little more than "go-fors" for the General staff in those assignments. *(I never liked putting the politics of career advancement, ahead of doing the best job I could in the positions I held. I had made my own career decisions based upon truth and loyalty to the USAF mission, always believing that the promotions would follow based on my performance. Was my judgment proven wrong, or was it just "that I had already fulfilled my destiny"?)*

After USAF Retirement — Upon retirement, I was offered a position by Boeing Military, which was my top-most contractor ("employed-vendor") in my USAF career. Boeing based my offered salary upon what my qualifications and experience would bring in the civilian market place – <u>but deducted my USAF retirement salary from their offer</u>. I informed them that I earned that retirement pay and it did not belong to them, and I declined their offer, "with prejudice".

E-Systems, Greenville, TX (1981 – '84) —

I subsequently was offered and accepted a Program Management position at E-Systems in Greenville, TX (July 1981). In my active duty position as C/KC-135 WSM, E-Systems had been my second most important sub-contractor vendor – now I was their employee. But I avoided any activities that involved the C/KC-135 fleet programs. My next three years saw the very satisfactory completion of a Top Secret program, which designed and built systems hardware and software then installed and calibrated the modification on the entire fleet of thirty four USAF E-3A AWACS aircraft with a new ELINT "electronic support mission" (ESM) system (analogous to the WWII Enigma Program). E-Systems had invented and developed this system for the NSA, based upon intelligence and technology that they had exploited through the USAF RC-135 fleet systems (which they had also developed, installed and maintained on the RC-135 fleet, over several decades). My position there was as "Co-Program Manager" responsible for structural airframe modifications and systems installation of the electronics suite on the USAF AWACS fleet, in partnership with the Systems design and development "Co-Program Manager". This was a $45 million contract. At the completion of the AWACS contract, I found myself employed at full salary, but with no job to do as the next round of contract bids was awaiting US budgetary funding and contract award. Out of overwhelming boredom, for 40-hours per week on duty with little or no work to do (except "make-work"), I began to search for new employment (in the fall of '84).

Golden Opportunity, Waco, TX (1984 – '85) — In mid-1984, a unique executive management opportunity arose from Mr. AB S — the same American Air Lines executive (now retired from AAL), whom I had come to know from the KC-135E program creation effort. My position was joining his small venture-capital funded technical firm in Waco, TX, which was involved in the development and FAA Certification of "hush-kit" engine nacelles to be retrofit to meet new environmental noise standards on commercial P&W JT3D fan engines as used on commercial DC-8 and B-707 aircraft. Most of these remaining assets were owned by small international companies where competition would not permit the purchase of fleets larger than two to six aircraft, and where operations would be largely outside of US regulations.

This new start-up venture-capital firm was owned by Mr. AB S and manned by, one Boeing retiree (technical consultant) formerly involved with and having access to all of Boeing's 707 Quiet Nacelle prototype engineering, development and test data, plus loan of one of their test prototype nacelles. (Boeing's technical prototype work on a 707 noise-cancelling nacelle design had been terminated due to Boeing's internal business conflicts between improving older 707 airframes and producing, and marketing new aircraft designs). The remainder of the firm's management were AB's son ("Production Manager for the Hush Kit program" who was an oil company wild-cat operator, with no aviation experience, nor aviation (FAA) production management, nor engineering background), and AB's wife (as "Chief Financial Officer" for the new firm), in addition to a work-force of independent part-time contracted engineering staff with specialization in design and manufacture of aircraft manufacturing tooling (for building the special nacelles.

I was hired initially as the VP for Subcontract Management and subsequently elevated to VP of Engineering and Tooling. My employment contract had a very lucrative annual salary (nearly three times what I had been earning at E-Systems, plus a $15,000 bonus for each aircraft modified. At the time of my employment, AB had already successfully sold kits for an initial 20 aircraft on contract with one million dollars each in down-payments deposited). That amounted to a $300,000 bonus for the first year of production, with more to follow based upon successful program continuation. (A big "if"!) I had recognized the high potential for the firm to fail, due to its lack of a proper formal business plan, and proper depth of qualified staffing in aerospace management, not to mention potential pitfalls from nepotistic conflicts, and a subcontractor-based engineering labor force that was more inclined to disloyalty to the job completion, and greater loyalty to deliberate and continuous redesign effort, to keep their positions needed and filled.

As a result of these concerns, I had negotiated my employment position with a well defined job contract that had protective provisions to provide me with 24 months of salary guaranty, placed in trust, to protect my income should the program fail to produce a marketable B-707 FAA certified product (and a separately funded second program for the somewhat similar DC-8 nacelle design).

Unfortunately, my contract was with Mr. AB S's. firm (ATS, Aviation Technical Support), not with the Financial Groups funding the two separate programs. I later discovered, meanwhile, Mr. AB S, the owner of the firm continued with outlandish marketing expenditures *[like purchasing and refurbishing a 707-300 aircraft for flight test and marketing, generating expensive and premature marketing brochures, travel activities, display graphics-packages and desk-top nacelle models, while entertaining potential future customers of small fleet owners, and hunting for venture capital to support either or both programs]*, while his non-aviation-experienced son over-rode internal efforts to coordinate continuity and integration of design, and FAA test requirements.

ATS B-707 Test Aircraft (Before Hush-kit Nacelles were installed)

Before the first year of my employment was past, I had generated over a million dollars in cost efficiencies (for which I was never recognized or compensated) within an already negotiated Gulfstream subcontract to build the nacelles (on our tooling designs – tooling designs which I discovered could never be satisfactorily completed). During that entire time I was commuting weekly between my family and home in Dallas (Rockwall, TX) to a rental house and office location in Waco, TX, over 100 miles away, while Mr. AB S drained the accounts of working capital with misdirected, unrealistic marketing efforts, a new office building and other premature business expenses.

The first project (the 707 program, which my job contract was based upon) went into bankruptcy. The second (the DC-8) went into FAA noise testing on prototype nacelle inlet components, and was faltering, with new separate venture financing being sought.

My inability to overcome inadequate management priorities, nepotistic decision priorities, and a faulty (or non-existent) business plan was in great danger of failing, so I implemented an employment-contract fall-back to depart the sinking ship and invoke my 24-month salary protection, only to discover that the protective trust of my contract had never been funded, and realization that the pending total bankruptcy would nullify any potential for payment of my unfunded trust. Under advice of legal counsel, I walked away from a law suite — that I was guaranteed to win by my contracted employment agreements, but could never collected, because of the bankruptcy — and took a "lesson-learned" lump on the head. All of my excellent background experience had never exposed me to Personnel issues and employment risks! I departed with a pre-paid new car, and the earned salary for that initial year of employment.

Unemployed, Back in Rockwall, TX (1985 –'87) — I found myself unemployed for about 18-months, back in the Dallas location from where I had worked at E-Systems, in Greenville, TX. At age 49, I was now looking for upper income technical management or marketing positions at a time when the job market was shrinking and there were typically about 100 applicants, for every potential aviation executive job opening, nation-wide. And neither my age nor my diversified experience was working in my favor. The job demands available were oriented more toward highly focused specialties than diversification and extensiveness of technical management experience.

My resume included potentially marketable skills as an Aero Engineer, my Program Management and Commercial Safety Management skills including Industrial, Aviation, Nuclear, Munitions, and Base/Plant-level categories, my Commercial Pilot License with Instrument and Instructor ratings, and turbine engine plus reciprocating engine ratings, as well as DC-3, B-707-300, and B-720 (KC-135 equivalent) Type Ratings, with over 3500 hours Heavy-Jet qualification, experience with flying VVIP government and senior civilian corporate leaders, not to mention my advanced user-level computer skills, and Top Secret clearance certification. This meant that at my age and salary expectations, I was "over-qualified" for most available entry-level positions, with too short a remaining employment window (by virtue of my age seniority), to justify a company's interest, particularly those unfamiliar with the value of diverse military assignments and diverse management skills.

As one example. American Airlines, at that time, was advertising a new program to hire 4,000 new pilots. With corporate headquarters in Dallas, I made application with them. I sailed through the pilot physical exam, their required Boeing-727 FAA Flight-Engineers Exam, and the B-707 flight simulator flying skills test. My competition (in this interview session) were two dozen "30-somethings", a generation of multi-engine non-military pilots – mostly with just barely the minimum of 2,000 flight hours, mostly in turbine powered light twin-engine commuter aircraft. On the second interview session, after completing all the previous pre-requisite qualifications, I was informed that American AL was not interested in hiring flight-engineers, or copilots. And despite my superior demonstrated skills and experience, that if I was hired on probation, as every new-hire pilot was — even if I accepted the least desirable domicile assignments (New York, or Chicago) — because of airline pilot union rules of simple majority position, rather than skills and/or qualifications, that they would anticipate it would take me 12-years to successfully work up enough seniority to achieve "Left Seat" Captain's status. At this point I would not achieve Left Seat status, prior to facing mandatory FAA retirement at age 60!

While unemployed, we had been living off of my USAF retirement pay (which was only 40% of my previous USAF active duty income, and less than 25% of my previous E-Systems salary). During this period of unemployment I also had part-time employment supplementation at menial positions, including self employment doing multi-level Amway-type multi-level marketing and selling automotive-installed early-vintage cellular phones, before they had become pocket devices, (plus Pat's part-time real estate sales income) and we were rapidly depleting our retirement nest-egg. Also working against me was the fact that at the time we moved to Dallas in 1981, mortgage rates were at 12.5% interest. After becoming "formally" unemployed for several months, new interest rates had come down eventually to 7%. Even though I was able to continue making mortgage payments at the higher rate without delay or default, the mortgage companies said I was unqualified for refinance – even though the reduction in rate would reduce my monthly mortgage payments by over $400 (30%), and further improve my loan risk. Talk about "Catch 22"!

GE Aircraft Engine Marketing, Cincinnati (1987 – '92) While job-hunting during my nearly 2-years of unemployment, I attended several local Job Fairs over the period, and left several resumés with various corporations. One day in 1986, while still residing in Dallas, I received a phone call from the HR Department of GE Aircraft Engines wanting to set up a visit to Cincinnati for job interviews, all expenses paid. This was one of a very few interview appointments or follow-up calls from over 200- resumés submitted or mailed out. I happily accepted. During the trip, numerous executives within the Military Marketing Dept., including the Department Manager interviewed me. During the visit, the Dept Mgr asked me if I knew how I was selected for an interview. I did not, but suspected it came from one of the Job Fairs where I had left a resumé. The position I had left the resumé for at GE was in flight test, and was more suited for a Commercial Airline pilot, than a military pilot. So I was of no interest to that department. But Col. Charlie D (Retired SR-71 pilot, whom I had "rescued" from Hill AFB on an SR-71 landing recovery, and also knew well from the KC-135R Source Selection activity), worked in the GE Military Marketing department and had seen my resumé and recommended I be interviewed. I then had the opportunity to meet with Charlie and talk informally about my desires and interest. I was out-briefed and told that further communications were forth coming within the next week. After returning home, and reviewing the total events, I received a letter of interest for a position. I formally thanked GE HR by letter and informed them that unfortunately I did not see a good match for my skills, interests, and capabilities. (I was not anxious to move back to the "snow belt", and there was some potential legal USAF conflict-of-interest with the still ongoing KC-135R re-engining program, at GE in Cincinnati).

About three months later, as my prospects and finances were becoming more desperate, I received a phone call from Col. Charlie D. He asked me if I was ready yet to move to GE in Cincinnati? He told me that GE was transferring him back to Omaha (where his family had remained, after his USAF retirement from SAC). He was transferring in the capacity as the GE representative and office manager at the GE Field Office, for SAC. His vacated engine marketing position in Cincinnati, which did not have a KC-135 connection, would be available, if I was interested. I agreed and an acceptable position, salary, and benefits package were negotiated, making me a senior Military Transport Engine Marketing Manager. I relocated to Cincinnati in Oct '86 with a temporary apartment 6-month lease, and began house-hunting. Meanwhile, Pat and family remained in Texas to get our home sold in a very depressed real estate market. Pat was successful in selling it within about 6-months, and soon joined me in Cincinnati, with our youngest daughter (Melissa, age 18) and family pets. Our oldest (Caryn, age 20) remained in Dallas to complete her Court

Reporting training.

I was assigned several projects to begin familiarization with my new position. One was an initiative of CFM-56 re-engining the NATO AWACS fleet, with follow-on program to re-engine the USAF AWACS fleet. Another was to assist in generating support for re-engining the current Presidential 707 fleet with CFM-56 engines, based upon the original 707 CFM prototype that Boeing had fielded and then converted into the KC-135R conversions. And another was to develop a new production 707 CFM-56 platform for the newly developing JointSTARS acquisition, which was proposed by Boeing to be the same platform as the US Navy E-6 already in development, with CFM-56 engines and thrust reversers encorporated. A couple years later, with some limited success on these projects, I was asked to take over the unsuccessful 12-year effort at GE to initiate and succeed in marketing a program to re-engine the fleet of 23 RC-135 reconnaissance aircraft (complete with thrust reversers and dual generator packs on each engine, similar to the EC-135B aircraft) with a modified CFM-56 power-plant (with similarity to the KC-135R).

Marketing Potential & Results —

USAF AWACS, 34 Aircraft – This fleet had been in service for a decade before the NATO (European) AWACS became operational. Other AWACS system upgrades and modifications and USAF funding priorities proved to be greater than the need for upgraded engines, at that time. (i.e. No current USAF Funding, or priority requirement.)

NATO AWACS, 34 Aircraft, separately owned by numerous allies – This fleet was still very new at that time, and there was no demonstrated need, nor interest in upgrading the low-time well supported existing engines. Later production models (10 in UK and 4 in Saudi Arabia) were produced <u>with CFM-56</u>s, after the development of the CFM-56 upgrade was completed on new E-6 (707) airframes for the US Navy submarine detection fleet).

Presidential VIP 707 (VC-137), 2 to 4 Acft. – My efforts were successful in gaining support by the 4-star Commander of MAC and 89th Wing Commander at Andrews AFB, DC, on re-engining the original two pristine and low-time, high-investment VC-137s (known as "Air Force One", and spare). Political manipulation by Boeing (and the White House) caused USAF course reversal for two new Boeing-747, replacements. Suddenly the VC-137 Re-engine program collapsed when the Mac CC retired and the 89th Wing CC was transferred to Dover AFB on a new assignment. (Were these departures related to the political decision for new jumbo-jet Presidential aircraft? My guess was "Yes", with the support from the Presidential Offices.)

JointSTARS, 12-14 Acft – The original acquisition plan was for a new 707 (E-6B variant) airframe with CFM-56 power plants on the airframe. The JSTARS SPO negotiated the diversion of one in-production E-6B airframe out of the Navy production-line contract. The SPO purchased 5-engines (4 plus 1-spare) for that airframe, through my efforts. Since Boeing was trying to shut down the 707 production line (to concentrate on newer, higher-tech airframes introducing more efficient computer generated design and manufacturing techniques), they priced the new-production older 707 airframes out of reasonable cost, and the JSTARS program switched their initial program airframes to use some of the used 707 acquisition airframes (from the KC-135E program mentioned above). By converting to used 707 airframes, sufficient funds were saved to increase the fleet size to 16. Out-year JSTARS production was beginning to migrate to a new Boeing airframe based upon the CFM-56 powered B-737.

RC-135, 23 Acft — The prior efforts at GE on this fleet had been unsuccessful, because the prior marketing effort could not get deep enough into the cost benefits, due to the security classification on these numerous different mission applications and configurations. I was uniquely qualified and knowledgeable from my -135 WSM and 707 experience, and I was able to overcome these obstacles in a little over a year with very favorable outcome. First, I developed a computer spread sheet graphic display program that had over 20 assumption variables in a graphic chart algorithm -- depicting a time-line overlay of the aircraft conversion input, rate of conversion, the mod cost, the cost of fuel, the annual flight hours per aircraft, the maintenance hours and cost, for both the new and the old engine configuration, the improved fuel efficiency compared to the old, and other quantifiable mission efficiency benefits, etc. With this tool I could define a point (number of years) at which the total estimated costs vs. efficiency benefits would cross-over, thus defining the break even or pay back point. During a live presentation, using a laptop computer, I could project this chart onto a screen and as various audience experts would challenge any of the assumptions made, I could instantly input their preferred suggested values and the algorithm would instantly redraw the graphic chart. This was a very valuable and convincing tool, and amazingly also instantly showed the sensitivity of projected cost for each item in arriving at the cross-over payback point. Surprisingly, it proved that variation of any of the most dynamic and arguable parameters (fuel cost, annual flight hours, or increasing maintenance costs on the old engines), if varied even by as much as plus or minus, 30% in any one assumed parameter, only varied the payback point by about one year. The pay back point was always between 5 and 6 years from program production start.

Secondly, I knew of a SAC consulting firm in Omaha that worked with classified data on all the various RC-135 mission profiles, to assist SAC in mission operational planning and scheduling. I negotiated a subcontract (from GE) for them to do some representative generic, unclassified mission scenarios (with SAC approval) which analyzed and compared the efficiency between the original configured and the re-engine configured mission impacts — including improved tanker fuel economy allowing more fuel for offload, longer tanker range, operations off of more (shorter) airfields, benefits of fewer A/R, and more launch bases in range of target areas, and many other variables. Using both these tools together, I was able to provide very objective and convincing demonstrations of the cost benefits and a mere 4-year payback. These "marketing presentations" were provided to all levels of SAC, the Black Programs Office at AFLC, Office of Management and Budgeting–OMB, and the Pentagon, until all the questionable issues and parameters were well identified and understood, and all agreed, to the substantial and rapid reconnaissance enhancements of initiating the program.

Upon returning to GE after a week on the briefing circuit, and obtaining agreement of the program's go-ahead after many months of 60 - 70 hour work-weeks, I was summoned into my immediate boss's office and expecting congratulations on gaining USAF approval on the program. Instead, I was informed that I was being laid off for lack of work! This despite a subsequent strong endorsement letter from the USAF Commander of the Black Programs Office to GE's VP of Aircraft Engines protesting this action because of my critical involvement in making this a successful program. The lay-off direction was not reversed, the program management at GE was transferred to a civilian engineer, who quickly became "*persona non gratis*" at OCALC and the program was put on hiatus for nearly 10 years *(at substantial inflationary cost increases)*, before it was resurrected and implemented, in early 2000.

My Second and Final Retirement, 1992 — My forced second retirement at age 53, through lay-off at GE came after 5-years and 6-months employment there – just barely enough to have been vested in their retirement program, but not enough for full benefits. I received a minimal fixed pension for life (without adjustments for inflation or COLA), and sufficient to leave only about 30% in my pocket, after paying for policy premiums for Long-Term (Nursing Home) Health Care for both Pat and I, which has increased periodically, to currently use almost all of this small pension.

The final year at GE was one of extreme pressure and anxiety, which triggered a thirteen-year subsequent bout of progressive Atrial Fibrillation (AFib; heart arrhythmia). After having an AFib-induced dual cardiac bypass surgery (Feb '2002), I was experiencing continuous and very symptomatic negative life quality impacts from ongoing AFib–related congestive heart failure (CHF). Fortunately, by 2004, I discovered a world-renowned cardio-thoracic surgeon (and prior partner in developing the DaVinci Surgical Robot) in Cincinnati, who had spent nearly 10-years developing a minimally-invasive surgery bearing his name, the "Wolf Mini-Maze". <wolfminimaze.com/testamonials>. Dr. Wolf performed his procedure on me in Oct 2004 and freed me from my AFib, as well as the symptoms of CHF, and all need for any arrhythmia related drugs and blood thinners. This AFib-initiated ischemic CHF lead to the heart by-pass surgery, and was classified as related to Agent Orange from Vietnam exposure.

After leaving GE, I dabbled with a bit in consulting and home business enterprises (selling home air and water filtration systems), as well as providing executor assistance to my centenarian Great Aunt Grace and her physically handicapped husband, Great Uncle Harley, as they spent their last 4-years in a Florida nursing home together (from '92 – '97).

After their passing in 1996-'97, at 104 and 102, respectively, I became fully retired and pre-occupied by volunteer activities, including being a volunteer consultant and contributor on the EC-47 website <www.ec47.com>; the first President of our local Home Owner's Association: a named Member of the Order of Daedalians (at Wright Patterson AFB); Past President of the Ohio Chapter of the Silver Wings Fraternity; Senior Vice Commander of Ohio Commandery of MOLLUS (Military Order of the Loyal Legion of the US, an Abe Lincoln Civil War heritage organization); Vice-President of the Victory Aviation Aero Club; and First Vice Commander, then Commander (and now Past Commander) of the local West Chester, OH American Legion Post 681." I also spent several years (2004 – 2010) as a contributor and guest Testimonial Speaker for Dr. Wolf's AFib – Mini-maze Seminars, in Ohio and Indiana, and wrote articles on Internet websites on this subject, as well as many anecdotes on my experiences of my USAF career — abbreviated anecdotes that are expanded upon in this book.

CHAPTER 9
HINDSIGHTS (Epilog)

"Destiny"— At best can be identified only as a very broad and generalized objective (like "success", or "wealth", or "adventure"). Only through hindsight, can it be fully defined by looking back after-the-fact at what has been accomplished. These accomplishments are a function of academic education and life's experiences, mistakes made and one's reactions to these mistakes, and... much more.

As I look back over many years, I realize that the early death of my father during World War II (December, 1944, at my age 6), was the beginning of very formative events in my life. It redirected my upbringing to be "a man in the family" and relocated me from a carefree "Southern, Huck Finn" small town riverside environment, to the hostile big city environment of post-war Chicago. That event was certainly nothing that I selected or controlled. But it was the beginning of the events that have led my destiny ever since!

The next most significant event in my destiny was when I enrolled at the University of Illinois (Urbana Campus) in training as an aeronautical engineer.

This second destiny-changer came when I was forced to enroll in ROTC at the U. of I. and from there entered the USAF and completed Undergraduate Pilot training to gain my Wings. Under my choice, upon graduation, I planned to select an F-100 fighter assignment, but "destiny " had another plan for me; to take an alternate assignment from selecting a potentially deadly fighter assignment, to piloting the vintage C-47 in a Navigation Training (TC-47) assignment at Chicago's O'Hare Field, which certainly broadened my USAF experience, and began rapidly expanding my transport aircraft activities, moving forward first to the highly classified EC-47 assignment in Vietnam, then onto bigger and more complex aircraft. Destiny with guidance from an ever-present "guardian angel" perfected my knowledge and skills in aerial refueling in the 4-engine, heavy-jet KC-135Q with the SR-71, also developing extensive skills as an Instructor Pilot, and Wing Chief of Safety, and then into an international Exchange Pilot program in Canada teaching them the new skills of aerial refueling using the modified commercial Boeing 707 "stretch" as the tanker platform, and then finishing my career with management responsibilities for the logistics, maintenance, and life-extension upgrades of the fleet of nearly 800 USAF KC-135 tankers and all other -135 variant configurations, plus the USAF B-707 Presidential Fleet.

From that very first operational assignment in 1962 in the C-47, all the way through and beyond my USAF retirement in 1981, I was following an ongoing and intensive learning path, which progressively trained me and provided experiences that were critical to achieving a satisfying and challenging career growth, in each succeeding assignment. In each case, I made the choices of which selection to make, but I served in assignments that I could never have prepared for, with my own choices, mainly because I never knew they existed before I was offered or selected as a candidate for them. This factor is what gave rise to the title of my memoirs "***Soaring with Destiny***", and acknowledges the strong and ever-present hand of a guardian angel, or the hand of God (by any other name) on my shoulder, providing direction and protecting me from harms way.

In my perspective, the two most significant characteristics of my personal destiny, were ***communications*** (spoken, written, and perceived by attitudes and body language), and ***transportation*** (focused primarily on aviation). Both were heavily formed by *education*, consisting of academics and reality-awareness. These two significant developed skills added the blessings of broad experience and provided essential preparation to accept opportunities when they arose, and were combined with a strong blessing of creative analytical skills and the ability to think "outside the box". A little bit of luck, also provided a good convergence of opportunities, and gained expertise.

In my hindsight the years following the death of my father in WWII when I was 6, ***destiny*** was steered more by my self-determination for achieving excellence for getting the job well done, than by parental or family influence, or striving for promotion or financial gain. I believed that focusing on doing my best work on any task or job undertaken, would provide all the rewards of advancement and increased financial gain would follow accordingly — rather than focusing on promotion at the expense of quality of effort. Looking back at the bigger perspective, I believe I succeeded very well (but not without *some* disapointments along the way).

Hindsights: Safety of Flying Military (Transport) Aircraft — Over the course of my Military career, I spent 75% of my years involved in the cockpit with flying, piloting, and instructing. I spent the remainder in managing the development, the maintenance, the logistics (upgrades, modifications, design improvements in systems and aircraft structures) and communicating all of these facets with the operational users and maintainers. Communications and safety awareness spanned the entirety of what I consider a very successful and notable career.

As I look back from my current vantage point, I am totally amazed at the awesome nature of my experience with the flying safety and aircraft reliability of my USAF experience. Military flying has one of the highest perceived operational safety risks (arguably not to elevate this risk in regard to higher combat risks in any other military activity), due to the technical complexity, the performance parameters of the aircraft equipment, and the highly adverse environment in which it operates, coupled with the unforgiving nature and consequences when the "safety net" fails, and with the extensive requirement for excellence of and time spent performing demanding training, and the resulting performance from that training. As compared to the automotive environment, in an aircraft when an engine fails, a fire starts, a flight control malfunctions, or you run out of fuel, one cannot just pull off the road, abandon the vehicle, and look for assistance.

Looking at the bigger picture — assessing the number of individuals involved in designing and manufacturing the vehicle, its components, and its ground support and inflight systems, are in the 10's of thousands, or even 100's of thousands — this generates an awesome picture. Combining that with the numbers of those maintaining it, and providing the spare parts and consumables (fuel, oil, breathing oxygen, hydraulics, rubber seals, etc.) raises the personnel by another order of magnitude. These millions of people span the range from highly educated scientists and engineers down to the lowest paid and least educated persons that keep the dirt and dust minimized from the precision components and warehouses. Each and every one of these potential participants, no matter their pay or education level, can cause a single weak link, which in-turn can unintentionally bring an "aircraft weapon system" down in a catastrophic accident.

Yet in my career – as an example – I flew in a group of aircraft (the twin-engine propeller-powered reciprocating-engine C-47 family) *that was originally designed and flown 5-years before I was born.* In seven years, I accrued over 2,700 flight hours (double that in engine flight hours) – and flew about 325,000 miles, equivalent to 13 times around the earth at the equator. (Equatorial circumference = 24,900 statute miles). I had no background on these numerous vintage C-47s in terms of hours flown on the airframe, or how many times they had been overhauled, repaired from major incidents, or damage. (My experience in the C-47 consisted of three TC-47s, more than a dozen EC-47s plus short experiences in about a dozen other variations of the C-47). And these were – by today's standards – very simplistic aircraft (even by "Rube Goldberg standards") … "obsolete", is the operative adjective. But in all my experience in the C-47 family, I experienced only ONE true in-flight engine failure, and only a couple instances of sub-system failures that were serious enough to be considered "potentially life threatening". When compared to automotive vehicles, even these old aircraft were three to five times more complex than automobiles, both in design and maintenance, and in the training required to operate.

From the C-47s, I passed on to the KC-135 tanker. It was the very first USAF "operational" 4-engine jet transport aircraft, and was fitted with the earliest turbo-jet engines (which had no attached fan sections and required water injection to boost take-off thrust). At the time I began operating the KC-135 aircraft, they had been "maturing in service" for about 14 years. I flew these for ~2,000 hours (8,000 engine flight hours), and encountered only two or three engine failures in-flight, maybe 5-aborted take-offs due to engine performance deficiencies before take-off, and even experienced one inflight engine failure that was not determined until after landing, when it was discovered on post-flight ground inspection, that the engine had suffered more than one compressor blade failure that had a "cascade-failure" with debris moving aft through the length of the engine so that upon inspection daylight could be seen from the tail-pipe forward. Yet the engine had continued to operate without vibration or noticeable engine instrument indications to the end of the flight.

This aircraft and mission reflected a level of complexity more than 10 times that of the C-47 (... aircraft maximum weight 12 times greater than the C-47; cruise speed, five times greater; nominal max. altitude five times greater and training time for crewmembers initial qualification, more than 10 times greater). I then transitioned to flying the converted Canadian B-707-300 commercial aircraft for another 1,500 flight hours, which represented 6,000 engine flight hours and another ten years newer (upgraded) reliability and performance and a total of 2–million flight miles (77 times around the circumference of the earth), and another order of magnitude in flying, with no incidents of either engine failure, take-off aborts, or systems failures that were potentially life threatening!

Was this just "luck", or divine intervention? I believe it reflected both. But more so, I believe it rather reflected the high quality of training, maintenance, and professional personnel at all levels of their operation. Again, this reflects my personal experience, and is not intended to reflect every pilot's experience, but rather to reflect on the ultimate overall professionalism, safety, reliability, and performance of USAF (and Canadian military people) and policies – which I helped to instill and educate into those under my career leadership, responsibilities and qualifications. Now that is certainly another measure of my ***DESTINY***.

Hindsights: Flying Transports vs. Fighters —

Piloting (and flying in general) is a lot more hard work and physical and emotional stress, than fun and glory. Much of the considerable joy of flying is the sharing of the experience with others, be they aviators or friends, or passengers and family. Multi-engine aircraft typically are crew-served and carry along a number of co-participants who closely share those experiences. (This observation is not intended to demean the experiences of those flying single-seat aircraft, but merely reflects my personal experiences).

In my quest for adventure in life-fulfillment, I rode a motorbike, and then a small motorcycle in my teens. After that it was automobiles and convertibles in my 20's and 30's. I added water-skiing powerboats in my mid- to late 30's, by which time I was also flying in command of a 4-engined, 333,600 pound, Mach 8.4 (550 mph) aircraft with life and safety responsibility for over 175 passengers (at times) and crew of up to ten, plus additional refueling receiver aircraft equipment totaling a multiple aircraft value approaching 100's of millions of then-year dollars. The motorbike and motorcycle were more analogous to flying a fighter aircraft (by virtue of being a single-person oriented activity), where the big transports vastly increased the sharing with dozens and even hundreds simultaneously.

In the USAF, there has always been a certain competitive relationship between pilots and navigators that creates minor dissention and acrimony at times. A large percentage of navigators wanted to be pilots from the beginning, but were frequently downgraded to the "perceived lesser position" as navigator, due to an eyesight deficiency, or other lesser physical abnormalities, and in many cases just because at the time of entry, there was a reduced pilot need and they were shuttled to the "back seat". As a result of my particular assignments – with the exception of pilot training – <u>every flying assignment I had happened to have a primary role involving the use of navigators</u> (training them, being mission critical in the combat reconnaissance mission, critical mission responsibilities in aerial refueling rendezvous, and global mission operations).

As a result, I have a great respect and rapport with navigators, then and to this day. Their participation on my crews and operations were critical, and highly technically involved. And they saved the day and our lives on more than one occasion, as an extra set of eyes and expertise during complex activities that could often be very distracting to the pilot's responsibilities. Unfortunately, they have been mostly replaced by highly sophisticated electronics systems in today's military (and more so in commercial) aviation. Unfortunately, these robotic replacements for those highly trained air-crewmen, are sorely missed from the cockpit environment. Yet some of my best military friends (including Navigators) were, and still are among my closest.

Hindsights: Military Vs. Commercial Flying—

Flying the Canadian Military Boeing 707, in their traditional air transport passenger and cargo rolls (excluding the aerial refueling missions), were as close to flying in heavy-jet commercial aviation as one could get. The schedules and routes were all essentially repetitive, canned, and regular – *point-to-point* and return. The aircraft and equipment were modern and current with the standards of commercial airlines fleets. The procedures used by the crews, were the same as those taught to commercial airlines standards.

I arrived in Canada with substantial military aircraft experience in the KC-135, the predecessor of the Boeing 707. The two airplanes shared many common characteristics beyond their similarity of appearance, even though the KC-135 was a decade-plus older and, slightly smaller, and less sophisticated, due to its older technology. Many of these commonalities were shared structural design, and early versions of similar systems, as well as aircraft performance characteristics. My Canadian counterparts were trained initially under contract by Boeing, in their commercial training center in Seattle, WA. Boeing was in the business of selling commercial airliners, and their aircrew training was oriented toward teaching their crewmembers confidence in the hardware and maximum passenger comfort. Military operations (and most non-Boeing owned instructors), have a somewhat different focus of concern; Maximum performance in extreme conditions and potential combat operations was their focus.

As an example, after the initial contract with Boeing Commercial expired (3-years from aircraft delivery and 1-year after my arrival), the Canadians transferred their training contract to American Airlines in Dallas, TX. I experienced annual training with both contractors. Boeing taught their course using 4-axis full motion flight simulators, but the older 707 aircraft simulators at Boeing, were very rudimentary in their visual outside references, which were only visible to the left-seat pilot and were based upon video cameras shooting optical images of model buildings and landmarks attached to an 8-foot wide conveyor belt, which was anything-but elegant or life-like. Crude in contrast, to American Airlines, which had updated full motion simulators with highly refined computer generated graphics visible to both pilots with both straight ahead and peripheral vision imagery, projected on a hemispherical screen, making it possible for a pilot to accurately (and realistically sense) flying the simulator with almost no reference to instruments! The AAL simulators could realistically simulate the entire sequence of system failures or degradations that could impact the aircraft and safe continuation of flight. Do it wrong, and the simulator would actually "crash" with all the sounds and flashing lights, like total reality — a much better simulation – and these simulators, could actually be used by the National Transportation Safety Boards to simulate and define accident causes.

More significantly, when the Boeing program-generated simulator emergencies (engine failures, system failures, flight control problems, etc.), their instructors taught only the primary failure response and answered "student's" questions about related failures with very little detail. (i.e. When an engine fails or is shut down, the aircraft also loses the electrical generator and hydraulic pumps from the failed engine, which cause additional alarms and related systems to operate differently, or not at all.). Boeing's instructors response to a student's challenge typically was, "The Boeing aircraft is well designed and lasts a long time". American Airline's took the pilot all the way to the bottom of all the inter-related failures.

Secondly, I found that my Canadian counterparts had been trained to similar standards as I had been initially at SAC, and had *not* learned to fly the complete scope of the flight envelope. Only after certifying through the SAC Central Flight Instructor Course (in my previous assignment) was I really capable of flying the aircraft with complete knowledge of its performance and limitations.

Another example I encountered in Canada was that they were taught "passenger comfort rules", like no banks in excess of 10°-15°, so the passengers never felt any significant G-forces; and no idle power, speed brakes deployed, "jet penetration descents" from above 20,000 feet, because they were noisy, bumpy, and "unsettling to passengers". Yet these procedures were typical military requirements during formation flights and tactical operations.

When I demonstrated this last mentioned penetration procedure, my Canadian counter parts balked and said they never were trained like that at the commercial airlines facilities; that the FAA had never certified the airplane for such procedures. In other words, they were unsure if and how the aircraft would perform under those conditions. This failed to take into engineering reality that this implied a potential failure risk would occur if commenced at 21,000 feet, or even 20,100 feet, because it was officially tested only below 20,000 feet. (Where, in fact the actual design limit parameters are designed with a 150% or greater structural margin, on all critical components).

Because of these differences in training and experience – and the primary focus on "passenger comfort" versus "getting the mission done" – I found that the aircrews tended to rely on external and automated canned systems more heavily, than on experience or common sense. And the flying was not nearly as diverse and challenging as what I had previously experienced. After flying the routine transport roles for several months, I found that I was getting bored with the repetitive and very conservative operations.

These differences also had to be overcome, when we started to do tactical military aerial refueling operations, where commercial practices and precision formation discipline, and aircrew communications were non-existant. This was the most demanding to design, teach and instill on the aircrew members conducting the A/R operations, until they became automatic habits required for safety and organization.

Hindsights: "Mission Oriented" Vs. "Money Oriented"—

Transitioning from a 20-year career in the USAF, to a post-retirement aerospace corporate program management, or marketing environments, I observed and was often challenged by the significant differences.

As a USAF officer I had learned (both in formal training – and by example in the field) how to manage people and available *resources*. But this experience was never focused on "bottom-line dollar management". We were intensely aware of the value of property and equipment by magnitude of cost, as well as people resources by skill and availability numbers, and had a focus upon "preservation and good stewardship of resources". But emphasis on bottom-line cost was seldom ever used as a decision parameter (except in the budgetary process of needs and priorities). The decision basis was predominantly focused upon conservation of resources and best use of the limited resources available —*And the higher mission.*

In the military, officers and managers were encouraged to share "peripheral information" gained through external outside contacts, to forward it on to others when it was outside one's direct responsibility, and was appropriate to support the higher cause (of the military "Mission"). Conversely, in the corporate world it appeared that many department managers and technicians alike felt that "knowledge was power", and therefore should be kept to one-self, for job security. This was conspicuously apparent in large corporate "program management" tasks, where the program or project manager was responsible to be the bridge between customer and internal team members.

For example, if the Project Manager requested details of coordination to help resolve corporate versus customer issues, (for example during proposal competition bids) it was approached (using an analogy for simplicity) that the manager or middleman was to put the problematic issue on the "top of the fence", and the individual technicians would do their work in private "behind the fence" and return an answer "to the top of the fence" with a result or recommendation, but often with little or no insight to the recipient into the details. Therefore this "project manager" was often left unable to satisfactorily answer to either his boss or the client how the recommended solution would impact the broader picture, and he was often unable to provide further suggestion to other technicians for a more integrated and complete reolution of the concern. Said another way, "teamwork" was often flawed, or less fully analyzed, in the corporate workplace.

I also found in the corporate world – *I suspect largely from this difference in perspective on teamwork* – that my co-workers had no desire to get together for a social gathering and some camaraderie, after a strenuous workday, or work week. In fact, I perceived some real disdain for this form of stress relief and team interaction, which I had always found provided very positive motivation and active personal relationships in the military management of projects.

Hindsights: What Changed the Course of My Career? —

At the time I made my first available-assignment choice (May-62), I initially opted for an F-100 Fighter assignment. "***Destiny***" forced me to choose an alternate, at the last minute. I had an alternate decision already chosen to select a C-47 aircraft assignment in Chicago near families of both Pat and I. That choice was based upon speculative near-term changes in Air Force planning, and I felt my best candidate was the TC-47, at Chicago International Airport, Chicago. This aircraft category was "planned" to soon be replaced with a newer aircraft. The USAF was considering replacement of the primary Navigation Trainer, which then was the T-29 transport, with the DC-9 commercial twin-jet transport. The speculation was that the Reserves would get the retired T-29s to replace their older TC-47 Nav Trainers — which would ultimately become my revised alternate career path. However, limited funding after the Vietnam War delayed that procurement, and the early model Boeing-737-200 "Gator" entered and won the competition, several years later.

The final procurement choice of the Boeing 737-200, in 1971, procured 19 aircraft (and was well after I had finished my Chicago and Vietnam tours). Had the replacement for the T-29 taken place in the originally anticipated time frame, within a couple years of my first operational assignment, then the TC-47 would not have been the springboard for my career with its subsequent Top Secret ***EC-47*** assignment – which provided my "ticket in-hand" security clearance that got SAC's attention for my KC-135Q (SR-71 tanker) also a Top Secret assignment. This issue combined with the fact that I also had the "Vietnam combat tour behind me", was a major consideration in gaining the new assignment. If what I originally based my decision upon, rather than what actually occurred, I probably wouldn't have had the substantial qualifications from the TC-47 O'Hare assignment behind me to advance to the Top Secret SR-71 at Beale AFB, CA, near Sacramento. (And thus we wouldn't have been in Chicago to adopt Caryn in 1965; nor in California to adopt Melissa in 1969, while operating with the SR-71!

Yes, my "questionable" decision to select the transport pilot role, when my first-choice fighter assignment fell through, was proven the right decision for me! And I feel it was guided by my "Guardian Angel", to keep me out of harms way. And my unexpected elevation to Instructor Pilot during my SAC experience proved to be the area, which I found most emotionally rewarding. This also became a critical stepping-stone in my over-all career advancement.

Hindsights: Stepping Stones to Advancement —

In each assignment I had, I always focused on first learning my primary role, and then getting up to full capability in that role, with competence. In my first assignment, it was just good fortune that allowed me to stay in the TC-47 in Chicago for 5 years. Following that assignment, official policy limited my Vietnam Assignment to 1-year, and separation from my family. All following assignment were much more complex in nature and required one to two years minimum to become "fully competent".

A saying in the military is, "Never volunteer for anything". Good advice if it was asked for someone to volunteer to be the "Point man" in a combat patrol, which translated as "the target of the first enemy bullet". But I always tried for opportunities to learn and gain comfort in many different knowledge levels, even when it took me out of my comfort zone (like public speaking, or lecturing before a crowd, or becoming a Logistics Engine Manager). This open-minded attitude broadened my skills and created higher self-confidence. I tried to always look ahead to the long term in making assignment choices, or requests, trying to capitalize on my past experiences and looking to what new challenges I could add to and profit from. After pilot training, when it looked probable that I wouldn't get my "fairy-tale" assignment (single seat "go-fast" aircraft), I chose the alternate that I felt provided the best conditions for growth potential and maximum exposure to USAF operations. I had more than a little help from a ***Guardian Angel*** in making that choice! I amplified my skills by volunteering for additional duties, where I already had interests or background training (Flight Safety, aircraft structures and mechanics, teaching and training acquired in Advanced AFROTC), throughout my career. Each new assignment capitalized on my prior experiences and operations. I volunteered for Flight Safety as an additional duty (both at O'Hare in the TC-47, and again in Vietnam in the EC-47) to pass on my experiences, engineering skills, and training to others. My ferry flight experiences provided valuable applications and lessons in safety-oriented decision-making.

My already-obtained Top Secret clearance, from the EC-47 assignment, combined with already acquired combat related operations were the keys to my volunteer selection to the SR-71 Aerial Refueling assignment, when combined with my already acquired total flying time and Senior Pilot Wings. My limited Instructor Pilot time in the two C-47 assignments also gave me an advantage in SAC, even though the aircraft I had previously flown and instructed in had absolutely no commonality with heavy jet-tankers.

My Safety experience in two unique operational situations with two different configurations of C-47 opened the door for my brief, but highly noteworthy SAC Bomb Wing Safety Officer assignment. And gained experiences with SAC combined with more formalized Instructor Pilot training and total acquired flying hours, made me first choice by HQ USAF between three other candidates for the assignment to Canada to develop their aerial refueling operation in the semi-familiar Boeing-707 refueling operations. And "***Destiny***" provided me two other assignments to choose from, if I preferred. Finally, volunteering for a position in the fleet logistic management unit for the KC-135 "weapons system" put all of the technical experience of inflight refueling in both boom and hose-and-drogue operations, combined with my aeronautical engineering (major in structures) at a critical intersection with USAF needs.

After my Canadian assignment, "***Destiny***" steered me away from routine SAC Squadron Operations, and Systems Command assignments. None of these assignments were planned, nor sought in advanced by me. They just seemed to come up at the exact right time in my career, and finding me with just the right set of experience, skills and management and leadership to step right into them. Certainly, each had their unique transitions that I had to learn and experience, but they each became a significant focal point in my military career. I was also fortunate to be allowed to stay in each assignment location and unit for 3 to 5 years, so that I could build reasonable competency over the first third of the assignment and then work at near-100% efficiency for the duration of each, with increasing responsibility "well above my pay grade" and rank status.

And the Most Important Hindsight of All ... Spiritual Enlightenment —

As I reviewed my experiences, extolled in substantial detail above, I realized that the most important thing I had learned through all of these experiences, was the realization of how and where ***my destiny*** had taken me. There appeared to be some form of a ***Spiritual Component*** in all these experiences. The Creator with HIS guiding angels had blessed me so many times with HIS silent guidance, and with the many blessings HE bestowed upon me from birth. HE blessed me with a strong curiosity about how things work and an intuitive ability to figure them out. HE blessed me with, and guided me to refine an ability to think critically and "outside of the box". I developed those skills (through HIS many challenges and guidance) to be able to examine "the forest" (as necessary, to gain sufficient overview), and then focus that view to examine "the trees" and foresee the consequences of changing its components far beyond the obvious. HE guided me to learn "cause and effect". HE gave me the ability to look at an unfamiliar subject that had a fault or issue, exam it to determine the nature of the problem, and define a sometimes-innovative solution to resolve the situation(s). HE also blessed me with the ability to explain or teach these observations to others. These led to my love and skill for instructing and leadership.

From my mind's-eye view, eight miles above the earth, through my cockpit's windows, I saw all the glory of God's nature: Powerful and towering white and gray clouds, surrounded by beautiful hues of blue sky and cotton-puff formations, tinted by the colors of sunset and sunrise; The inky black sky over the North Atlantic at night surrounded by millions of stars often with no detectable horizon, and lights near where the horizon should be, which could not be determined as whether stars or surface vessels. The beauty of the Northern lights in their rainbow of gossamer colors on apparent gauze curtains; Night flying in summer or winter over cities illuminated with white and yellow diamonds of carpeted ground lights spotted by occasional rubies, emeralds and sapphires of vehicles, signal lights and neon signs; The beautiful mountains, lakes, rivers, and oceans of the world, bordered by the patch-work quilt of fields, prairies, hillsides and mountains; And the miniature lightning bolts of St. Elmo's fire, at night, crackling from the static-electricity of microscopic particles of water or ice impacting on the exterior of the wind shield, or the circular rainbow centered on the cockpit (or viewer's position), cast on the airplane's shadow on the tops of a flat cloud deck below, commonly called "a pilot's rainbow". These were just a few of the spectacular breath-taking sights of God's grandeur of flight! As John Gillespie Magee Jr,, said in his famous 1941 poem, *High Flight, " ...I've put out my hand, and touched the face of God".*

All of this was encompassed by the sensations of flight; the occasional bumps of turbulence; The silky sensation of flying in close formation with other aircraft; The challenging sensation of a low visibility approach and then breaking out under the clouds just in time to see the runway; The feel of 80,000 pounds of combined thrust accelerating a 333,600 pound airplane from zero to 140 knots, taking off in only slightly more than a mile of runway. And the chance to visit and observe over 50 different locations and countries around the globe. Most of this would never have been experienced, had I never chosen to be a career transport pilot. Much less likely, had I not been "guided to avoid" the path of a "combat fighter jock".

My many experiences with over 6,500 hours of logged flight time gave me the appreciation of the world from high above its surface, the awesome nature of actively operating in 3-dimensional environments and fast speeds, of controlling powerful machines having thousands of horse-power and speeds up to near the speed of sound, the grandeur and diversity of cultures around the globe, and the importance of separating common sense TRUTH, from agenda-driven propaganda. These were a combination of experiences that probably relatively few other individuals would ever be able to experience in a lifetime. Seeing, feeling and experiencing all these events made me more fully realize that there was a much higher entity that had created the combined complexity and wonder of it all!

DESTINY'S Thread—

Talk about ***destiny!*** I have truly soared! My career, and my destiny can be seen as a series of steps, not just by chance, but by a greater "plan" **(not my own),** which placed me in exactly where ***destiny*** wanted me, at exactly the right time, when a new requirement had just come onto the scene! During my 20 years of military service, I strived to give far more than I received, and this was marked by the contributions I made to the USAF mission.

While in SAC, I trained between 30 and 50 heavy-jet tanker pilots, providing them with flying skills, systems understanding and a strong perspective of safety in their flying. I followed that with providing one of the United State's primary allies ... the Canadian Armed Forces ... with their first real exposure to professional aerial refueling, which brought them into the global scenario for supporting NATO during the Cold War. In later years I initiated a unique program of using over 150 salvaged commercial transports for relatively low-cost cannibalization of their power plants and more advanced systems to re-furbish an obsolete fleet of vintage KC-135A aircraft with greatly improved reliabilities and fuel efficiencies, adding "equivalent increases in refueling booms" during the 1990s Iraq War. This program created a calculated savings estimated at more than $15 Billion in modernization for these weapons systems using assets from retiring later vintage donor aircraft. Now that is what I considered a more common sense "bang for the tax payers buck".

These initiatives created and implemented, combined with my combat tour in Vietnam earned me the following major recognition and awards — The Distinguished Flying Cross (DFC), seven-

Combat Air Medals, two- AF Commendation Medals, two- Meritorious Service Medals, a Vietnam Service Medal, a Vietnam Campaign Medal, two-Presidential Unit Citations, two-AF Outstanding Unit Awards, the National Defense Service Medal, an Armed Forces Expeditionary Medal (for Korea), a Cold War Recognition Medal, and the Canadian Chief of Defence Commendation. They provided me the opportunity to successfully support the USAF mission at very high, and also international levels. During my final eight years of duty I served in job capacities fulfilling the responsibilities and job descriptions of Full Colonels and a Canadian Brigadier General, while actually serving at the lesser ranks of Major and Lt. Colonel.

I retired from the USAF in 1981, with a Command Pilot rating (with final flight criteria achieved during my Canadian Assignment), and with the rank of Lt. Colonel, which was awarded on 1 June 1977, at the Oklahoma Air Logistic Center, following my Canadian assignment. I could never have achieved all of these accomplishments without the grace and guidance of my Creator and Guiding Angel(s), nor without the values, experiences and guidance of my father and mother, nor without the wonderful support and military life-style flexibility of my loving wife (of 58 years), and my wonderful family. ***Destiny*** and ***God*** have certainly blessed me, kept me from harms way, and guided me all the way on my path through all these experiences. And I am also very thankful to all those others (both mentioned and unsung) who shared with me the benefits of their knowledge and support.

This is the *destiny* I experienced, lived, and accomplished —
This is my story, and I am sticking to it! —

— Chuck Miller
email: av8or.usaf@gmail.com
Feedback, comments, and suggestions welcomed.

CAF Boeing 707 with Two CF-5 Receivers over North Atlantic

ABOUT THE AUTHOR

Chuck Miller was commissioned through AFROTC as a reserve 2nd Lt. after obtaining a BS in Aeronautical Engineering at the University of Illinois in 1961. This was followed by T-37 and T-33, all-jet Pilot Training, where he earned his Pilot Wings and accumulated 260 hours of flying time. His first assignment was flying the TC-47 Navigation Trainer at the busiest airport in the world, O'Hare International Airport, Chicago, in support of Air Force Reserve navigator proficiency training. While at O'Hare he was offered a Regular Air Force Commission as a 1st Lt., and spent 5 years while logging nearly 2000 hours of flight time. Then off to Vietnam, ferrying a Top Secret and highly modified EC-47 (1 of 45), from New Hampshire island-hopping the Pacific to Vietnam. He served in Vietnam from March '67 to February '68, where he logged another 1500 hours flying 115 unarmed, low altitude combat electronic reconnaissance missions. He then transferred with his Top Secret clearance to SAC and became a KC-135Q tanker pilot supporting the SR-71 "Blackbird" special global operations for 5-years, ultimately becoming Chief Instructor Pilot for the base and then Wing Chief of Safety. Based upon his unique qualifications, he was selected in 1973 by HQ USAF for a special category Exchange Pilot assignment with the Canadian Armed Forces, to develop their NATO inflight refueling role with modified Boeing 707-320C tankers and CF-5 fighters, adding another 1500 hours to his log book. He spent 3-years there, successfully bringing their refueling capability into full proficiency and reliability, for which he received a unique 4-Star Chief of Defence Staff Commendation. He was then reassigned to the Oklahoma City Air Logistic Center in the C/KC-135 Logistics Management unit where he rose to the position of Weapon System Manager for the fleet of 750 aircraft, plus the Presidential VC-135 and 707 fleet. In that capacity he was responsible for the C/KC-135 structural integrity program, wing reskin program, played a principal role in the KC-135R (CFM-56) re-engining program, and was the originator and architect of the KC-135E re-engining program using refurbished commercial 707 engines and components for over 160 C/KC-135s, and saving over $15 Billion. He retired in 1981 in the rank of Lt. Col. as a highly decorated USAF officer.

Major Chuck Miller, USAF, in 1974
While assigned with the Canadian
Armed Forces